Portrait of a Partnership

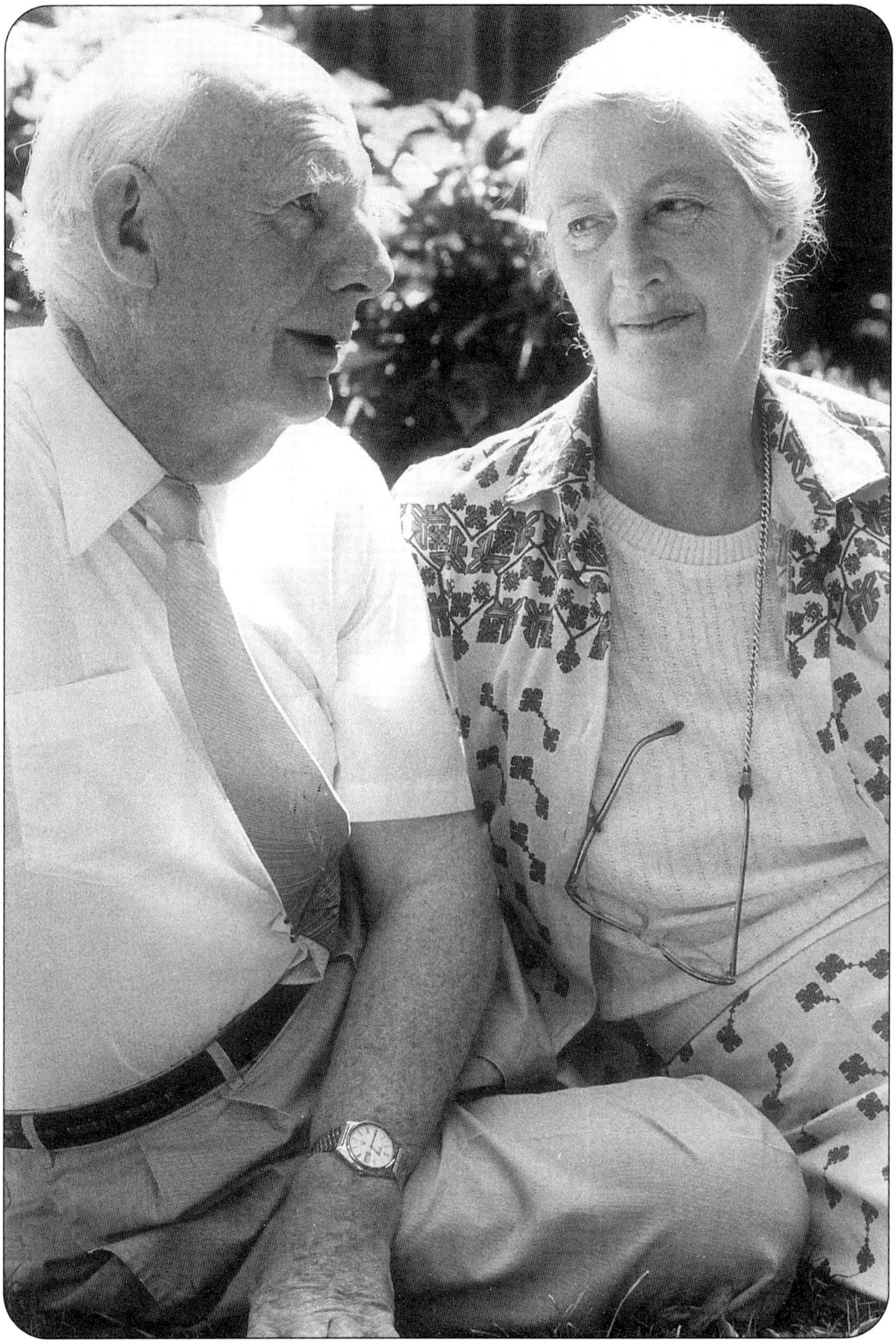

Portrait of a Partnership

Mora Dickson

ROBERTSON PUBLICATIONS

© Mora Agnes Dickson, 2004

Robertson Publications
Tomchulan, Old Crieff Road,
Aberfeldy, Perthshire PH15 2DH

Designed and Typeset in Minion by
Pioneer Associates, Perthshire
Printed and bound in Great Britain by
The Cromwell Press, Trowbridge, Wilts

A CIP record for this book is available
from the British Library

ISBN 0-9547327-0-7

The right of Mora Agnes Dickson to be identified
as author of this work has been asserted in
accordance with the Copyright, Designs and
Patent Act (1988).

Contents

PART I Early Days

CHAPTER 1	**Alec**	3
	Home and School	3
	Oxford	5
	Saar Plebiscite	10
CHAPTER 2	**Mora**	14
	Home and School	14
	Art College	17
	War	19
CHAPTER 3	**Alec**	21
	The *Yorkshire Post*	21
	Berlin	24
	Czechoslovakia	25
CHAPTER 4	**Mora**	29
	War 1939	29
	6 Troop No 2 Commando	31
CHAPTER 5	**Alec**	36
	The Phoney War	36
	The King's African Rifles	38
CHAPTER 6	**Mora**	45
	War 1942–43	45
	Orkney	45
	YMCA Shandon	49
CHAPTER 7	**Alec**	54
	East Africa Command	54

CHAPTER 8	**Mora**	60
	War 1945	60
	Nymegen	60
CHAPTER 9	**Alec**	70
	Uganda (BOAR)	70
CHAPTER 10	**Mora**	75
	1946–47	75
	Moffat	75
	London	76
CHAPTER 11	**Alec**	83
	Ghana	83

PART II Coming Together

CHAPTER 12	**Nigeria and British Cameroon**	91
	1948–50	91
	British Cameroon	96
CHAPTER 13	**Man O'War Bay visit**	99
	1950 – Man O'War Bay	99
CHAPTER 14	**Mora**	109
	Calabar, Itu, Uburu	109

PART III Team Work

CHAPTER 15	**Marriage**	121
	Moffat – August 1951	121
	Man O' War Bay	122
	Mount Cameroon	144
CHAPTER 16	**Interim One**	151
	11 Morningside Place	151
	Iraq 1955–56	155

Contents

CHAPTER 17	**Interim Two**	182
	Edinburgh 1956	182
	Austro-Hungarian Frontier	183
	Edinburgh 1957	190
	Bela Horvath	190
CHAPTER 18	**Interim Three**	193
	Sarawak 1957	193
	Padawan	197
	Budu 1957	204
	Baram River – The River of No Return	212
CHAPTER 19	**Interim Four**	223
	Edinburgh 1957	223

PART IV True Partnership

CHAPTER 20	**Acacia House**	227
	Mortlake 1957–58	227
	Letter to *The Times*	232
	The Year between	233
CHAPTER 21	**VSO**	234
	Voluntary Service Overseas 1958	234
	USA 1961	249
CHAPTER 22	**Sequel and CSV**	255
	Community Service Volunteers 1962	255

Dedicated to

DAVID GREEN
(Director of VSO 1990–1999)

and

ELISABETH HOODLESS
(Executive Director of CSV from 1975)

PART I
EARLY DAYS

CHAPTER 1

Alec

Home and School

'Mine was a home on an upstairs-downstairs model,' wrote Alec Dickson looking back after 40 years. Born in 1914, he was the youngest of three sons and an older sister, living in a large and lovely house on the edge of London. 'There was a glorious garden, with a view over treetops to the horizon which, on a summer evening, moved me even as a small boy. Servants who cared for me, brothers who were dear to me – as they are now – and parents who seemed to me the quintessence of loving kindness'.

Norman Dickson, a civil servant originally from Glasgow, had done well for his family. He was a hard working businessman, respected in international circles. His wife, Anne, also from Glasgow, passed on to Alec not only his red hair and physical appearance, but an open, loving and romantic temperament. Looking back on his inheritance, her son was far more conscious of what was lacking in him as a boy. 'The first picture I asked my mother to give me was the famous one of Jack Cornwall (Boy First Class as the Navy expressed it) standing beside his gun at the battle of Jutland, with a look of infinite sadness on his face as the ship's ammunition and his own blood ran out. If only it could have been me, I thought illogically. Would there be a time in my life when I might be brave?'

Those nearest to him he took for granted, as indeed most young children do. His father had worked in remote places, helping to build railways in Siam, Nyasaland and the Argentine. At home Norman Dickson left much unsaid. It was not until he was dead that his youngest son regretted the questions he had never asked his father what adventures he had experienced. What had his home life in southern Scotland been like? How had he compensated for an almost total absence of formal schooling? With their mother likewise few questions were asked about her early life. But, in one respect, the family was fortunate on both sides. Their parents brought with them into the affluent background that the young inherited, a wide kith and kin that remained, in the Scottish way, close and affectionate.

Alec Dickson was a self-absorbed child, taking for granted the pleasurable atmosphere that surrounded him. His mother made a home sunny with contentment, whether outside or in.

Then, quite suddenly, all this ended, almost without warning. Certainly with what seemed shocking suddenness, he followed his brothers to public school, Rugby in Warwickshire. He was eight years old.

The shock was devastating. He failed to understand why his loving mother had cast him out of the home that had sustained and swaddled him until now, nor why his despairing letters were met with a refusal to bring him back, and the transformation in his brothers from friends and accomplices to distant upholders of an adamant law and order. There was the prevailing threat of punishment, the suppression of Christian names and the coldness: coldness of dormitories; coldness of showers; coldness of relationships between masters and staff – between boy and boy. The intentional exclusion of any deep friendships lest they go beyond the platonic – for reasons which were a mystery then to most of the boys. The total lack of any form of the affection which up to now had permeated his home and the wider circle of friends and relations.

Alec Dickson became known by his contemporaries as 'Gloomy'. He recognised the name to be appropriate. He had the sense that he was no good at anything. He suffered from the misery of the mediocre. As time went by he would scan the columns of the newspapers towards the end of the holidays, hoping to see a paragraph announcing that Euston Station had been destroyed by fire. Alas, instinct told him that some alternative method would be found to return him to school. He had already learnt that under no circumstances was any emotional feeling to be shown.

By chance he had lost a Christian name. Dickson minor's seat in chapel was under the picture of an old boy, already dead – Rupert Brooke. All Alec Dickson's crushed romanticism responded to this beautiful memorial profile and to the poetry that surrounded it.

'If I should die think only this of me
That there's some corner of a foreign land . . .'

Once again some inner longing for sacrifice – perhaps an act that would set him apart from the mob – seemed only possible on the battlefield. Too late, alas, too late. He steeped himself in the life and poetry of his idol, amazed that his idol had survived Rugby School, and eventually won the Rupert Brooke Essay Prize. Throughout adolescence he cherished a conviction that only on the battlefield could courage and sacrifice be exercised, a belief reinforced by the Team photographs that lined the walls of his House – half of whose young subjects were already dead.

He knew himself to be insignificant within the school community. He excelled in nothing – languages, science, art, sport, music – though he loved the latter and found consolation when this was discovered by a music teacher who encouraged him to learn the clarinet. Gradually within himself a reviving spirit told him that he must choose a way of life that avoided competition: that opened a door towards doing things that nobody else had thought of doing. This resolution edged him in the direction of being alert for chances and ready for any opportunities that came along.

In later life Alec Dickson used to say that Rugby had formed him – he did not mean it as a compliment, yet he had benefitted from the experience. In the sense that the French use 'formation' for the effect that schooling is intended to make, public school had formed him. Everything he did later or tried subsequently to achieve was shaped to avoid what he himself had experienced in those years.

In his last summer holidays, the weeks between Rugby and Oxford, chance took over. A friend had recommended that he go to a family in the Black Forest. In a remote rural village which could not have been further removed geographically or in spirit from Berlin, when Von Schleicher the German Chancellor was removing the last obstacles to Hitler's coming to power, a retired Colonel and his family treated their young guest with great kindness. Their house was named 'Dar es Salaam', the capital of Tanganyika.

Suddenly Alec Dickson was absorbed in Germany – the country, the situation and the people. When he reached Oxford this absorption was to take priority over his studies, influence fundamentally the next few years and bring him lifelong friends.

Oxford

At New College, Oxford, Alec Dickson began to feel a person in his own right, in contrast to the nonentity he had felt at school. Academically he was not distinguished, to the despair of his Modern History Tutor, Professor Ogg. It was 1932 and the modern history that enthralled him revolved round what was happening in Germany; but anything subsequent to 1870 was held to be too close to the present day to be studied with adequate detachment. When, in an essay on Cardinal Wolsey, Alec Dickson pointed out to his Tutor the topical relevance of a speech made by Goering the day before, he was rebuked. 'No, No, Mr Dickson, I beg you! A character in history must be judged in the light of his experience and surroundings – in the spirit of his time – and not judged in relation to a speech made 400 years later'.

It was the immediacy of events in Central Europe there and then, about which the public in Britain knew next to nothing, that so passionately aroused Alec Dickson's interest.

He flung himself into all the extra activities that excited him. He became Hon. Secretary of the University German Club and of the Conservative Association; a member of the exclusive Raleigh Club which dealt with matters concerning the Empire and attracted very distinguished speakers; and Assistant Secretary of the League of Nations Union. On vacations – and perhaps not only on vacations – he travelled widely in Europe, particularly in Germany and Czechoslovakia. In the autumn of 1933 he had an article accepted by the *Yorkshire Post* on his experiences, while they were still voluntary, in a German Arbeitsdienst Lager (Work Camp).

New College had a considerable number of German students at this time. The names of those who went back when the great rift came and died for their own country can still be found on the College 1939–1945 War Memorial.

A casual conversation with one of those German students that summer of 1933 led to an invitation to go skiing at Christmas.

'Where do you live?' 'My home is in Prague. We ski in the Bohemian Mountains'.

It seemed then as though a magical door of discovery was opening. In terms of History and Current Affairs he would learn at first hand the realities of relations between Czechoslovakia and the Sudetenland; the old links with Austria-Hungary; the intentions of Nazi Germany. But the manner of that learning was to touch deeper springs within Alec Dickson. Staying in a mountain hut in Bohemia, with his friend Willi Fiedler and his young companions from Prague, Alec Dickson was introduced to the romantic origins – the mystique almost – of their Sudetendeutsch Youth Movement, the Wandervogel with its pre-1914 origins, not yet affected by Nazi influence, although already differences were appearing. Here were young people, politically innocent themselves at that time, infinitely musical and ready to open their hearts in friendship in a way that Alec Dickson had not found in the colder climate of school.

To return in the darkness after an all-day skiing expedition, which was Alec's first experience of the sport; to spend the evening singing folk songs, this made him aware of a new dimension of human relationships. The unabashed romanticism that moved these young people – and Alec Dickson himself – held an almost lyrical quality.

Deep down, though, he was aware that the loyalties of these youngsters could, and very likely would, betray the Czech Republic. They sang no Czech songs – only the songs of old Bohemia, of the old Austria-Hungary – songs that led back and, alas, forward to the heart of Germany.

On the way home Willi asked Alec Dickson if he would stay with his family for a few days. They arrived in Prague on the evening of Christmas Day after a miserable train journey. The Fiedler family had no room for a guest as the house was small and simple. The six-year-old brother had whooping cough and was very ill. Alec Dickson stayed with the grandmother in a nearby street. The food was edible but not enough. A friendship was made with Willi Fiedler that stood the test of time and bitter experience.

Midway through his first term at Oxford Alec Dickson had been visited in his rooms at New College by a German fellow student, Hermann Wallich, who was clearly distressed. He had just heard from his father in Potsdam that the younger brother, Walter, was being tormented at school. The boy had said no word to his parents, but could be heard weeping in his room at night. There was Jewish blood in the family and it was already clear that, with Hitler's rise to power, anti-semitism would increase. The question was, would Alec Dickson help to get Walter out of Germany into some boarding school in Britain? Alec Dickson did not hesitate to say 'Yes'.

At that time it was not difficult to get Walter out of Germany. The trouble lay in securing his acceptance in a British Public School. He had not taken the obligatory Common Entrance Examination. He was older than the correct age for entry. He lacked the background of an ordinary English boy. He did not play the right games. It was made clear to Mr Dickson that he was asking for rules to be overlooked. This was not a strange concept to Alec Dickson. However, eventually Bradfield in Berkshire said, 'Yes'.

Walter came to Bradfield, where his progress was outstanding. He won an English prize, which must have been a cause of mixed feelings among his British peers. He was happy. Alec Dickson kept in touch with him and the Dickson home was always open. Walter won a scholarship to King's College, Cambridge, but life for him was not to be without tragedy and disaster. As mob violence in Germany against the Jews and their property increased, Walter one day heard that his father, in a courageous act of self-sacrifice to save his wife and family, had left home and thrown himself to his death off a bridge in Dusseldorf.

In spite of his naturalisation papers application already being in the pipeline and assurances from his university college that they would give him shelter if war broke out, when it did, in the panic after Dunkirk, there was a knock one late evening on the door of Walter's student lodgings. Two policemen gave him ten minutes to get ready. He was to be interned on the Isle of Man as a potential enemy alien and later, on an unescorted liner, to be transported to a remote lumber camp in western Canada.

Walter joined the steadily growing band of Alec Dickson's friends. Those friends came from a wide range of backgrounds and sometimes they brought their families with them. Class, gender, generation, nationality did not matter. What did matter was that as individuals, as people, they were ready to respond openly to any gesture of genuine friendship. To give back as well as receive – as Alec Dickson himself was doing.

Amongst those who were to influence Alec profoundly was Alec Paterson, one of three Prison Commissioners at the Home Office, a man of drive and dynamism. He had fought in the 1914 war. The experience had greatly affected him and had led him, with the Rev. Tubby Clayton, to found Toc H, a club for survivors of those terrible years. The name was based on a certain signal of the Morse Code.

At the Home Office, Alec Paterson, known as A.P., quietly struggled for greater humanity in every aspect of the Prison and later Borstal Services. He had imagination and inventive force, a missionary rather than an administrator, who would say 'It is through men, not through buildings or regulations that our work is to be done'.

A.P.'s way with the young was visionary. Alec Dickson's older brother Murray was already preparing to join the Borstal Service as a Housemaster. Alec Dickson became a Prison Visitor at Wandsworth Prison and in 1935 was to act as personal private secretary to A.P. at the International Penal and Penitentiary Congress in Berlin. A.P. became not only a friend but a patron, the forerunner of a pattern which was to become increasingly important in Alec's life.

In December 1940 Alec Paterson was asked by the Home Secretary to undertake a special mission to Canada, to interview the aliens of enemy nationality who had been sent there by the United Kingdom for internment. His task was to sort out those whose sympathies were genuinely with Britain. When the time came, one recommended for repatriation was Walter Wallich, who eventually landed as a Major on the beaches of France on D-Day.

In the spring of 1934, his son having had a full year of university discovery, Norman Dickson was clearly beginning to feel uneasy that so little time was being spent on study for a degree – the purpose of his being at Oxford – and so much on activities not directly related to academic work. He came down to Oxford to ask some pertinent questions.

Alec Dickson, perhaps thinking that his father had not been entirely convinced by the subsequent discussion and perhaps because he found it easier to put his thoughts in order on paper, wrote a letter some days later. It began

Dear Daddie,

I want to explain what I am doing here, as you asked me. If one has set one's heart on gaining a First it means one must give up all idea of taking part in University and College activities and all that goes by the name of University Life . . .

Well, I have chosen not to take that course.... As you know I am reading Modern History. It used to be imagined that History was one of the easiest schools here. But now that so many people take it, the standard is as high as anything else. It is indeed a matter of whether one can obtain an honourable second or not. Now is it worth my while swatting out my guts to get a second, when, in my opinion, my energies and time might be more profitably spent. I think no. I have quite made up my mind to be a journalist. What is essential is a good background of historical learning and an all-round knowledge and an acquaintance with most branches of modern life, wide interests, and a broad mind.

By doing what I am now, I am doing my best to acquire these qualifications. The activities of the various clubs I belong to really do give a broad education. Participation in the life of the College and University genuinely does broaden one's outlook and increase one's knowledge and capabilities.

Last week I presided at a lunch given by the League of Nations Union at which the Foreign Editor of the *Daily Herald* spoke. On Friday I dined with Sir Philip Sassoon, before he addressed the Conservative Association, and I shall also do the same with Winston Churchill next week. On Tuesday I have a meeting of the German Club in my rooms when I shall read a paper on 'War Guilt'.

I would maintain that all these activities, and going to lectures, concerts and meetings on art, politics, foreign affairs and music etc. are of more use to me as a future journalist than pure academic learning.

I think you know me well enough to be assured that I am doing some work. Finally I must unashamedly confess to a great liking for spending hours in talking to other fellows in their rooms at night. What practical use one gets out of this is doubtful, but I do know that one seldom gets an opportunity again of having such interesting arguments, from Hitler to the nature of happiness in afterlife. I suppose this wrangling and talking is the most typical part of Oxford life.

I should just like to say one word about the vacations. I can either shut myself up for six weeks and read solidly for eight hours on end, as my brother (Murray) did. I can waste away time in theatres, cinemas, sports etc. or I can go abroad!

I am convinced that all the time I have spent abroad, especially in Germany, will be of use to me afterwards. A foreign language is always useful. I can understand and read German perfectly and I hope soon to speak it fairly well. Needless to say, the travelling there and my friendships with German youths of my own age I find extremely enjoyable.

Moreover, the Easter vacation, which I spent touring the Midlands, inspecting factories, slums, housing developments, docks, coalmines and prisons taught me a great deal, for which I am grateful.

I try, when I have the time, to write an article on something like the Work Camp System.

And if I don't get a second in History, I hope you won't be very disappointed but realise that I haven't been altogether wasting my time and your money.

>Your Loving Son
>Sandy

Norman Dickson must have accepted his son's apologia, for he began immediately to get in touch with his influential friends, sending them a copy of the letter and seeking possible contacts in the journalistic world.

In January 1935 Alec Dickson still had two terms to go in the idyllic setting of New College. In May he would be twenty-one and in June came Finals – the examination that determined his academic rating, the yardstick by which many employers would assess his worthiness for a job. He was attacked by nervous agitation and despair, by the stark reality of possibly having to face humiliation before his Father.

Saar Plebiscite

He had begun to prepare and revise the neglected studies when he was invited to spend a week at a castle in the Saarland owned by the von Stumm family. The journalist within him jumped at the chance. Ulrich von Stumm, his own age, was an ardent young nationalist, too prudent to espouse openly the Nazi cause while at Oxford, but with his heart set on the return of this tiny territory – so fabulously rich in coal and resources – to Germany. Politically Europe's hot spot, it meant much to French pride and power to retain and control: repossession meant even more to Germany.

To be present, residing at the castle throughout the Plebiscite, put Alec Dickson in a position to undertake his entry into the world of foreign correspondence. On the fourth evening of his visit, working hard in the bedroom on what he liked to think of as his first 'Despatch,' he was interrupted by Ulrich, with no other object than to show friendship and discuss the two political meetings they had just attended. He put out a hand to glance at the typed sheets beside his friend, 'Is this for a newspaper?' 'Yes. The *Birmingham Post*.' Alec Dickson replied truthfully, for this was the paper he hoped would accept his article.

'Excuse me,' Ulrich said, as he left to speak with his father, a senior official in the Foreign Office in Berlin.

The following morning early, Alec Dickson was asked to leave the castle. He was held to have betrayed Ulrich's friendship and abused the hospitality of the family. What he had written was what he thought; that 'Heim ins Reich' was the destiny of Saarland to the danger of Europe. On his return to Britain, however, having remained in the Saar though not in the castle, until the Plebiscite was over, Alec Dickson was to find that front page coverage had been given to his articles in the *Birmingham Post*: 'From our special correspondent'. And a letter from his father expressed as much pride in the achievement as his son himself. He had made it – on his own – writing on a crisis point in Central Europe.

He came back to what was practically a nervous breakdown. In order to get any sort of degree he must concentrate on his academic work as he had never done. The *Birmingham Post*'s acceptance of his articles now made this even more difficult. The possibility of becoming a foreign correspondent hung enticingly before his imagination. Seizing opportunities was one thing: deciding which opportunity to seize was quite another. Alec Dickson was good at the first, but decision-making in the quiet of his own room he never found easy as alternatives went up and down in the balance, each in turn assuming a beaconing glitter. Fortunately, and perhaps surprisingly, he had a sympathetic Tutor in Professor Ogg. Alec Dickson's temperament was not to retreat into isolation but to look for sympathetic help.

In August 1935, when Finals results were published, Alec Dickson had managed to get a Second Class Honours Degree. Norman Dickson wrote warmly from the Leopoldina Railway Company Ltd, Rio de Janeiro, with many congratulations and no doubt much unexpressed relief.

Before the results were even known, Alec Dickson was already back with the engagements that interested him so much more.

It was in August that he went to Berlin as Alex Paterson's personal private secretary at the International Penal and Penitentiary Congress. While there he inspected a concentration camp, the only foreign delegate to do so; spoke in German on Berlin Radio (criticising the German Prison System); visited Thaelmann, the Communist Leader in goal and addressed meetings of the Hitler Youth. Writing a number of articles, he was beginning to get published by papers such as the *Manchester Guardian*, the *Spectator*, and the *New Statesman*.

In the same winter of 1935, Alec Dickson went for some months to live in a South Wales depressed area, Glamorgan. He was there in October at the time of a 'stay down' strike. At this period the situation in the Welsh mining areas was desperate, appealing to all Alec Dickson's humanitarian instincts. An article written by him appeared in the *Spectator*. When told it had been accepted, a manager with whom he had become friendly wrote to him: 'Thank you for your letter, but it has frightened me. I had no idea you were getting copy for an article. I hope it has been so compiled as to conceal the identity of the colliery and its manager.' He need not have been concerned.

In every crisis of his life it was his mother to whom Alec Dickson turned. Norman Dickson was detached from too close family ties: Anne Dickson was interested in every aspect of the daily affairs of her sons, especially the youngest. She was a prolific correspondent, perennially hopeful that Alec had inherited this trait. In fact he had, but the pattern was different. Where his mother longed to have the gaps filled with at least a postcard, he preferred to wait on an accumulation of news and then to send a budding booklet. Once, on hearing that a cousin had failed an important test and had not the courage to tell his own mother, Alec Dickson wrote: 'I bet I couldn't keep my mother in the dark about an exam of mine for very long!'

She was expected to be active, not only as a confidante and sympathiser, but also very close to a personal slave; entertaining his friends, keeping him informed of important events in the capital when he was not there and, in respect of the article in the *Spectator* which was an important one for his career, sending copies not only to friends and family, but also to anyone known to them who was at all influential.

In the winter of 1935/36 Alec Dickson decided to add French to his languages. It had become apparent that only the major papers in Fleet Street felt it worthwhile financially to maintain correspondents in the European capitals. The provincial papers relied on Reuters. It would add considerably to his prospects if he spoke two major languages well – he could read and write French, but was tongue-tied when it came to talking.

He started with a course at the British Institute in Paris but did not find it useful. Too many of the other students were British; too many intelligent Frenchmen enjoyed speaking English so he moved on to Geneva. As for speaking French, there were good days and there were also black days when 'I couldn't get myself to speak the confounded language'. He missed the joyous friendship of the Bohemian mountains.

He missed too not being in England when George V died and his parents went to Windsor to see the funeral. So much more was going on in Britain than in sleepy Geneva. A job offer had come from the *Western Mail*. He refused it; probably because he felt it too far from the centre of activities. An agency was anxious to have him on its books but advice from his father was against this. The *Yorkshire Post* had agreed to take him on in February in what seemed to him a rather half-hearted way. His own feeling was that Leeds was not what he had hoped for. He anticipated a dull life there. The last weeks in Switzerland were spent in a hectic round of visiting – including German friends, and ten days at home before he reported to the Editor of the *Yorkshire Post* on February 28th – or, as he put it to his mother, 'as the very last grain of sand allotted to me runs out and I am chained for life'.

CHAPTER 2

Mora

Home and School

Though our roots on both sides were in Glasgow, my family, the Hope Robertsons, had moved out of the city to a small town, Moffat in Dumfriesshire, when I was six months old. My brother Robert was three.

Our mother Mora Sloan, whose first name I inherited, was the eighth child in a family of thirteen and close kin to endless cousins. Her father, a Glasgow businessman who had in his time pioneered The Institute of Chartered Accountants, enjoyed bicycling and skating up Loch Lomond in the Trossachs and on the local pond followed by as many of his seven daughters as were of an age to be physically active.

It was our mother who made the decision to move out of the city. Daddy, Laurence Hope Robertson, had suffered a bad nervous breakdown before they were married for which she blamed both Glasgow and his father's office. After that our father was never in robust health. Our mother was determined to replace the desperate fogs, long lingering winter illnesses, problems and turmoil of her native city with the calm of daily life in a small town, the hills and the rain of the countryside. With us we took Nannie, engaged when I was ten days old. She was to become the mainstay of our family.

Moffat

In Moffat two more sons were born, at home as we all were. Laurence, named after his father – nicknamed Larks because of his cheerful adventurous nature – and Alastair, arriving on my fifth birthday and therefore special.

We were a close happy family, Christian and teetotal, blessed with a multitude of relatives living within easy travelling distance – at one time with eleven unmarried aunts – in two generations.

Ours was very much a masculine family. Our father was gentle, bookish, a good craftsman. The country suited him. Our mother became a pillar of the local community. She had always wanted to be a boy when she was young, envying her own brothers being able to wear trousers. Of a generation hampered by long skirts and corsets, she had nevertheless become a good golfer and skater. Her sons' sporting activities delighted her. They delighted me too. Known as 'Wee Mo' because I carried my mother's name, I became admirer, supporter, helper and long leg fielder in games of cricket in the garden. Always at my brothers' beck and call – or excluded from male games. We lived in a house full of books. I don't remember ever learning to read or being restricted to childrens books and was never sorry to be alone. From a young age I was sure that I was going to be a painter.

The Colvin Fountain, Moffat

We grew up in a conventional way, going to the seaside for summer holidays, family picnics in the hills where the duty of keeping the campfire going was hotly contested between Mummy, Nannie, and the odd accompanying aunt.

Family Christmas parties in Grandfather's house in Glasgow were enormous and for me intimidating, at least until the compulsory solo turn by each grandchild was over. Skinny and timid, with no public talents, I was reduced to an embarrassing rendering of a Highland Sword Dance, though my older brother had been known once to refuse to recite a bloodthirsty highland lament if he were not allowed to wrap himself up in one of the drawing room curtains. For Larks and Alastair when their turn came, the duets on the piano, accompanying invented ribald songs about the younger aunts, were always received with generous acclaim.

Then the first crack in our contentment came. At nine, Robert went to boarding school outside Edinburgh. We, who were younger, loved and admired him, accepting that he could cope with any adventure. It was when the time came for Larks to follow that I felt bereft, suddenly alone with Alastair, who was my baby. He and I were left to bicycle each morning to a village school behind our house, meeting on the way the challenge of a neighbour's bad tempered and aggressive Pekinese.

My father was determined that his only daughter should have the same educational advantages as his sons. He and Mummy began to search the length and breadth of England to find a boarding school that came up to my father's high standards – the only school in Scotland having failed this test. Without sisters, I looked forward to making friends. The family closest to us had four boys and two much older girls, so my brothers were well supplied with 'buddies'. Lacking in self-confidence and very shy, I had few friends of my own age.

After a disheartening search, one afternoon my parents drove up to a school on the coast of Suffolk. My father, who in this decision was the dominant partner, took one look at the grounds and said, 'This is it'.

The reason was the layout; a flat and open campus beside the road, a wide drive without gates led into the grounds. My father's recognition of freedom was vindicated when he discovered that the girls were trusted, if there were two of them, to go down to the nearby town by themselves and not, as in other schools, in a crocodile with a teacher in charge. Of course my parents knew that the school had a good academic reputation but that was not my father's first priority. Just after my thirteenth birthday in April 1931, I went to St Felix.

For me it was not a fortunate name...

As children we had never been further out of Scotland than Carlisle, the English border town which once a month had a renowned market. A flat country was beyond my comprehension. My mother and Nannie, who up to now had made all my dresses (as she knitted all my brothers' jerseys and school stockings), spent many anxious hours discussing the clothes list. Neither of them had any experience of this kind of girls' establishment. It was a summer term and they decided to make all my cotton dresses with long sleeves because of the skinny arms about which I was very self-conscious. My one physical asset was a waterfall of dark hair in two plaits down my back. Daddy was adamant that it should never be cut. A woman's 'crowning glory' he used to call it.

What in rural Scotland would have gone unremarked was immediately conspicuous in the community of the school house to which I was assigned – especially as the shingling era was just coming in. My neighbours in the dormitory longed to chop off my hair. Efforts were also made, not so gently, to persuade me to trim the long sleeves to short, but I was more afraid of the reaction of Mummy and Nannie when they saw me again than I was of my tormentors.

I knew I was no good at sports. This was a school that played cricket. At least fielding out in the grass at long leg was familiar. I would rather have been behind a bush with a book but I had tried that and knew that the school did not approve.

There were refuges. Classrooms were one. I enjoyed learning. In the early days when I was miserable, the middle-aged man who kept the house furnace going would let me sit in his bunker occasionally and talk. Several storeys further up in the school building the Art teacher, Miss Blott, gave me the freedom of the Studio, not because she had any respect for my talent but somewhere she recognised a kindred spirit.

Yet a determination to survive arose. The accent quickly disappeared – never to return. People got used to me and I to them. In the autumn term new girls arrived and I became just one of the crowd. I made two resolutions which later seemed to me very strange. Mora Hope Robertson would play in the First House hockey team and Mora Hope Robertson would one day be Head Girl. By default I managed both. The school gave me self-sufficiency, though not yet self-confidence.

In the bad winter of 1933, unexpectedly, my father died. For every one of us, including Nannie, the family balance changed. At the time probably only Mummie and Nannie realised this. Our mother, a strong, stoical woman in tragedy, was left with a profound grief and the responsibility for three sons; Nannie, because knowing he was dying, my father had begged her to stay on and look after his wife. Preoccupied with school, living a divided life, it took us some time to realise how the scales had shifted.

Nothing in my school experience had changed a determination to go to Art College when my education ended. It never occurred to me that university might be an option; it did not occur to many girls in the 1930s. When our elderly academic Headmistress suggested that Oxford might be a possibility I was astonished – and alarmed – in case I might be deprived of my dream. Besides I knew I was not clever.

The end of my school life, however, gave me one unsought triumph. In my last term I became by seniority Head Girl which meant that I was officially consulted about the gift which a rich parent of three daughters, the last of whom had left the term before, intended to present to the School. Summoned to a meeting with senior staff and the parent, I was told that he wished to give a handsome pair of wrought iron gates. Asked my opinion, I told the story of *my* father and said, 'If the school had had gates I would never have been here'. So he gave a swimming pool instead.

Art College

When I came home from school for the last time, it was to rejoice as I crossed the border into Scotland. I had not then realised that I was not the only one who had changed.

It was a shock to discover that my mother had waited for me to finish school and settle down with her. Sometimes she referred to my painting as a nice 'hobby', a word which aroused in me real anger, especially as one of her own sisters, Aunt Chrissie, had gone to Glasgow College of Art. But Aunt Chrissie had never left home afterwards.

During the months before I went to Edinburgh College of Art a recognised pattern became clear. My brothers would go out – Robert was already at Cambridge, preparing for the Colonial Service, going on holiday with his own friends. But it was taken for granted that I had come back to settle down in the traditional manner. A 'hobby' was a safe way of describing my long-time obsession: with marriage and a family it would take its rightful place.

It was also apparent that the relationship between Nannie and my mother had changed. They shared, as they did with no one else, particular memories of life with Daddy and the growing up of the family. But my father was dead: home no longer the primary focus for the children. There was an uneasiness within the alliance of the two women. Each had their separate mini-establishment in the house. Nannie was waiting for the next generation of babies, meanwhile she accepted stoically the role of housekeeper. My mother took it for granted that Nannie would always be there and valued her, but found it difficult to deal with her in her new role. My arrival home eased the tensions that had grown between them.

I was shocked when my mother said that she was going to rent a house in Edinburgh for the winter months when I started College. I would not need to go into 'digs' and she would be near her two younger sons. It would be easy to go to their school sports and functions. Of course Nannie would come too.

In spite of everything, Art College was a revelation. The common themes, painting, drawing, sculpture, crafts, in an atmosphere where those things were thought important and could be talked about with friends, opened up new horizons. I lived in two different worlds and became good at juggling with them: going back to Mummie and Nannie in the evenings, talking with them of events I sometimes felt I had long left behind, keeping Fridays for cinemas or expeditions with friends, growing in self-confidence because they laughed with me, enjoying jokes and serious discussion. The smell of oil paint enamoured me – it was not something that could be used at home. To be a real practicing painter at last was a dream realised. I was coming to see myself as a portrait painter. Then there were the additional adventures of other mediums to explore and learning to weave as my compulsory craft.

The University had a fencing club. One day their coach asked me if I would be interested in joining. The discovery that long legs, skinny arms and height could be assets instead of disadvantages changed my physical perceptions.

Edinburgh had the first Chinese restaurant in Scotland. For three of us our weekly lunch there introduced us not only to the skill of using chopsticks but to an exciting touch of the Orient so different from our Scottish background.

To have friends with my own interests and opportunities to range far and wide in talks, released unexpected avenues of speculation and questioning. My mother, whom I both loved and feared, was a stoically silent woman when it came to the more profound things of life.

War

I was happy and came to feel at home in Edinburgh but the outside world impinged more and more upon that cheerfulness. My mother had lost a brother in the First War, now three sons must have been constantly in her heart. Perhaps the prospect of Robert going to Tanganyika was not as saddening as it might have been. At least there he would be safe. But for her two youngest, still at school, things were different.

One or two of the male students could be heard talking about war. The constant subject of gas, the weapon experimented with in 1914–1918, hung over us, undiscussed. Wattie, our gardener in Moffat, a veteran of that disastrous conflict, spent resting time in our greenhouse coughing his life away.

George V was dead. He had been on the throne all my life. There was a consciousness of change – and for my generation a feeling that it would be good to have a young King. But there was an uncertainty about the monarchy though publicly there was silence. During the holidays in Moffat we danced, played tennis and tried to look the other way.

When the news broke, it was voices on the wireless that connected us to reality. Stanley Baldwin, heavy and profound with the weight of all the elders of the kirk. By the time Edward VIII came to the microphone to say that he was abandoning his country for love it was too late to have taken his side even if we had wanted to. And there were other things that affected us more closely.

Certainly I had become afraid. We knew now how unready we were, as a country, to face a war. There were whispered conversations in Moffat of digging trenches, or shelters, in gardens. The grocer, it was rumoured, was hiding away extra stores in his cellar for the favoured. Things looked bad. I had a year more at Art College, where Art remained a priority for staff and students, but at night courage deserted me and timidity took its place. When the Munich crisis came, and another voice on the radio told us that there would be 'peace in our time', none of us believed it.

It was a beautiful summer in 1939. We prepared for war – and could not believe it possible. Gas masks were issued and fitted by our policeman, leaving his bicycle at the gate and loitering up the path swinging the cardboard boxes under the laburnum tree as though the visit was of no particular consequence.

In differing ways the village got ready. We watched each other limbering up with fear, amusement or scorn. Some actually dug trenches in unlikely places – it was a relief to air our wisdom though, in truth, we none of us had the least idea where, or how, or even why we should do those things. Men got together and talked of defending their families and homes. We all had an idea that the sky would be filled with German parachutists shortly after war was declared. Many years later my mother told me that she had made lethal arrangements for me if this prospect became a reality. I was mortally offended, even when the necessity was over, that she had not trusted my own courage and ingenuity in escaping an unimaginable fate. Though she may have been right.

On the first Saturday in September our mother took us all to Dumfries where we sat through two full film programmes in two different cinemas while the sun blazed down outside and Nannie at home quietly contrived blackout screens for all the house windows and coped with newly issued ration books. We knew now that war was inescapable.

CHAPTER 3

Alec

The *Yorkshire Post*

Alec Dickson was most fortunate to get the job on the *Yorkshire Post* in February 1936. He had thought that life there, away from the capital, would be placid and pedestrian, and had wondered how he could stand it after the tensions of Prague and the stimulations of upheaval in Central Europe. Until the final moment of commitment he would have jettisoned the opportunity if any offer had come from Fleet Street.

He was quite wrong – and he admitted it.

The *Yorkshire Post* agreed to take him on as a member of the Editorial staff. Almost immediately on arrival the *Yorkshire Post* itself became involved in a number of critical situations.

A few days after his coming, having established himself in the Toc H hostel, become a blood donor and Acting Assistant Scoutmaster with the 13th N.W. Leeds (St Michael's) Troop, Alec Dickson walked into the office to find that a fire had broken out during the night in Bradford, eleven miles away, at the offices of the *Bradford Telegraph and Argus* – a rival paper. Within an hour, Arthur Mann, Editor of the *Yorkshire Post*, had telephoned the *Argus* Editor to say, 'Bring your editorial staff and compositors here; print your paper on our presses until the fire damage is repaired'. Competition between the two papers might be intense but fellow publications must not be allowed to perish. Staff, as they arrived, were instantly alerted, extra room was found in corridors, every facility was shared with ready goodwill and professional cameraderie.

Assistant Scoutmaster Alec

This event, and the unfolding of the next few months, changed Alec Dickson's view of his Editor. Stolid, a man of few spoken words, Arthur Mann on first acquaintance was a grave austere person of whom most of his staff were afraid. But crisis brought out his virtues; absolute honesty, respect for the truth and for his readers, and a dogged perseverance in the face of criticism. His junior member of the editorial staff grew to admire and revere him. After a month Alec Dickson asked the Editor to allow him to run a Scout Troop in Burley, a distinctly poor area. This would have to be in office hours. Who would deputise for him? The boys were working class, mostly in apprenticeships, one only at grammar school and he was regarded as a 'wunderkind'. Reluctantly the Editor agreed, setting a time when his junior editor had to be back in the office. A full hour beyond this, Alec Dickson would rush back to the paper, sweating from a game of British Bulldogs in the Scout hut, and grab his pen to continue the line of thought in his article.

The next crisis was felt nationwide. Coming back to his office one evening from a meal in the canteen, Alec Dickson's eye was caught by the proof of a Leader which had just been set in print. It was entitled 'A Bishop and the King' and took note of a sermon preached by the Bishop of Bradford that day. A few moments later the words were being repeated on the Press Association wire to the *Yorkshire Post* office in London – and were being noticed by every other paper in Britain.

The Editor's Leader began in a style typical of the *Yorkshire Post*'s editorial stance; 'It is fallen to the Bishop of Bradford to express the misgivings of His Majesty's subjects who have been acquainted with affairs of State and with international opinion . . .' In effect the *Yorkshire Post* in the face of months of national press silence, was saying that Edward VIII must go. Arthur Mann was at heart a fervent monarchist; the full title of the *Yorkshire Post* in this era of Conservative government was the *Yorkshire Post* Conservative Newspaper Company. The Editor was putting his own paper's reputation on the line when he grasped the opportunity to break a long held national press silence and inform his readers of the gallivantings of Mrs Simpson with the man assumed to mount the throne in a few months. After deep thinking and anxiety, he had reached the conclusion that such an outcome would bring no good to Britain and the Commonwealth. Since *The Times* on the one hand and the *Daily Mirror* on the other were not prepared to break press silence, then – in the national interest – the *Yorkshire Post* would.

The next morning there was a note from the Editor on Alec's desk. He was instructed to prepare a biography of the Duke of York. Six days later the Duke of York was recognised as the King-to-be.

In his very first job, at the age of 22, Alec Dickson was excited to discover that he had joined a paper whose Editor had the determination to take what he considered was the right side for the *Yorkshire Post* rather than the popular side. For following the Abdication crisis, came the more subtle challenge of Appeasement, with a Prime Minister convinced that the peace of the world depended on Britain reaching agreement with Hitler and Mussolini.

During the time he was in Leeds, Alec Dickson wrote over fifty leading and a number of special articles and was 'at the stone' every night for a year to see the leader page away. Nevertheless, the lure of Fleet Street working as a Foreign Correspondent remained, reignited by mounting alarms in central Europe. In May he applied to the *Daily Telegraph* for a job.

He was accepted – and learned instantly what he had given up. At the *Yorkshire Post* he had been Mr Dickson, a member of the editorial staff, with free entry and a welcome to any room – proof readers, the compositors room, the editorial sanctum. In the *Daily Telegraph* he was Dickson, in an atmosphere felt to be cold and cynical, confined to the reporter's room.

Working on general reporting in the London office until July 1937, he was then sent to the World Scout Jamboree in Holland as a Special Representative of the *Telegraph*. The *Daily Telegraph* had taken an interest in the Scout Movement from the very beginning. It was in their paper that the first reports of the Movement were published. Opened by Queen Wilhelmina, in the presence of the Chief Scout Lord Baden Powell, she addressed 28,000 scouts from 21 nations.

Though the *Telegraph*'s Special Correspondent was bitterly disappointed by the way the paper treated his articles, probably because of the sub-editing, they appeared continuously each day. He had tried to represent the excitement, the colour and warmth. The News Editor had told him to write bearing in mind the *Daily Express* rather than *The Times*. So he did and they cut it down to dry, expressionless sentences. Alec Dickson heard however, through a friend, that the London Office was very pleased with what he had written. Towards the end, the *Telegraph* published a Supplement which was delivered by air and the subject of a great many congratulations – especially from Baden Powell. The Special Correspondent had managed to meet the great man.

Alec Dickson left the Jamboree on August 6th having been told to report to the *Daily Telegraph*'s office in Berlin that evening. The Chief Correspondent was going on holiday and he was to work as Assistant Correspondent to the Deputy until October 1st. He walked into a crisis with the expulsion of *The Times* representative (who had a stroke soon after he got home and died) and an exceptionally virulent campaign against English correspondents in the city. Once again, Alec Dickson was where he most wanted to be – at the hub of European affairs.

Berlin

The first weekend he went on a hike with the Hitler Youth. He did not view this as simply a journalistic opportunity. His attitudes had changed. 'It amused me at Oxford to write as I did then, caustic and satirical, but not now,' he wrote to his mother. 'Sleeping in a barn, bathing in the lake, I thought as I walked. German youth may carry a Bismarck Marshall's baton in his rucksack – but, and no less important, he carries also a Beethoven or a Brahms baton as a musician.'

Before he became overwhelmed with the work of the *Daily Telegraph* Berlin office, Alec visited the Wallich family in Potsdam. They were very nervous, rightly, that he telephoned so much from their house. He did not realise yet the reality of their situation which was to become shockingly clear in the autumn of 1938, after Kristallnacht, when mobs attacked Jews and their property in every city. It was shortly after this that the father walked quietly away from his home and threw himself off a bridge in Dusseldorf into the river.

Alec Dickson also met in Berlin his friend from Oxford and the disastrous visit to the Saar at the time of the plebiscite and they were reconciled. Ulrich was now in the German army doing two years' service. This experience had done for him what all Alec Dickson's arguments could never do. He had had enough of it all.

The young Deputy correspondent and his temporary assistant in the Berlin office of *The Telegraph* were now working very hard. 'I don't think any other office in Europe can have had so much to do as this one,' her son wrote to Anne Dickson with some natural hype. 'First the Nuremburg Conference. That lasted a week and we both had to work day and night: in the evening listening to the speeches on the wireless in German, taking down the important bits, translating them, putting them into decent English and then telephoning them to London.'

Then there was a week long 'blackout' in Berlin and an air raid practice. The *Telegraph* staff wanted to send a story to the London office on how the city looked from the air, whether any lights could be seen. Alec Dickson had been trying to visit a friend and his family in Hamburg so the very next day he flew to Hamburg and then got a night flight back to examine the 'blackout'. He felt uneasily like a spy.

Mussolini's visit, when it came, practically broke a diminished staff, whose job was not just to read the German papers but also to find out what the German press did not print. Alec Dickson went to the stadium on the last day of Mussolini's visit to hear the speeches and see the vast military tattoo. It was breathtaking and sinister. There were a million people there. In the middle it rained cats and dogs and at the same time he was wishing he had been in

Czechoslovakia when President Masayrk died. He regretted missing a first class story.

By nature Alec Dickson was a freelance, not content to be restricted to one employer. He had sent an article on the Jamboree to the *Manchester Guardian*. They accepted it and asked permission to hand it on to the *Glasgow Evening Post*. Now, from Berlin, he was being asked for an article by the *National Review*. But he was also well aware that freelance work was precarious and financially unrewarding.

When the Chief Correspondent came back to the Berlin office, Alec Dickson returned to London and the routine work of a reporter. In February 1938 he was sent again to Berlin to report on the German Motor Show, a job which he found both frustrating and humiliating. In April he was off once more, this time with a friend, to explore the Polish Soviet border. It must have been becoming plain to the *Daily Telegraph* that their junior reporter had other things to occupy him – and his talents – unconnected with their more mundane daily chores.

Czechoslovakia

Having in a rash moment severed his connection with the *Daily Telegraph* Alec Dickson found himself without a job, the *DT* having accepted his notice. It happened to be at a time when it was virtually impossible to get employment as a correspondent. Humiliated by his own naivety and ambition, his despair was all the greater when he reflected on the build-up going on in Central Europe. With Austria now annexed to Germany, Nazi pressure on Czechoslovakia was daily increasing. This was the one area outside Britain of which he had knowledge and about which he cared deeply. Could he manage to represent a Czech newspaper? What he could not do was sit at home and mope.

The decision was made. Alec Dickson would strike out on his own. He sat down and wrote a simple message to a friend, a member of the Wandervogel – another Willi – with whom he had skied in Bohemia. Willi's home happened to be in Brno, the heartland of Czech industry and therefore likely to be the target of Nazi pressure. The message announced that he was coming to spend a few days in the city. He put on shorts, stuffed pyjamas and jersey into a rucksack, bought a 3rd class ticket to Prague at Victoria Station. He would be his own reporter.

In Brno Willi welcomed him. The Czech army was preparing for mobilisation. With Willi as fluent in Czech as he was in German and protected by their youthful appearance, they walked together through towns and villages, past barracks, encampments and improvised defences. They could not have been nearer to the heart of desperate military activity. The talking was left to Willi, for it would have been folly for Alec Dickson to engage troops or local people in conversation.

A moment came when Willi said quietly, 'You must go – at once. The Czech radio thinks the Germans are about to invade'.

Alec Dickson caught the Air France plane, described as the last out of Prague, and on it he began to draft articles. Four provincial papers he had contacted before he left Britain had said they would accept work 'From our Special Correspondent' – the *Birmingham Post*, the *Western Mail*, the *Yorkshire Post* and *Kuryer Codzienny* of Cracow, also the *National Review*. The date was September 28th 1938 and, more significantly than Alec Dickson's Despatches, was the nationwide broadcast by Prime Minister Chamberlain announcing that the Four Powers had met in Munich and agreed upon the secession of the Sudetenland to Nazi Germany. As the Prime Minister observed, 'peace was too important to be endangered by Czechoslovakia, this small country of which we know so little.'

Within hours of Alec Dickson's arrival home, over the telephone, an authoritative voice from Military Intelligence was enquiring about his knowledge of Germany and of his German fluency. He was then asked to report with his passport and a small suitcase at Croydon Airport, destination Prague, role British Observation Officer on behalf of H.M. Government as the German army advanced into the Sudetenland and the Czech army retreated.

The experience was alarming, humiliating and short-lived. Supplied with a Union Jack armlet, Alec Dickson and a companion paid a lot of money to a nervous Czech taxi driver to convey them to where they believed the advancing German troops might be located. They rounded a bend in the road – and there was the German army, in divisional strength, moving towards them.

'What is your business?' barked a staff officer. Alighting from the taxi with as much dignity as they could muster in the circumstances, Alec Dickson asked to be taken to their General. 'Your papers?' Suddenly it was apparent that a rubber stamp placed in their passports at the British Military's Office in Prague that morning was not going to stop an armoured division.

The General to whom they were taken knew of no understanding reached at Munich about British Observation Officers. With icy courtesy they were escorted back to their taxi and a relieved driver sped back to Prague. They were to return by the next plane to London and to keep their mouths shut. The episode was closed.

But not for Alec Dickson. A telegram was handed to him by the British Embassy. It was from Sir Walter Leighton, proprietor of the *New Chronicle*, who was already voicing indignation about the consequences of the Munich

Agreement, the abandonment of the Czechs and the cruelty of the plight facing thousands of refugees. He was raising money for aid to them. Would Alec Dickson help by contacting Miss Doreen Warriner at the Hotel Alcon in Wenceslas Square, Prague.

Doreen Warriner had been Lecturer in the Economics of Agriculture at the School of Slavonic Studies at London University. She reflected all that was admirable in Quaker Action dealing with situations of disaster. She inspired Alec Dickson with a daunting combination of political skill and positive concern. She became a firm friend.

The Czech nation felt betrayed, but in that deeply despondent winter of 1938 those most endangered were the German-speaking Sudetan minority who had not sided with the Nazis but remained staunch democrats.

On his first day under Doreen Warriner's direction Alec Dickson found himself going round some of the refugee camps established for Sudetan German Social Democrats who had had to flee from the territories occupied by Hitler's Army. He was accompanied by the Leader of the Sudetan Social Democrat Party, Wenzel Jaksch, a man surveying total collapse. Alec Dickson stood beside him as he bade farewell to working members of his Party in a dank, disused restaurant in temporary use as a 'camp'. Wenzel Jaksch confessed one hundred per cent defeat: told his audience how he and they could still have gone over to the Henleinists a few months before and thus saved their jobs and their homes. They all agreed that they preferred the physical misery they were now enduring rather than be subject to the Nazis.

Though a Lord Mayor's fund had been raised in London, on the ground in Prague any results were non-existent. The Quakers and Doreen Warriner's group however were working quietly, organising relief often out of their own pockets. It was not physical misery but the mental depression and dejection that was most demoralising. This affected Alec Dickson too: the knowledge that every effort to maintain freedom and democracy in Central Europe had been betrayed, that the bastions were down and everywhere the doctrine of cruelty and force prevailing was devastating.

For a few there was the possibility of getting groups out, with much difficulty and some danger, across the Polish frontier. Twice Alec Dickson escorted such groups into Poland and on to Gdansk, the port on the Baltic where it was arranged for onward travel by ship to Britain. Then the Polish Consulate in Prague refused permission for the next transport of refugees which Alec Dickson was to have accompanied across Poland.

When it was clear that there was no longer a role for him working with the refugee groups, Alec Dickson said 'goodbye' to Wenzel Jaksch and Doreen Warriner and to the Czech Scouts who had befriended him. He reflected on the fact that he had been bequeathed a nature that had enabled him to enjoy friendship and loyalty with young people growing up in such vastly more difficult circumstances than himself. He connected this with the satisfaction that could come from writing articles and having them published, which might alter public opinion or affect the thinking of those in authority. This was a turning point. It seemed that in youth service, in work that brought relief to the anxious and frightened, there was a reciprocal satisfaction – not only in the work but in his own God-given gift of friendship.

Returning to Britain in early 1939, Alec Dickson both wrote and spoke to audiences in England about the situation in Eastern Europe as he had been involved in it, while anticipating, as indeed the whole nation did, the now inevitable war.

CHAPTER 4

Mora

War 1939

Sunday, September 3rd, was a beautiful day. On the wireless the voice of the Prime Minister, Neville Chamberlain, announced that Herr Hitler had been given an ultimatum which was to expire at 11am that morning.

Our church service began at that hour. As we walked down the road, a small aeroplane droned across the sky, a forerunner of things to come. The Minister had provided a wireless. The church clock struck eleven. We all sat in breathless silence. The village siren went off, an unfortunately timed practice. Mr Chamberlain's voice told us that the nation was at war with Germany.

Moffat's war, civilian at that stage, began next day. Evacuee children from one of Glasgow's worst slums, the Gorbals, arrived by train, some with their mothers. Frightened, exhausted, totally adrift without the city streets, two or

A Moffat farm

three hundred staggered under escort, up the High Street from the station to the local school. Round their necks dangled their labels and their cardboard gas mask boxes. They carried small broken suitcases or stuffed brown paper bags.

There had been previous visits from billeting officers and local planning by the WVS. But faced with a multitude of unknown children, many weeping, others in family groups, the older children clutching the little ones, pandemonium on both sides was very near the surface. The WVS had gone round the village knocking on doors , making lists of those who would be willing to take one or two children or more. Rumours were rife. They would have to be disinfected; lice would be everywhere; their mothers kept coal in the bath. The latter showed a total ignorance of living conditions in the Gorbals, where no family owned a bath.

Laurence, with others, provided a ferry service for pregnant or overburdened mums. Alastair, now sixteen, roared about on his new motorcycle delivering messages, seeking news, and reporting to all and sundry how the allocation was going. They were exhilarated by action. I helped to deliver children whose hostesses had not turned up at the collecting point – some of whom banged their front door shut when the reality of their commitment turned up on the doorstep.

As the day wore on, hot, disorganised and harassed workers, surrounded by distraught, often leaking, children – the leftovers, many of whom had become stubbornly belligerent, refusing to be separated from their smaller siblings – the afternoon descended into chaos. Workers went off home exhausted with more abandoned evacuees as their 'guests' than they had ever visualised. We took back to Nannie a family of seven and their mother, resolute in their solidarity.

Then, contrary to all our expectations, the Phoney War spread its insidious effect across the country. Some mothers appeared to reclaim their families, the expected catastrophe of bombing raids over Glasgow not having materialised. The mother of our family went home to look after her man, taking her youngest with her, feeling that she would rather face what disasters were to come with the neighbours in her own home environment. Presently she sent for the rest of the children too.

Laurence left for Cambridge University. After a year there he joined up and found himself eventually in the Army in India. Alastair, still at school, joined the Royal Air Force at 17. I went back to get my Diploma at Art School. Then, with some apprehension of the unknown, I offered my services as an Auxiliary Nurse at a hospital that was overcrowded with Polish soldiers who had been wounded in the calamitous overrunning of their country and, after perilous escapes, had left behind their families and everything they possessed except a gallant spirit which would not admit that they might never go back.

It was I who failed, increasingly discovering a squeamishness that was uncontrollable and led to fainting at even the sight of a simple injection given or blood sample taken.

Summer of 1941 was beautiful. I found myself at home, in a vacuum, while considering the next move. Dunkirk and the Battle of Britain had told us that now we were alone facing the German Army across the Channel and the North Sea. On the wireless another very distinctive voice, that of Winston Churchill, inspired us to believe that alone we might be but not defeated; ready to repel any invasion on every shore or seaside town, from the air, mountain or plain. The village Home Guard who had been left behind, walked over the hills at night, inadequately prepared, anticipating enemy parachutists. We were remote from the realities of Dunkirk and the momentous battles in the air until day by day news began to trickle through of local young men lost or wounded, aeroplanes shot down or ships destroyed.

6 Troop No 2 Commando

One day our doorbell rang and I went to answer it. On the step were two men, an Army Sergeant and a Captain in khaki battledress. The Captain saluted me courteously and asked to speak to my mother. When she came he explained that his was a new unit, 6 Troop No 2 Commando. Their training was intensive. There was no time for spit and polish or ordinary regimental fatigues, so they were to be billeted in private houses. Could we take two?

My mother was hesitant although already she had billeted a Polish Count, Captain of a Cavalry Regiment. Captain Michael Burn, looking around, said he would make sure she had NCOs and he himself would guarantee their behaviour. I said quickly to her, 'Yes. We must take them'.

Still not sure, she asked, 'How long?'

Captain Burn replied, 'Oh about three weeks'.

Later that day, handpicked, Sergeant Bill Wilson and Corporal Peter Harkness, complete with weapons and kit, arrived on our doorstep.

The Commandos had been formed after the cataclysm of Dunkirk with units whose primary purpose was to undertake raids out of embattled Britain – to harass the enemy on mainland Europe. The men recruited were chosen for character, temperament, resourcefulness; trained to think for themselves, every one able to organise if higher ranks were killed. Moffat loved them. The thought of an aggressive future, however minuscule, lifted the community's spirits.

Bill, son of a Glasgow policeman, and Peter from London with a girl in

Chiswick, took possession of my mother's drawing room and her best spare bedroom with a quiet assurance and good manners. Their Captain had picked them specially for this assignment and they were determined not to let him down. They came and went in their own time, we never knew where, though the men of the Home Guard reported strange doings on the hills at night. Bill and Peter were self-sufficient. Sometimes they took their food in the town's canteen; sometimes they asked Nannie if they could have a meal at a certain time, giving her rations. As both sides became acquainted we grew to respect and like each other.

On my side the attachment was stronger. I knew, without proof, that it was for my sake that their Captain had chosen his best to be billeted in our house. Having lived a respectable, sheltered, middle-class life with no special male friends outside my own kin or close family, this Unit, lacking any class distinctions, and especially Bill and Peter, changed my social perceptions and prejudices radically.

The time came when I knew without being told that 6 Troop thought of me as their Captain's girl. I was well aware too that their own confidence in and affection for their Captain (known privately to them as Micky) placed a responsibility on me to be worthy of their regard. As a civilian, Michael Burn from London had been a writer and journalist, not very tall, blue-eyed, hair with a curl, charismatic.

Once a week 'hops' were held in the village hall. Mostly the music was provided by a gramophone. Sometimes a piper from the local band came to play for Scottish reels. Between officers and men no distinction was made, as had been with other Army units. All 6 Troop came – and with my Captain I was there too. For the first time in my life I mixed uninhibitedly with the local boys and giggling girls having a joyful night out from serving in the shops, running the garage, delivering the milk round and otherwise keeping the town ticking over – and found a new freedom, sharing with them my Captain and Tom and Morgan his officers, as he did me with Bill and Peter and the rest of the unit.

The long summer nights in the High Street were dark with blackout restrictions but lit by moon and stars. In intervals, aware of disapproving glances from some of the elderly men enforcing blackout regulations at the door, my Captain and I went out to walk in the balmy air, holding hands. He gave me a confidence that I had never had. I knew that when he took me home my mother would still be awake, noting how long before the car door banged shut, greeting me in her dressing gown with a valid excuse – to her – for being up and awake. She liked Captain Burn, she never questioned or distrusted me, but I knew she was uneasy about the changing times.

Bill Gibson was a dark, dour, quiet Scot. It took time and the knowledge that grew with living in our home before he began to reveal the man underneath – gentle, kindly, brave and warm. He and his father, a widower, were close. Bill was the most trusted man in 6 Troop; once given, his word was never broken or retracted. On his side, Bill felt that his Captain could do no wrong and that no harm would come to any man of his command who kept within the charmed circle of his personality. At the same time Bill was afraid of death and knew that death lay just ahead. He had another great interest, a strange one for a man of his background – music.

Peter Harkness was the opposite. Smaller, golden haired and cheerful with a ready tongue and quick wit, he found life an adventure, lived eagerly in the present and gave generously of his friendship and kindness. At first when they came to squat in our drawing room it was Peter who talked. Bill just grunted. But these two men were devoted friends. Both trusted and relied on their Captain whom they thought of and talked about openly as 'Micky'.

It was their Captain, my Captain, who worried about his responsibility for their deaths. His prayer, 'Let me bring them back unharmed' was one that he knew in his heart to be hopeless. But mostly, though the future lay just beyond the horizon, he did not think about it. He gave all his men a lightness of spirit and a breadth of comradeship that set them apart from the common run of men, because they knew that the ordering of life was no longer in their hands but in the safe keeping of a man they trusted. For me the feeling for my Captain had gone a long way beyond casual affection but I knew that for him his men came first. Perhaps my understanding of this released and enhanced what he gave me back.

But it was not always training. The three weeks extended unnoticed into a month – then two. In the continuing sunshine Bill and Peter sat sometimes in the garden, where we talked and watched Nannie knitting bulky oiled seamans stockings and my mother took over her stint in the village canteen. I painted Bill's portrait, then Peter's. One weekend my Captain's London girl came up to see him and in our garden I also painted hers. I knew then that I had no capability for jealousy. I also knew that 6 Troop No 2 Commando and myself shared something that she never could – a profound mutual understanding born of a short complete experience of life and death.

Then one day we woke and they had gone from the house with no indication of their destination. We all knew that 'Careless talk cost lives'.

Some time later my mother got a letter, signed by both Bill and Peter but clearly written by Peter. Surprisingly, they gave an address – a Youth Hostel in Keswick in the Lake District. It apologised for the long delay in writing. They were all finding life pretty good, climbing, walking and keeping remarkably fit, though very scared of the climbing 'which is on occasion most unpleasant'. Peter had more or less got over his fear of heights. 'But Bill, I am afraid to say, does not appear too keen about it, no head for heights, but carries on with other, just as strenuous, if not as risky, work'.

They had heard from me that Alastair had got embarkation leave. He was to cross the Atlantic on the *Queen Mary* en route to Phoenix, Arizona for training, though we did not know that at the time. They sent him regards and happy landings. The letter ended, 'we are always with you in spirit and wanting to be back with you'. I too had a letter from Bill; 'Dear Mora . . . we have not as yet been very fortunate with our billets but hope to rectify that in the future – one can't expect to find The Lodge (the name of our house) everywhere one goes. Micky told us he wants the whole troop to go back to Moffat for the weekend en masse'.

By this time I was on an airfield in SW Scotland, working in a Church of Scotland Hut for 'Rest and Recreation'; cooking sausages, eggs and chips for healthy young men. I knew now that this was the job for me, having discovered from the experience with 6 Troop that, though food was essential, the young men of the RAF also needed the encouragement, affection, comfort and laughter that I was capable of giving them. This became known among senior management as MHR's 'peculiar talents'. This was not meant as praise.

Shortly after my arrival a young pilot in training, contemporary and namesake of my brother Alastair, was killed trying to avoid a farmhouse during an aerial joyride. The reminders were always there alongside the laughter, jokes, parties, baked beans and the washing up. For twenty-four hours we all mourned. We did not forget. But neither could we afford to alter the daily routine. To live in the present was the only option, and the present could be happy as well as sad.

If he was in the canteen, the prerogative of helping with the washing up belonged always to one airman. He was older than the rest. He hated life in the RAF. When I was transferred he handed me a small book of his poems – he was John Gawsworth. Another group of friends included 'Trot' and 'Algy', married, each with a baby girl. Like Bill they lived with death. But none of this prevented evening sessions in the canteen from being hilarious.

That year Trot did not come back from a raid over Germany and Algy was lost over the Moray Firth.

A month later at the end of March, the news came that No 2 Commando had taken part in an assault on St Nazaire to destroy the submarine pens from which British shipping was being disastrously threatened. Then a dark cloudy picture appeared in a local paper of a small group of British prisoners being marched along the dock at St Nazaire. Among them I recognised Michael Burn, my Captain. I knew then that Bill and Peter were gone and most of 6 Troop with them.

The raid had been a disaster. Most of the Commandos never got ashore.

Bill and Peter died in a hell of burning oil. My Captain's hell was of a different kind, agony for the many he had not been able 'to bring back unharmed'. He spent the next three years in a prisoner of war camp in Eastern Germany. It was only later that I found out its name was Colditz.

By this time I was stationed at Glencorse, the Royal Scots Barracks outside Edinburgh. I walked the hills with a friend, weeping, not for one but for many. Offered leave I could not go home to Moffat.

In June I had a letter from Bill Gibson's father to whom I had sent his son's portrait. He was still clinging to a hope that his son and Peter might yet be alive, though a last letter from Bill, written from the ship that carried them until they were off the French coast, had given him no hope. 'Well Dad dearest, I'll close now. Don't worry and don't be too unhappy, remember what you always told me, to keep my chin up. I'll have done what little chance has made my duty and I can only hope that by laying down my life the generations to come might in some way remember us and also benefit by what we've done'.

Then communication with the Oflag was opened – and a long wait began with only the slender uncertain thread of censored letters to keep hope alive.

I was posted to the Orkney Islands and the Royal Navy. Of course, as with all the others, life had to go on.

CHAPTER 5

Alec

The Phoney War

For Alec Dickson September 3rd 1939 – the Declaration of War – was not the great watershed that it might have previously been supposed to be. The Government was discouraging volunteers. Men were told to wait for the 'call-up'. But for Alec Dickson waiting was always painful. In the earliest days he had joined a Scottish Regiment and been commissioned into the Cameron Highlanders. They had already left for France. He went round knocking on doors – the Foreign Office, Military Intelligence – and came away muttering 'Surtout troop de zele'.

During the months that followed there were minor appointments at the edge of intelligence. Unstretched intellectually, disliking the orthodox Army routines of Aldershot which cast a dark shadow of school, he retreated into thinking – planning memoranda which might spur senior officers into action.

By the summer of 1940 the Germans had conquered seven nations in Europe by political penetration and organised treachery. The formation of the 'Austrian Legion' in the mid-30s had harassed the Dolfuss and Schuschnigg governments and the formation of the Sudeten Freicorps had similarly harassed the Czech government. Britain knew to its cost what it was to face with forces trained only for 'straight' fighting; an enemy which employed guerilla tactics and sabotage for the Boer War and Ireland had provided this experience.

Alec Dickson felt that the British were forgetting their own history. They should have been thinking in terms of a new specialist force, recruited and trained for a particular purpose, the instigation of revolt behind enemy lines and interference with Germany's war effort on the home front. Within the United Kingdom there were now thousands of exiles, Poles, Czechs, Norwegians and many others; men who would gladly take part in the downfall of the Nazi regime. Furthermore, these men would bring expert knowledge of the waterways, the electrical systems, telephone apparatus, railway communications, industrial installations and topographical layout of practically every important town in Central Europe. Instead of suspecting foreigners as being potential saboteurs of our armies' preparations, they should be regarded as possible saboteurs of the German military machine.

One of the determinants behind this thinking may have been the fate of the boy Walter Wallich who, in his first year at Oxford, Alec Dickson had helped to get out of Germany into a school in Britain and was now languishing in an internment camp in the Isle of Man.

Alec Dickson tried to get his memorandum onto the desks of senior officers in the War Office. It sank without trace.

Erasing proper and place names, titling it 'An Army of Pre-occupation', he sent the manuscript to a prestigious political quarterly, 'The Nineteenth Century'. It was published two weeks later. He waited for trouble from Military Intelligence or at least some attention but nothing happened. He yearned for a call to action. That call came in January 1940.

A memorandum from the War Office asked for volunteers who could ski. No actual place names were mentioned but it could only be that help was to be sent to the Finns, then at war with the Russians.

Alec Dickson was not a good skier. He had greatly enjoyed the friendships that had been created with young Czechs and Sudetan Germans during holidays on the magnificent mountains of Bohemia but he was not physically adept. Falls and minor injuries were frequent and a serious accident to a Scout friend had made him conclude that skiing was a dangerous sport. Nevertheless, he volunteered instantly to escape the dreariness of the stagnant war; to ski in a cause so challenging. Hurriedly he found himself sent to Chamonix with a unit that bore the bogus title of the 5th Scots Guards, to train alongside the Chasseurs Alpines.

Senior officers rapidly had to contend with the discovery that a number of scallywags had volunteered who had never seen a mountain. They had put in three days training when the order came to leave at once for Glasgow.

When Alec Dickson saw the funnels of the ship awaiting them there, the SS *Stefan Batori*, not only the flagship of the Polish merchant fleet but bearing the name of Warsaw's No 1 Polytechnic where warm friends of his had been at school, he was consumed by a sense of excitement and drama. No sooner was he on board than a bugle summoned the unit to the ship's officers saloon. Finland had signed an agreement with the Russians that morning. Quartermasters were to see that all the superb skiing outfits were returned to Lillywhites in London's Piccadilly. The Winter War was over. They were to return to their units.

But now the possibility of dealing with a German invading force was real enough. There wasn't a coastal hotel or clutch of clifftop chalets that was not commandeered by troops awaiting the arrival of the enemy. To belong to a fighting regiment, The Queen's Own Cameron Highlanders, was a proud place to be. The NCOs closest to Alec Dickson were fatherly in the extreme lest his inexperience of soldiering should humiliate the platoon.

At night when the codeword 'Cromwell' was flashed, indicating that the enemy had been sighted, the unit stood-to in full battle dress, staring into the night along their little strip of shore in East Yorkshire. Months later it became clear that 'Cromwell' had been a mistake.

In his naivety Alec Dickson had assumed that part of his responsibility was to instil into the men, especially those from the East End of London, a feeling that they were all Cameron Highlanders. On the contrary it was those from Tower Hamlets and Upminster who asked daily when they were going to be issued with kilts. One afternoon Alec Dickson walked into the village and bought a brush and a pot of luminous paint. Very carefully, on the inside wall of each pillbox, he painted the words 'A Cameron ne'er can yield' so that they glowed in the darkness. This led to a demand to learn the regimental song. To his shame, their officer had to admit that he knew only a line or two. His face was saved by the fact that the older NCOs knew no more than he did.

Every piece of equipment was in short supply, every item of uniform precious. When the Colonel, attended by the Battalion Adjutant and Quartermaster, was to inspect the Company on a bitterly cold day, the Company Commander told the Sergeant to 'conceal' a private in Alec Dickson's platoon who had no overcoat, by 'moving' him as soon as the Colonel had 'done' the rank in front so that he would not be seen. For the Company Commander, the object of the inspection was to present an image of perfection to the Colonel. For Alec Dickson, a non-professional, the object was to pinpoint an imperfection which only the Colonel could remedy. Alec Dickson hissed at the private, 'Don't move'. Two seconds later he confronted the Colonel and that evening a truck arrived from battalion HQ and delivered an overcoat. Alec had a bad fifteen minutes with the Company Commander on the theme of loyalty.

These days were to be shortlived. It gradually became clear that there would be no invasion. The whole of the forces now within Britain were in flux. The fear that gripped many young officers was that somehow they might miss the actual experience of warfare. So the War Office did not have much difficulty in getting two hundred of them to join a draft bound for Mombasa, Kenya – among them was Alec Dickson.

The King's African Rifles

Following Mussolini's entry into the war and the Italian invasion of Abyssinia (later Ethiopia), the Italian forces had captured British Somaliland, French Somaliland and threatened Egypt, the Sudan and East Africa. Potentially they had the ability to close the Red Sea and cut the lifeline to India and the East.

To destroy Italy's growing East African Empire, forces were converging in Kenya to meet the threat, from the Sudan, South Africa and the King's African Rifles, recruited from the East Africa territories, Kenya, Uganda, Tanganyika, Nyasaland (Malawi) and Northern Rhodesia (Zambia).

The outward bound draft were told that officers were needed for those African troops. No account was taken of the large white settler population in Kenya which had moved into situations of authority in 1939. From their first landing in Mombasa there was friction between the junior officers of the new British contingent who would be expected to lead Africans into battle almost immediately and were despised by the long-rooted settler higher command who claimed that only they understood the African. Alec Dickson, who took with him (as do all human beings) an individual temperament, had a nature demanding of action and was often hasty in his judgements. He was not to find life easy.

Arriving at last in Mombasa after a long sea voyage, the group continued by train to Nairobi where they were confronted by a breezy group of British officers whose task was to sort them out and assign them to units of East Africa Command. Alec Dickson learnt that he was to be with the 1st Battalion, The King's African Rifles, an elite unit already in action against the Italians.

For weeks on the long idle journey, when he had made an effort to learn Swahili, the lingua franca of East Africa, he had wondered what his first encounter with African troops would be like. Now he was to find out. The Regular Army Major in charge of the company greeted him sardonically: 'So you're here. I'll show you your men'. Thirty-two Askari, clad for battle, stood at attention before him, staring straight ahead. 'You're likely to be going into action in the next 72 hours', remarked the Major, adding no further word of explanation. Their new young officer remained silent but looked more closely than ever at his Askari. From now on his life would be in their hands and to some extent theirs in his. Then the Major delivered his parting shot: 'By the way, none of them speak English!' He turned on his heel. It was not Swahili those troops spoke. It was Chinanja, a language of Nyasaland.

The Major had referred to 'your men'. That was not how the Askari saw it – rather it was this young officer who belonged to them. The Medical Dresser of the company was the only one who spoke English. A mission trained Nyasa, intelligent and skilled, Philip was pleased when 2nd Lieutenant Dickson asked him if he would be willing to answer questions in Chinanja for an hour each evening. It was agreed. Alec Dickson began to acquire a good simple vocabulary, to be able to surprise and delight his platoon with the occasional colloquialism. He also acquired his first African friend.

Even before Italy had entered the war, this battalion, the 1/1 KAR, had been constantly in the forefront, enduring exacting conditions, fighting not only Italian troops but wild Abyssinian irregulars. Unfortunately, the very day the fresh platoon reached 1/1 Battalion it was withdrawn from the line and went to what Alec Dickson considered the most devastating of military time-filling occupations – garrison duty in Italian Somaliland.

The time that followed, spent guarding a large estate with a friendly Italian community, was not what Alec Dickson had come to Africa for. Indeed they found themselves not in any way guarding the Italians from escaping but from raids by predatory Somalis. Not being a professional soldier, neither a drinker nor a gambler, he did not fit in to the life of a colonial army mess – nor indeed did he try. He concentrated on his men and on acquiring their languages, enlarging his understanding of their background and their customs. This was not an occupation approved of by his brother officers.

He found the troops simple minded, warm hearted and loyal. Their training, based on that of the British soldier, was short and ludicrously inadequate. They often failed to grasp what the 'Bwana' wanted done and had a total lack of personal interest in the campaign. Their own tradition of tribal fighting, 'bush' sense, and their particular capabilities were totally ignored. This knowledge, gradually accumulated, was to prove valuable in the months to come.

Meanwhile, 2nd Lieutenant Dickson spent time and energy trying to get himself transferred to active service anywhere. A Mediterranean North African Front was stirring and he heard a rumour that his regiment, the Queen's Own Cameron Highlanders, would be there. Intelligence beckoned. He wrote urgent letters to anyone he knew who had influence – the War Office, Commanding Officers, influential civilians – many of which never arrived and many that did were often of no help to his reputation.

It then became clear that the Battalion was concentrating for further action. Orders came that the battle for which they were intended was the Battle of the Omo which would open the road to Gimma, the last big Abyssinian town held by Italian forces. In fact it turned out to be the final large scale action of the campaign.

For Alec Dickson it was a completely satisfying encounter. The territory was a tremendous gorge, with mountains rising 2–3000 feet on either side of a raging torrent with a great blown-up viaduct bridge. A serpentine road wound down and then up. The KAR were on one side of this immense chasm with the enemy on the other. The object was to cross this roaring river – under fire or not – then to scale the opposite side and capture the town.

A zigzag descent to the river under enemy fire when least expected; a twilight crossing on a temporary rope bridge supplied by the engineers; a long upward march in silence; the enormous cliffs scaled to the top of the plateau to face machine gun fire, Lieutenant Dickson gave the Nyasa tribal war cry 'Sokole'. The Askaris, forgetting everything they were ever taught, began to fire wildly in all directions. The company charged across the plain. Out from beneath a clump of trees leapt an Italian battery gun crew, hands above their heads. The platoon dashed round the corner to find a battery commander with all his staff and a white flag.

At that moment an aeroplane swooped down, apparently to machine gun the KAR. The troops scrambled into the bushes trying to display their identity sign. At the fourth swoop a message was dropped. No apology but directions to where the enemy now were: 'Hurry and good luck'.

Returning in the evening with no KAR casualties, ten lorries, 80 prisoners and piles of ammunition ended a satisfactory day though in the mess there was much amusement at the enemy's lack of heart for battle, and not just because they were locked into E. Africa without hope of reinforcements. Around Italian lines, particularly after dark, crept the Shifta, guerilla fighters who saw themselves as patriots. Wild long-haired men, their bodies festooned with ammunition and a smile that frightened even the British, to fall into the hands of the Shifta meant for Italian officers and NCOs death by mutilation. Small wonder they preferred to surrender.

This was the biggest action the battalion had been in and the final one of the campaign. With a large number of Italian prisoners and no officer on the British side speaking that language (or feeling inclined to try out their French), Alec Dickson suddenly found himself in demand as an interpreter, a role that he welcomed as it brought him into contact with interesting senior officers on both sides. On one occasion it transpired that the Italians had surrendered owing to an extreme shortage of food. However, after the official surrender and the replacing of the Italian flag with the Union Jack, the official party was invited to lunch with the Italian General. Profound apologies were offered for the food and wine. 'The best I've tasted since leaving Nairobi', Alec Dickson wrote to his mother.

After the ceremonial surrender truck after truck drove the Italians hundreds of miles to remote POW camps in Kenya. Alec Dickson's unit began to disintegrate. He was recalled to Nairobi. His platoon bade him goodbye. Now, as he reflected on their staunchness and kindness, the recognition grew that he and those young Africans had grown to like each other and that this was going to be important for his contentment of mind during the next few years. 'Pitani Bwino' ('Go well',) said his orderly, clasping his hand. 'Ambuye Akale noi' ('May God be with you'.)

Recalled to Nairobi in August 1941, having received automatic promotion to full Lieutenant, with little idea of what might await him but aware that because he had some knowledge of an African language there was no possibility of transfer to any other theatre of war, he was both excited and apprehensive about the next step. It was to work in the Kenya Information Office – 'lent' he was told by Intelligence, to whom he had been transferred on arrival in the capital.

Then three incidents occurred – the first disagreeable, the second frightening, the third, fortunately, of a different nature.

He was suddenly instructed to appear at a Court Martial where the accused was a young British officer whom he had got to know, months before, at Aldershot and who had asked for Lieutenant Dickson to act as Prisoner's Friend. From the beginning, Alec Dickson believed that the Court Martial was prejudiced and his evidence in favour of the prisoner totally discounted, to his great distress the prisoner was found guilty, dismissed the Forces and sentenced to imprisonment in a Nairobi goal.

Three weeks later on October 1st, when Alec Dickson was sitting in the public room of the Kenya Information Office, the door was flung open and the officer in charge of the Base Depot announced that he was under arrest. As he was driven away he asked what the charge was. No answer was forthcoming then but in the next few hours he was given to understand that the order for the arrest came, in a ciphered message, from the War Office. He was detained under close guard, growing increasingly alarmed, remembering the hostile questions that had been directed at him during his friend's Court Martial three weeks before – especially in regard to his experience of Central Europe.

After 48 hours he put in a written protest, pointing out that his being held for more than 24 hours without a charge was against military law and King's Regulations. He began to make a list of everyone he had known in Germany, Austria, Poland and Czechoslovakia.

After five days imprisonment he was marched before the Depot Commander and told curtly that there was no charge. Humiliated and enraged, he demanded a Court of Enquiry to clear his name. After three weeks he got a copy of an unsigned minute saying that it was regretted that Lt Dickson had been arrested owing to a mistake in the deciphering of a telegram from London and in consequence a cipher clerk was on a charge for negligence. Alec Dickson was never to know what lay behind this brouhaha. For an incident which could have had disastrous effects on his reputation and career no apology was ever received.

A few weeks later Alec Dickson was called to the Military Postings Office. Not unnaturally he went with mixed feelings. What was to happen to him now?

'Have you a camera?' was the first question. This could have been a trick because on active service it was forbidden to possess photographic equipment. However the next remark was, 'I do hope you have.' It seemed best to him to admit that he had a Zeiss camera purchased in Nairobi from a shop trading in goods bought off Italian prisoners of war.

The interrogator was a retired Provincial Commissioner from Tanganyika, now serving as a Liaison Officer with East African forces. In Tanganyika there had been little response to recruiting appeals from certain tribes. It was now seen to be important to spread among the rural people some understanding of what war meant. The suggestion was that, with the aid of Lt Dickson's camera, a record might be made of what happened to young men from the villages who became soldiers. It was an idea after Alec Dickson's own heart.

Two days later he and the Liaison Officer left Nairobi for Arusha in Tanganyika. With them in the truck was a young soldier, Kisarishu, belonging to the Warusha, a branch of the Masai.

At lunch with the Senior District Commissioner they told the reason for their journey – that Lt Dickson intended to tell the story of Kisarishu from the day he left his village and became a recruit in the KAR.

'Where is he now'? asked the SDC.

'He's gone to visit his family'.

'You've let him go? And you think you're going to see him after lunch?'

The DC laughed harshly. 'When I think of the trouble we went to three months ago to round up these youths for the Army. You'll never see him again!' The Liaison Officer fell silent. Alec Dickson envisaged the angry laughter that would greet him when reporting back to Army HQ that they had lost their man.

The evening before, when they had left Kisarishu outside his family home, he had been attentive to instructions. He was to report beside the big tree in front of the District Office wearing what he would have done when he was a civilian villager. At the time arranged, Alec Dickson stood alone beside the tree, his heart sinking. Suddenly a soft voice said 'Effendi' ('Sir'.)

There he stood, his body oiled to copper colour, earrings, a 6ft spear in one hand and oxhide shield in the other. Shorn of his pigtail by the Army, yet here was a 'moran', a warrior.

'The Story of Kisarishu', booklet and posters published in English and Swahili, fulfilled the expectations of the Government of Tanganyika and were ultimately published by the Ministry of Information. The photography had been to represent Sergeant Kisarishu as a figure of nobility, of loyalty, deserving of admiration. The photographer had indeed seen him as he was depicted. At the end of those few weeks Alec Dickson did not return to his depot. An idea was taking shape in his mind: he saw a role for this man, of more importance, in another setting.

The momentary sense of triumph aroused by the successful campaign against the Italians had now given way to alarm and foreboding. The Japanese had entered the war and were carrying all before them: Pearl Harbour, Dutch East Indies, Hong Kong, Singapore, Malay, Burma. Suppose a Japanese fleet veered across the Indian Ocean making for Mombasa which, at that very moment, accommodated two British fleets? The military/strategic implications of such a possibility seemed real. What would be the impact on African public opinion? Did they at all conceive what the war was about or what defeat could mean? Had we, the British, formed any ideas of what the civil population's role might be?

Alec Dickson put his thoughts down in a memorandum. 'The Story of Kisarishu' had brought home to him the limitations of the written word – of posters too – in a country overwhelmingly rural and predominately illiterate. A human impact was needed, and that could only come through seeing and hearing. The 'doing' could only be done by Askaris.

He sent his memorandum through the Head of Intelligence to the Commander-in-Chief. Lieutenants are not expected to correspond with Generals but in fact there was a reply, 'If Dickson thinks he can do it, let him try'.

CHAPTER 6

Mora

War 1942–43

Orkney

Orkney was different from the rest of Scotland – that is once the frightening journey across the Pentland Firth was over. Notoriously rough, with the meeting of northern currents from two seas disputing the passage round the tip of the Scottish mainland, it could also be the secret seaway of enemy submarines.

The posting was to the Church of Scotland Hut on Flotta, a tiny isle within the enclosed stretch of sea called Scapa Flow, bordered to the north by the largest island of the group known to Orcadians (confusingly to outsiders) as the Mainland.

The Flow had been thought to be an invulnerable shelter for big naval ships, until in 1939, not long after the war began, a U-boat penetrated one of the narrow open passageways by stealth and torpedoed and sank a battleship, the *Royal Oak*, lying unwarned and relaxed at anchor offshore. The submarine then stole away as it had come. Caught unawares, there were over a thousand men on board. Suddenly confronted with the realities of war the whole of Britain was thunderstruck. A Scapa hiding place, thought impregnable, was revealed as badly flawed. Confidence evaporated. Alarm generated a belated alertness.

Flotta, like the rest of the Orkneys was treeless. Our R&R Hut for crews off battleships and cruisers stood above the shore facing the Flow. Near us was also an enormous NAAFI (Naval Army Air Force Institute) catering for food and recreation – host at intervals to visiting dignitaries and famous entertainers. We did not suffer from the rivalry, indeed in every way they were on a different scale. But as well as the basics, we provided friendship, quiet if needed, an atmosphere not too far from the informality of home, to the men who came ashore in their leave boats after midday.

They were the sailors – disciplined in work hours – toiling in the bowels of the ship or on dangerous decks where routine took the place of thought. But in hours of leisure, substitutes to engage the mind were few; musings about things left behind and boredom took their place. On land, still castaways, but often with less to do, were the anti-aircraft gun crews, those who tended the barrage balloons and the elite technologists, the signallers. In each of those groups there were men who had skills, the fortunate ones; the sailor whose hands were dextrous in carving driftwood, as traditionally they might have carved bone, or could mend or sew or weave with string or rope. Some in all sections were sustained by music, or writing, or keeping a diary.

We who staffed the Hut were three, all women. Elizabeth, a sculptor who managed the office and kept in her apron pocket a small block of wood and a knife for carving, with which she brought alive exquisite little animals; Phil, a widow whose husband had been shattered at Dunkirk and died later; myself, with a heart in an Oflag in Germany.

For us Flotta was as much an enclosed community as was each ship for its crew. Kirkwall, the capital on the mainland, was not easily accessible. I have no memory of visiting it until the war was long over. Occasionally we went to Stromness, a little town on the north shore of the Flow to which a regular ferry ran. But somehow life for us remained on Flotta and I soon came back.

We lived and worked and slept in the Hut. For all of us, staff and customers, the kitchen resounded with laughter and cheerful conversation. Isolated, we created our own world, looking towards the needs of our sailors, simple or complex, and putting on hold our own deepest concerns. Only at night, each in our narrow room, did we meet memories and sorrows.

From the moment we woke and stirred up the sleeping stove, until exhausted we went to bed, the big naval ships were in sight. Swinging gently to anchor on calm days, rotating with wind and waves when storms lashed across the unprotected land, the clanging of bells and other domestic noises vibrated now and then across the air. We used to make jokes with their crews that the battleships never went to sea. Were they too precious ever to venture out of the safe haven of Scapa or had the disaster of the sinking of the *Royal Oak* made the Admiralty decide to keep them penned up, used only as a threat? Yet we knew, as everybody knew, that one of the vital jobs of cruisers and destroyers was to safeguard the convoys to Murmansk on the Barents Sea, a work of great danger undertaken with the knowledge that any man overboard, for whatever reason, would survive only a second or two in those icy seas.

We rarely saw the ships leave to act as shepherds to the merchantmen – or return. Some mornings they were no longer at anchor, another dawn they were back and the men who had been missing for a time were knocking on the counter for extra sandwiches and indulging in riotous jokes about the things we had changed when they were not there to be consulted. But where they had been they never told us – and we never asked. Nor did we seek to know if any friends had not come back.

One day, however, while the months slid slowly by, everything changed. We woke to find that the largest battleship, *King George V*, the centrepiece of our view, had gone. The weather was appalling, howling wind and drenching rain. At first we thought the ship was only invisible within the grey curtain of water. Then, as it paled and lifted, we saw her anchorage was empty.

A few days later we woke to music. Bands were playing on land and sea, sirens screaming, ships decks lined for a salute. The rain still streamed down, but as we strained our eyes, steaming slowly through the mist, dressed overall, crew lining every deck the *King George V* became visible. Through the crowds on shore the news ran like wildfire: 'the *Scharnhorst* is sunk', 'the *Scharnhorst* is sunk'. It was one of the few naval triumphs in those days and there was something to celebrate that evening in the canteen.

Flotta and the rest of the Orkneys had for me a visual seduction it was hard to resist. Enormous skies bestrode the land, giving to 'weather' a magnificence that I had never known. Colours of fleeting subtlety or dark brilliance lit the landscape. Even in a summer season the wind seemed always there, driving the huge cumulus clouds across the skies, racing the golden grasses on the treeless land, crossing or fretting the imprisoned sea. I had forgotten painting; when moved I now wrote poetry.

In the long daylight season, when newspapers could be read till midnight and in peacetime golf balls still be seen, dawns and sunsets were spectacular. When daylight shortened, the winds tortured the heavens black with thunder and riven by flashing lightning. In that season the *aurora borealis* performed splendidly.

All around us stretched the sea, promising only infinity; impersonal, indifferent to all our lives, our loves and fears, limiting each one of us to tiny, unremembered mites of land or on ships whose size meant nothing when the ocean fully revealed its immensity.

If at times we felt this, how much more did the sailors, for whom the sea held active terrors and deathly threats, feel? Routine did little to keep away the thoughts of home, the children growing up without their fathers, babies never seen and maybe unidentified, girls waiting or straying, friends in situations unknown with whom censorship and near illiteracy made communication virtually impossible. But the mail did arrive, not always frequently and not always with the expected letter. I had two men to support, one in an Oflag where increasingly what could be said grew more restricted on both sides, and my brother, isolated in the remote Rufigi Delta of Tanganyika, knowing that until the war ended, and perhaps not even then, he would not see us again.

I was happy and fulfilled in my work. I knew myself to be good at what I was doing and that it was both needed and valued. When the mail arrived, sent on by my mother, frequently my conscience was stirred by a whisper of betrayal. Ours was not a routine job. Every day there was essential work; cleaning, washing, preparing, setting out any programme for the day – maybe a gramophone concert in the quiet room, a service to be prepared, hoping for entries to the baby photograph competition or a quiz. There were bakeries or stores to be ordered from the mainland and received when delivered. In free hours walking about the island, perhaps with a friend from one of the land based batteries if the sun shone, going to a NAAFI concert or simply catching up on needed sleep if rain and wind battered roofs and windows. Each day unexpected incidents arose; a quarrel to be adjudicated, an accident to be plastered from the First Aid box, listening to urgent news, talking because human contact was what was needed, accepting help in washing dishes, quietly receiving confidences and knowing the trust that went with them.

The sculptor left us and was replaced, adjustments made, practical work rearranged. Friendships took longer and were not always possible but compromise was vital. Our community was too small and interdependent to survive without it. I took charge.

Then, without warning, HQ sent us an unexpected cuckoo in our nest. Until now we had been an entirely female staff. The newcomer was a young man, not long out of his training to be a minister. Maybe those in authority thought that a period serving in limbo would widen his experience. He was not an adventurous young man but from the beginning, he took it for granted that he was in charge while we worked. Naive and inexperienced, he sat by the stove, drank coffee, added up the accounts and, we suspected, when he was not visible, made contact with the Officers Mess. For us, conscious that we had been downgraded, compromise disappeared into the Orkney mist. As a unit we were against him, perhaps it was no wonder he sought the Officers Mess. He was not naturally gregarious. Our customers had enough men in their lives to take our side once they saw that all was not well.

There were no feminists then but for nearly a year we young women had been trusted and had run a successful business. We knew we were appreciated. The occasional letter from senior command when a ship left the Flow confirmed that. Had we been sent a young man who knew he was junior to us, ready to accept menial chores, he would have been welcomed. But this young man had no such idea. We gave him time – a month or so. Then I wrote to the top of the Church of Scotland Huts and Canteens in Edinburgh and made plain the damage that was being done to the whole atmosphere of our work by the new recruit, indicating that we would be grateful for his removal.

Some weeks later he was posted elsewhere. Whether it was his short stay that unsettled me, or that the remoteness of Orkney began to take its toll, when a letter from a friend suggested that I should join her with the YMCA Women's Auxiliary, which would give an opportunity of serving overseas if ever the invasion of Europe should take place, I answered 'Yes'.

The interview in Edinburgh before the changeover was cool. I was surprised to find that the Huts and Canteens were not sorry that I should take my 'peculiar talents elsewhere'!

YMCA Shandon 1944

The YMCA at Shandon on the upper Firth of Clyde was very different from Flotta in the Orkneys. Once a large Victorian private house, it was now a Hostel, mainly for sailors, beside the road above a bend of the river which curved round towards the City of Glasgow with its industries and shipyards – the target of enemy bombers. Beyond Shandon, hidden in the hills, lay the forbidden area of Gareloch, secret enough to camouflage what rested there and deep enough to shelter the biggest Naval ships in need of vital repairs.

On the road a mile or two below the YMCA was the small town of Helensburgh, landfall for crews on leave, however short. Helensburgh might not have much to relieve boredom but it had alcohol, and girls, both local and ATS, and modest dances and entertainments.

Buses ran to and from the limits of the forbidden area but their times were strict and early in the evening. There were often reasons why they could not be caught and walking was the only solution. Most of those who were the worse for drink knew that the YMCA had a regulation not to take them in if they were in that state. For me those late night incidents, when after a month or two I inherited the job of senior management, were a matter of concern. But on a cold, wet winter night with the only alternative the roadside ditch I never had the heart to refuse entry, even if all there was to offer was the kitchen floor. The sailors kept silent about those infringements of the rules but of course they became known. On the long summer evenings it was a different matter. At least the ditches were dry. Then I used my 'Nannie' act and sent them on their way with a good talking to.

In essence these were the same young men who had come ashore to enjoy our modest resources on Flotta but in reality the situation at Shandon was very dissimilar. Scapa Flow, for all its boredom and inaction, was a station always in readiness for potential activity. The seas surrounding those ships had been very dangerous ones even though the Flow itself was quiet. Routine jobs had to be immaculately performed. Life or death might depend on them the moment an alarm sounded.

In the hidden recesses of the Clyde lochs there were only crippled ships, resting and repairing after action. The men who worked on them were those with dockyard skills. Their crews felt their own routine jobs had little reality until once again they went to sea. Most of the sailors would have liked to go home until their ships were ready, especially the Glasgow ones, but this was wartime and unless it was compassionate, there were few extended leaves.

So we saw many more men, hard and cynical on the surface, restless after a long war of strain and family uncertainty, of concealed sorrows and broken hopes, seeking solace in alcohol which had not so easily been available on Flotta. Reminded constantly that they were back in Britain but might be idle for many months yet, in general they were the same ships' crews that I had known before; men who had appreciated then what we could give them and responded to it. I believed they would do so again.

For the first time since 1942 I went back to drawing. Each sleeping room in the Hostel (for four, five or six) was decorated over the mantelpiece with a silhouette of a different type of ship. It made a connection between the house and its customers. Sometimes one would demand a bed in a room with a particular illustration of a ship he knew. Most did not care, but they liked the silhouettes. It gave the rooms, in a house which had not been lived in for some time and whose walls had suffered from damp or flaking paint, a certain character.

The canteen side of the YMCA had a rota of respectable local ladies, not all of whom found the sailors they served with sandwiches or variations of eggs and baked beans, acceptable. Without those valiant volunteers we should have been hard-pressed to keep the catering side going.

The house was old and grey, unobtrusive. In the blackout at night some men were hard put to to find it but on short winter afternoons or long summer evenings our drive was filled with sailors, baggy trousers flapping in the breeze, hard round hats stuck on at every angle on fair, dark, red hair or on heads going bald.

The heart of the house was the high-ceilinged, old-fashioned kitchen with always a welcoming fire burning in the open grate. The centrepiece of this battered, comfortable room was an enormous Victorian black horsehair sofa, saved from a salvage dump and put in the place of honour before the flames. Relays of tired sailors had worn it threadbare. The two back legs had long since lost their castors due to the exuberance of one ship's company. There would be mugs piled on the wooden table and plenty of milk and sugar, in spite of rationing, stood ready. There were always steaming pots of tea and a tin of hot rolls. This was the haven from the world outside, where the men forgot they were numbers of no account and resumed their own identities and personalities. The kitchen lost its drabness and became alive with laughter and stories.

It was in the late evenings, when the house was quiet and most of our customers had gone to bed, that inarticulate confidences were approached. Jim of the long bony arms which he used to illustrate his difficulty in talking. One night, after an absence, he returned from compassionate leave to his home in London. His parent's house had been blasted by a bomb. His mum and dad were living in a shelter because his mum, aged 76, had refused to leave the site of her own home. When another bomb had fallen quite near, Jim had spent a long and horrible night delving in rubble, helping to extricate survivors, fighting flames, calming shocked nerves, then staggering back in the dawn to reassure mum and dad.

Then there was Joe, very young, who burst through the door one day accompanied by two more hardened friends. 'Tell her Joe,' they urged, 'Tell her, man!' Trying to disguise his pride and tenderness, Joe burst out, 'I'm to be an Uncle. It's the first you know'. His face shone, his friends, already uncles, did not treat it as a joke. Joe asked me anxiously, 'You an Aunt, Miss?' I shook my head. All three sighed deeply. 'I thought you'd give me lessons' Joe said, 'I've never been an Uncle before.' 'He'll make a fine Uncle, Joe will' said one friend, seriously, consolingly; 'He's started a Pluto already.'

Plutos were toy dogs made of wood and beautifully finished. In the long hours on board many strange and wonderful things were created by our sailors. Mats and rugs, toys, furniture, slippers, pictures, anything that could be manufactured out of little or nearly nothing. Material was scarce and dear but the difficulty of supplies never stopped any of our men. There was a craze for rugs. The rumour had it that a Welshman had unravelled his winter woollies, his long legged combinations and his thickest vests to make the father and mother of all rugs. Before the summer vanished and the Welshman could regret his pillaging, he was drafted to warmer climes leaving his rugs as a memento to his weeping wife.

An epidemic broke out on one ship, like measles, claiming victim after victim; sailors creeping along the decks, scissors in hand, ready to snip an inch off any material that afforded the possibility of adding to a rug. It was said that Jock had his blanket reduced to half its size. Pete had lost a seaboot stocking. The time came when the younger members of the crew feared even to lose their luxuriant hair. Some were said to sleep in their hammocks tied up like uncomfortable cocoons. Then the frenzy passed: rugs went out of fashion.

Sailors were the most conservative of men, never more so than where their amusements were concerned. For the great majority there were only two – beer or a girl. They never went together. The girls came to know well the drinkers and the dancers and what was to be expected from them. There was also a third section, quiet, secretive men who came and went, leaving little impression of their personalities. These were frequenters of the Dogs – we saw them only once a week, on a Saturday night. They were always polite; trooping in cold and silent off the late train. They would blow on chilled fingers and sit down by the fire with tea or coffee and a bun but they kept their secrets to themselves.

Once we had a bigamous wedding reception in the Hostel though we did not know it at the time. He was a cheerful man from Somerset with a good singing voice. In the two days leave he got before the wedding, his songs reverberated round the YMCA. He had arrived with all his worldly goods in a small battered suitcase and a haversack, supported by a grinning best man and two lesser friends. His rosy face was full of contentment. We knew his bride, a pleasant ATS girl stationed in Helensburgh. We were happy for the bridegroom and sympathetic. We knew he had been married before but his wife and baby daughter were dead, killed in some horrible accident which, naturally, he rarely talked about.

In spite of wartime restrictions we made a cake, iced and decorated with white heather and tartan ribbons. All the best pieces of china were collected together and the table polished till it shone.

The bridegroom emerged resplendent, the picture of self-satisfaction, the baggiest of baggy trousers, the roundest of round sailor hats crammed well down over his eyes. The bride had three friends, chattering and giggling. The little convoy came up the aisle unannounced. The bride put a hand on the bridegroom's arm. The white haired old minister spoke softly and quickly, anxious to be finished, and the whole group streamed out into the secular joy of sunshine. Someone had provided confetti. They walked up the drive to the YMCA in triumph. The bride was radiant now, the reception a complete success. Then they climbed into a car outside the door with a babel of good wishes and friendly greetings following them. They were gone.

It was months before Bob told us one evening that Charlie had been picked up by the 'civvy' police as he was coming off the ship to have some leave. 'Whatever for?' I asked. 'Bigamy', Bob said, 'Trigamy really'. 'Why didn't you say a word to us?' 'Oh well, you don't like to spoil a pal's fun' was the reply.

For me it was a shock, a disillusion that I took some time to recover from – thinking of the abandoned bride and wondering what I would have done if I had known.

One day, however, we had a tremendous surprise. I received a letter from the Captain of HMS *Nelson*, one of the ships that had been three months having a refit. The letter was one of warm thanks for all that the YMCA had done for her crew during that time. It contained a cheque for £100. Later that morning HMS *Nelson* steamed past our windows making for the open sea. Her crew stood lining her deck cheering and waving their hats.

Moved and delighted I wrote to Headquarters telling them about the cheque, saying I was thinking of spending it on one or two new wireless sets, perhaps even a gramophone. Two days later there came a reply. The cheque was to be sent at once to HQ. It was for them to make decisions about spending it. None of it ever came the way of Shandon YMCA which was where the Captain of the *Nelson* and myself expected it to go.

Once again we saw an unexpected sight being escorted down the river. This time it was not a ship. A square iron platform with what might have been large upturned metal legs at each corner, it bore no resemblance to anything we had ever seen. Only after the Normandy landings in June did we realise that it must have been a section of the specially constructed Mulberry Harbour on which so much depended.

Meanwhile, my personal life was changing. The intervals between the letters to or from Colditz had begun to stretch out. I was aware and guilt stricken about my inability to retain the reality of my feelings for my Commando Captain; for him too the magnetism had gone. I had a sailor of my own now – not a replacement but he filled the gap which, until I met him, I had not realised existed.

Then a week or two after D-Day, the invasion of the French coast, I heard from my mother that Alastair had been on leave. He had been among the RAF supporting formations and had described the astonishing sights as the troops disembarked from their landing crafts. A month later my mother telephoned one morning and asked me to meet her in Glasgow. There she told me a telegram had arrived at breakfast time to say that Alastair's plane had not come back from a raid over northern Europe. He and his crew were missing. Alastair was the pilot of the Halifax. It was not long after his 21st birthday. On April 20th 1923, my fifth birthday, he had been my present from my Mum and special ever since.

My mother wanted me to go home to Moffat with her for a short time. I was given leave but I could not do it. It was another betrayal. I needed to stay at work, to be within the community of Shandon where, somehow, such things were understood and I knew that my men would treat me with a warmth and sympathy with which many would not have credited them.

Mother had once told me that some of her relatives felt that it was not right that any young girl should be in my position, dealing with all those men. It had angered me. I was twenty-six. The two prevailing attitudes were that an endless series of flirtations must take place and that it was no job for me. Anyone could give out cups of tea. Of course cups of tea were important. But flirtations were non-existant and the job itself intangible. In this time of sorrow it was my sailors who comforted me.

CHAPTER 7

Alec

East Africa Command

'If Dickson thinks he can do it, let him try' was GC-in-C General Sir William Platt's message to Alec Dickson's superior officer. So Captain Dickson, whose promotion had after all not been affected by his mysterious imprisonment, began immediately to set up the Mobile Propaganda Unit, East Africa Command. One of his first recruits was Sergeant Kisarishu, a Masai from the Arusha area.

In July 1942 the Unit left Nairobi for Tanganyika (Tanzania). In the beginning it was only the hard necessity of providing recruits for the East Africa Command that had influenced HQ's decision to go ahead with the Dickson suggestion.

It was a small Unit that set out for this initial tour; a dozen Askari, three white men, one of them the South African cinema operator. Among the Askari, different Army backgrounds and language groups were represented, each man selected individually: a Northern Rhodesia (Zambia) candidate for the priesthood, the son of an Ngoni Chief, a houseboy from Limbe (promoted corporal for gallantry in the field in Madagascar), the twelve-year-old bugler Gabriel, a Musoga from Uganda, whose moment of glory was at the peak of a nine-man PT pyramid, Sgt Nyasulu, a magnificent singer of Zulu songs from Nyasaland (Malawi) and Ramazan Hasan, ex-Petty Officer from the Tanganyika Naval Volunteer Force at Dar-es-Salaam, who had perhaps the most difficult job, explaining the function of the Royal Navy to audiences who had never seen the sea.

By the time the MPU returned to Nairobi they had travelled little short of 4,000 miles and audiences were to be counted in hundreds of thousands. On the two following tours the Unit was expanded to twenty-four Askari and twelve trucks. They had learnt not to use the word 'propaganda' which Africans thought of as being 'lies' but to describe themselves as an Information Bureau, informing the people about the Army in which their sons were serving and how they might help the war in which the King's African Rifles were engaged.

The Unit was on safari for two-and-a-half years with periods of regrouping and refitting between tours. They covered approximately 60,000 miles through Tanganyika, Uganda, Nyasaland, N. Rhodesia (Zambia) and Kenya. Audiences came close to numbering three-quarters of a million, many of whom had walked very long distances from their villages to see this unprecedented spectacle.

Travelling was by no means an easy task – fording rivers, crossing mountain ranges, traversing deserts in enervating heat, negotiating bush roads whose red dust enveloped men and vehicles and into which both boots and tyres could sink.

In the evenings there was camp to set up, food to be cooked, latrines dug, exhaustion to be overcome, discipline to be maintained, a group composed of men recruited from heterogeneous backgrounds to be welded into a cohesive working unit, respecting each others singularity but sharing a common aim. As time went on it became clear that the men were moulded not so much by any training as by the work itself. They developed a fine team spirit, an atmosphere of mutual assistance, cheerfulness, communal self-sufficiency and confidence which impressed their audiences and enlarged the ideas of the latter as to what they might attempt within their own communities.

During the tours and in the intervals between for refitting, education courses were run. Some of the senior Colonial Servants seeing the Unit in action when it visited their area began to visualise possibilities of transferring some of the ideas being put forward into civilian practice when the war ended.

In March 1946 Alec Dickson had an article accepted by the *Geographical Magazine* entitled *Tell Africa*. He wrote:

> We would arrive in the fierce glare of noon, lorries laden with Askari, kit and exhibits, all covered with road dust, without any knowledge of where we were going to sleep or whether we should be greeted by tens or thousands.
>
> One day the Unit might be at Kota Kota, beside Lake Nyasa: another among plantation labour barely emerging from their primitive tribal organisation and suspecting witchcraft in our display: or at the Jeanes School in N. Rhodesia before one of the most intelligent native audiences in Africa: or the Copper Belt with 15,000 African miners yelling approval as at a Cup Final. If Africans only had come to our shows the task of holding their attention would have been difficult enough. But when from day to day were added Governors, missionaries, Afrikaner

miners, local settlers, Colonial Office representatives, and even Army Officers from Portuguese East Africa, the responsibility of evolving some common denominator of propaganda became very nearly overwhelming.

At 3.50 pm the circus commenced. The Union Jack tied to a Masai spear was planted proudly in the centre of the showground. As a dramatic opening a runner would appear over the horizon, an Askari, naked except for a loin cloth, carried a cut stick with a message in it. Panting he flung himself at the knees of the senior Chief. Meanwhile, far away out of sight, the sound of a motorcycle revving at speed was heard. In seconds the runner was replaced before the Chief by machine and crash helmeted rider saluting and handing over his message. The old and the new.

We made physical training the basis of our display for a variety of reasons. The demonstration of Bren guns and wireless receiving sets might astound our local audiences – but they were double-edged weapons, filling some of the more thoughtful of the Africans with a sense of despair at the inadequacy of their own potential contribution to the war. Such mechanical devices were the fruits of European genius but the physical hardiness, courage and dexterity displayed in gymnastics were something our Askari themselves contributed and for which they could be admired. One young African likened their tumbling and vaulting to 'lightning flashes in a thunderstorm'. Here, too, was something that schools and missions where physical training is still known as drill, could themselves emulate. Perhaps more important, it demonstrated the essential relationship between discipline and happiness.

Another item in our display was to show the development of the African soldier of this war, complete with Sten gun and battle dress, from the days of the tribal warrior. The appearance of the latter, magnificently apparelled with war paint, spear and shield, would be received with alarm by the women and children and with paroxysms of delight by the more sophisticated members of the audience.

But the show was not only weapons. It was one man's job to exhibit an Askari's daily food, together with his weekly ration of cigarettes and soap. An Askari cook demonstrated how vegetables grown in East Africa were prepared for the soldier's meal – and might be cooked at home. An Askari's full kit and uniform was on display. The crowd was fascinated by the safety razor. The full layout evoked the horror stricken question, 'What, does he have to carry all that?!', transport other than feet and heads not being known to those who asked. Another stall displayed hat flashes, badges of rank, the medals of various units to show the variety of talents that the KAR used – Signals, Medical corps, Pioneers, Gunners, Engine Mechanics, Forgers and so on.

There was social etiquette also to be considered. In order to bring home the idea of Unarmed Combat, the Army form of all-in wrestling, we adopted the most modern music hall technique of carefully rehearsed 'interruptions' from the crowd. Audience participation was also encouraged. Thus, so that the usefulness of a knowledge of self-defence might be apparent to all, we arranged that during the display a 'girl' should suddenly meander across the area, be molested by one of our Askari and promptly throw him with a ju jitsu grip. The local women were profoundly shocked by such conduct holding that submissiveness was a far more decorous attitude.

When the cinema broke down our Askari were persuaded to send home to their Chiefs for their tribal drums and spears and to practice tribal dances. Gabriel, the boy bugler, was taught to perform conjuring tricks. The Unit was rehearsed in little plays and sketches to be given round the campfire where the village children sat enthralled and the Chiefs pulled their skins and blankets a little closer.

Explaining the progress of the war to those who had never seen a map called for a special technique of its own. The contours of the North African coast was likened to the outline of a bull that had to be seized – Cyrenaica the hump, Tripolitania the nape of the neck, Tunis and Bizerta the horns. With these horns in our hands we could toss the head and gore Europe in the belly.

When the convergence of the First and Eighth Armies in Tunisia grew ever closer one old Acholi Chief, illiterate, but with his chest sparkling with the medals of bygone campaigns with the KAR, shook his head wistfully and sighed, 'Would that the Acholi were there to close the gap!'

But it was not in the formal displays or the technical impedimenta that the value of the work lay. The Askari were trained to go out in twos and threes on such spare days as there were to lecture on the meaning of the war to some school, to demonstrate the treatment of wounds in the field to some village dispensary, to teach Army methods of physical training to a mission class. One African clerk wrote: 'The Askari who showed these things were very good and gentle because a person couldn't know that they were soldiers' – a reflection on the way some Askari behaved when on leave.

Very early in the work it had become clear what counted was not what the Askari did or said during the show but what they said round the campfire at night as they answered the questions asked by the Chiefs and villagers. It was in trying to bridge the gulf between soldier and civilian – in showing that the Askari could be as disciplined in the Reserve as in the Regiment, and in reminding the villager of his obligation to the soldier – that the MPU probably made its most effective contribution.

In July 1944 Norman Dickson died in London. The letter that his son had written to him when he heard that his father was in hospital, full of gratitude and affection, did not arrive in time.

Alec Dickson had also celebrated his 30th birthday. He wrote to his mother: 'I constantly think of the irony that should confine me to the safest work in all Africa. I who was never content but when in the heart of things in Central Europe, I who tried so hard to get into the Commandos and other desperate undertakings. Well I've had to learn to lie as best one can on the bed one made. After such a ghastly start, I think I've succeeded in achieving a certain success with the work I'm on in East Africa, my Mobile Propaganda Unit.'

The MPU was leaving on what was to be its last safari, round Kenya in August. Before he left he had written a Report of the 1½ years work with the Unit, over which he took infinite trouble. It had been read with approval by both General Sir William Pratt GOC-in-C and the Principal Information Officer of East Africa Command Sir Geoffrey Northcote, a good friend. A copy had also gone to Sir Christopher Cox in the Colonial Office, London.

For Alec Dickson the strain of unremitting travel, continuous expectation not always fulfilled, a life without privacy in difficult conditions had taken its toll. In others in the Unit too, officers and Askari, the stresses were becoming apparent.

The night before the Unit left Nairobi, Alec Dickson wrote again to his mother: 'Kenya's the nearest of the Territories. But it is also the most difficult and stickiest. I've worked unceasingly to prepare the tour – overcoming the resistance of the Kenya government, winning the support of various military commanders, personally selecting every man individually, training them all myself, arranging every yard and every day of the tour – and yet I feel most dubious of its outcome. Like an invasion, we can plan for everything except chance and the human factor. It may sound conceited – but I know that everything depends on me. The keenness of my men, the spirit of the Unit, the sparkle of our performance all depend in a unique sense on my being able to put everything I know into the job. But if I go sick or lose heart – I know the show can collapse.

'It's flattering to one's self esteem to realise how much depends on one's own inspiration but the strain begins to tell. For months, literally, I've hardly had a couple of hours off – and never a weekend. I couldn't relax if I tried. My friends tell me I look like one obsessed with my job and my

Africans indicate that I'm growing very short-tempered. I think I am. This obsession with one's work has its dangers. One loses a sense of proportion and neglects one's family and friends. One gains the reputation of a fanatic. But what's the alternative? Better to burn the candle at both ends – and let the flame shine bright – than flicker along in aimless frustration. That would never be my way – as I know it has never been yours'.

As 1944 drew on and the news from Europe indicated that an end to the war might be in sight, those members of the Colonial Service who were already looking forward, began to see that the Army demonstrations they had witnessed might contain seeds that could be transferred to peacetime life in the service of mass education. Already two potential Governors had their eyes on Alec Dickson.

Secretary bird

CHAPTER 8

Mora

War 1945

Nymegen

We were in Lille, north west France, in May 1945, myself and a colleague, running the YMCA. We met while on overseas training in London and became a team. She was Welsh, I was Scottish. Though her nickname was Winks we later became known as Jock and Taffy.

VE Day in this French city was one of the saddest days of my life. For many of the troops also it was a time of mental turmoil and uneasy expectations alongside relief.

For me, Alastair's death within a year of the war's end, returned vividly as the tragedy it was. There were others too; Trot and Algy at West Freugh, who had become friends, young men each with a baby daughter at home; the other Alastair who had died from the sheer exuberance of flying and all those of 6 Troop No 2 Commando, especially Bill and Peter, who were lost in the holocaust of St Nazaire. These men and their Captain had taught me many things that were invaluable – and were to continue to be so.

At the end of April 1945 Colditz had been surrendered to American soldiers who, as they came out of a wood nearby, had been unsure of their reception. They could see that in the small town which had previously been shelled white flags were hanging out so they went there first. The grim fortress that was the Castle showed no outward sign of surrender. The first approach was made with caution. The prisoners watched from the heights. The prison gate was opened and a US soldier walked in, visibly alarmed to be greeted with rousing cheers by the community of prisoners.

Michael Burn, my Captain, and I met in London the night before I left for France. He had discovered where I was from my mother. A wraith in uniform, the Sam Browne belt barely holding his trousers up, so little flesh there was to grasp beneath it, the once blue eyes, grey now. He was coming back. I was going forward with confidence to the next job. We had an evening together but between us there was a sadness and a readjustment that was no longer possible. He went afterwards to Moffat and talked to my mother, apologising for his own inadequacy, saying he was going to Russia . . . perhaps when he came back . . . but for me there was no fresh waiting, no going back. When later I heard that he was married I was glad.

The YMCA in Lille was situated in the centre of the town. Above the door a huge red triangle told any service man who passed by that here they could find a cup of tea and a genuine welcome. It was a very big canteen, busy from early morning till 10 at night, with a constant stream of customers passing by. We too were in transit. With D-Day over we were to be transferred to Holland.

Meanwhile, our days began at dawn. In the two hours before the doors opened all the problems of the coming day had to be coped with; how to explain to French staff that there was a lot to be done and talking would not do it; how to get cakes from the baker; telling a stray soldier the time of the next train into Belgium; ringing the Garrison Engineer for more light bulbs or a new W.C. There were quantities of sandwiches to be made, buns to be buttered, a thousand and one questions to be answered in French, English, sometimes Dutch or Polish. By 11.30 the pavement outside was packed with British uniforms, seemingly materialised out of thin air, where fifteen minutes before only civilians had occupied La Grande Place.

The Army was patient and courteous. There was only a chair to bar the door but nobody dreamt of pushing it aside until one of us removed it. Then they streamed in – Pioneers, Gunners, Engineers, Signals, Airmen. With beaming smiles, 'How's life?' or 'How are you doing?' in all the accents of the Empire. They joked about the difficulty of supplies, the shortage of soap, the strange French smells, how to get a bottle of Chanel No 5 to take back to the girl friend. But they rarely grumbled. Their good humour and tolerance was amazing and touching.

There were those who wanted more than tea and a bun: the man who came to ask how he could get his wife to Czechoslovakia, another who wanted a good red dye – his wife was going grey and she did not like it. A long discussion about the wisdom of marrying a French girl. Could we translate a letter from her into English? 'It's funny. I can understand her all right when she speaks but when it's written down I'm beat!'

Sometimes in the evening there was a dance upstairs, sometimes a cinema. The Scots element hoped very much to have a bagpipe concert but was firmly suppressed by the Welsh and English. Lille at this time did not offer much entertainment. Sunday evenings there was a short service. Three days a week a good French orchestra played in the canteen, French lessons were on offer or a whist drive.

Suddenly, late at night, the canteen could be filled with Air Force blue, RAF crews from Germany on their way to Calais on leave with two or three hours waiting for transport in Lille. Everyone talked constantly of when they would be demobbed. They spoke of children they had never seen, of wives and sweethearts from whom they had been a long time separated. We gave time to listen, however hard it was to spare. One day a soldier remarked, 'Do you know – I was only saying to my mate last night what a difference it makes having someone to talk to.' Perhaps that was in itself our major contribution.

The time came for us to move on. Our instructions were to take over the YMCA at Nymegen just south of Arnhem and the bridge over the Rhine which had seen the last disastrous action of the Parachute Regiment in September 1944.

Winks, by now a close friend, was the driver. She was also in charge of all catering while I looked after the programme. There were no barriers between us and we worked closely together as a team.

Nymegen was an important staging post on the main route between Hamburg and the Channel ports in what had now become the British Sector of a divided Germany. The area was garrisoned by Canadian troops.

The YMCA, situated on a major thoroughfare, the Oranjesingel, was in a very large four storey house with a small courtyard in front and a hall behind. It was drab and dilapidated. One or two stray bullets had knocked holes in some of its inside walls and German troops had pictured the Herrenfolk round a few of the rooms. Our job was to create an established Centre serving the busy passing military traffic as well as the soldiers settled in the town and the surrounding district.

The Canadian Army Headquarters were in a wood near Apeldoorn beyond Arnhem. Winks and I drove out there together to ask for help and found a young Captain sitting in a tent smoking. Apparently women in the wood were unknown and excitement ran high. The Captain said 'Look at this now! What can we do for you?' We replied, 'We have a very dirty and disreputable canteen and we'd like to paint it'.

'O.K. girls,' said the Captain, 'It's paint you want. How much?'

We looked at each other. We had never painted a house before and confessed shamefacedly, 'We don't know'.

The Captain was delighted, '150 gallons? Cream, green, blue, yellow? Collect it at Nymegen tomorrow?'

So we did, with men to do the painting, plumbing and any other job we needed.

Thus began our friendship with the Canadians. They were to prove marvellous benefactors, always generous, ever cheerful, naturally unselfconscious. We were to owe to them the material success of our Canteen.

One day their Colonel, David Rosser, came in to look us over and said that it was about time our YMCA was advertised. What about a sign – a really big one, not like the small one we already had? Three days later the Canadian Military Police called on us and told us that the Colonel had ordered a sign and it was ready for delivery. So we became the proud possessors of an enormous sign, 6 ft x 6 ft, decorated with the Scottish Saltire and the Welsh Dragon – from whence arose our nicknames with the troops – Jock and Taffy.

Food was the next problem. We served about 800 to 900 men a day. A long search began for a baker who would not be tempted to sell our flour on the black market. When found, Jos Tiemessen was a treasure. Jos and special rations enabled us to keep the canteen more that adequately supplied.

Nymegen had suffered greatly as a town, both people and buildings, in a way that Lille had not. The people welcomed us quietly. They were courteous and helpful when we called on them but they had their own problems which we did not always recognise.

Our work absorbed us. The war was behind us. We were well looked after by the Canadians. When there was any technical hitch we rang up the Colonel and he sent down his Staff Captain Ken to deal with it. We had space and resources to expand activities for the men.

The town was close to starvation. We had excellent Dutch staff, especially a helpful and silent young man, Pieter van der Meuwe, who looked after our business and financial affairs and a PR/Secretary, Cune van Vorst Tot Vorst, of good family, who confided nothing but was very efficient with correspondence and office arrangements. Help in the kitchen, canteen and general household was undertaken by local people, including a first class handyman always in demand. It took us time to realise that the meals we supplied them with were often a lifeline and with that realisation, that tiny extras might help a family. We did not know, until the reality impinged on us, that there were those in the community who were now ostracised because they had had relationships with the enemy occupiers. We heard very distantly that some of the citizens were newly back from concentration camps – the survivors. Not until much later did we realise what that truly meant.

In the YMCA we set out to engender an atmosphere of welcome, warmth, cheerfulness and time for listening. The men of the British Army wanted to get home. As in the aftermath of all great contests, victory took time to assimilate, to recover from. The future looked flat, the moment for resilience had gone. There was even foreboding. Demobilisation could be slow and frustrating and what then? When others got their demob orders, or a group stopping off on their way home from Germany came into the canteen, the spirits of those left behind sank.

Very early we decided we would have a resplendent Christmas Party; the first peacetime Christmas when many would feel deeply that they were not at home. We started collecting, hoarding away everything that might be useful. From the Army Store we got jellies one week, hams the next. We kept chocolate biscuits and bits of silver paper. We enquired about Christmas trees and the possibilities of apples. We co-opted Ben the Education Warrant Officer, a man with humour and resilience. The thought of giving a party for four or five hundred men appalled us. We were sure the band would fail or the girls – issued with tickets by Pieter – would not turn up.

We managed to find two magnificent trees and spent hours stringing tinfoil stars on thread for decorations. The tinfoil was German anti-radar protection and came from the Canadians. Reinforcements arrived the day before the party. The Canada Club came with six or seven huge boxes full of streamers, baubles, paper chains and stars. One of us had bought mistletoe in Antwerp and there was abundant holly for sale on the streets.

We made jellies in every kind of receptacle, switched tinned milk into cream, put fruit salad in the well-scrubbed ashbin. Colonel Rosser supplied 100 litres of ice cream and his welfare parcels for the last six months containing soap, tobacco, chocolate, razor blades and chewing gum. We put them all in a wastepaper basket for prizes. A fat jolly Sergeant had consented to be Father Christmas. When the costume arrived it was St Nicholas but at least it had a beard.

Taffy and I were nearly nervous wrecks when the party finally began. We need not have worried. From the very beginning it was a tremendous success. Ben ran it and we were superfluous. We played Musical Chairs. We danced the Grand Old Duke of York and Conga all through the house. Above all, we ate. The youngest soldiers, long after the party was over, were to be found sitting quietly in corners with beatific smiles and huge plates of jelly, ice cream and fruit salad.

Our main resource lay within ourselves, every one of us, both staff and customers – and the Canadians. We asked for suggestions for a programme – and got them. Programming was difficult because it changed constantly with the men. One unit would play bridge and debate; another would only dance. A Pioneer, offered a quiz, said he preferred a Whist Drive. Dancing lessons were popular; classical concerts on an ancient gramophone and records; a table tennis competition sparked fierce rivalries. Every Tuesday and Saturday there was a dance. The dancing instructor was a volunteer. After two lessons one small soldier approached me: 'If you want to learn to dance, Jock, just come to me – I'll teach you!' Colonel Rosser, now known to most as David, was a tiny charismatic man filled with energy and humour. I was 5 ft' 10". He enjoyed dancing with me, especially polkas and gallops, to the enormous entertainment of the rest of the company, including the Dutch girls – all docketed and ticketed by Pieter, with no collaborating relations or unseemly connections.

Every now and then we would consider that both the men and ourselves needed a fresh interest. Then we had competitions: Baby competitions, Poetry competitions, Glamorous Girl competitions. We put up a notice and awaited results. The Baby competitions were always a tremendous success – even the scruffiest soldiers seemed to have beautiful babies. The Dutch would exclaim over the good looks and plumpness of British babies after the half-starved weans of Europe. A fever of poetry writing spread through the units when that competition was announced. Men came in with dreamy eyes muttering couplets. All the entries were anonymous.

Priority was a vision. Even before coming to Nymegen, Winks and I had wanted to produce a magazine. So we put up a notice: 'Wanted! Editors, Contributors, Sponsors, Friends, for a Magazine!' The result was surprising. The Field Bakery gave us Jim, who had apparently always hankered to produce a magazine. He was difficult and temperamental but he worked like a navvy, pulled strings everywhere, got a paper allocation from Amsterdam, discovered a printer, prodded, edited and pushed. We were appalled when we found the web into which our lighthearted notice had entangled us. There was a great deal of work but the men loved it. For Jim it was like a child. Don and Frank, the Engineers, did the donkey work – typing. Frank was an authority on medieval architecture and looked forward to a vehicle for his articles. The selection of contributions was heatedly fought over. Rex wanted to include pin-ups. John, a practicing Anglo-Catholic, tried to get ribald cartoons and hymns accepted. Ron, a peacemaker, an ardent Methodist who took the Sunday services if the Padre failed us, was the final arbiter of what went in and what not. I sent poetry and had it accepted, but there was another ambition long nurtured.

'What's that?' the group asked, looking apprehensive.

'That you agree to take me on as your Agony Aunt and give me a column'.

So 'Priority' was born and 'Aunt Aggie' (the only use I ever found for my disliked second name) took her place in the public arena.

She was a great success and had her fan mail. It was not unusual for a soldier to come up to the counter and say, 'Can I speak to Aunt Aggie? My heart's broken'. Or we answered a query from the Canadian Provost unit about their Sergeant Major: they thought his affair was not progressing as it should!

'Priority' flourished. There were three good issues and then the Army took over. Jim went to Germany and so did Frank and Don. Ron went home to work on the docks. The entire Editorial Board was swept away.

In September 1945 there had been a different call on our ingenuity. On the anniversary of the surrender of the bridgehead at Arnhem a memorial was to be unveiled and a wreath laid. One day, very shortly before the ceremony, I came back to the YMCA to find that a message had been left for us. The Parachute Regiment wanted the wreath for the Memorial and could it be made in the shape of their badge, Pegasus, the Winged Horse, on a maroon ground? An officer would call for it at 8 am the next morning. We viewed this demand with some dismay. Nevertheless it was a challenge.

I spent the afternoon making a design of the badge, a pale horse on a dark purple ground. Meantime our Dutch handyman was converting a pile of old wood strips into a 3 ft square frame onto which chicken wire was nailed. Taffy and Pieter were out on the town searching for dark purple-red and white dahlias. How much money we were expected to spend had not been mentioned in the note nor had the officer left any way of making contact. At 10 pm when the canteen closed and everyone went home we started to recreate in flowers, on the chicken wire frame, the Para's Pegasus Badge.

It seemed that we would never succeed. Flower heads dropped out of the wire mesh; making a romantic rather than a tattered picture seemed impossible. However, at 4 am, when we stood back bleary eyed to look at our work we were stunned by our own success. At 8 am exactly a young Lieutenant arrived. He took our wreath without a word, saluted and climbed back into his jeep. From him, or indeed officially, we never received any thanks.

By a strange coincidence, which was later to have repercussions, my brother Alastair's plane had been shot down in July 1944 near the small town of Heerde not far north of Nymegen. Two of Alastair's crew had escaped by parachute before the plane was too low for the remainder to have any chance. The bodies of my brother and four of his crew were found in a wood by the Dutch resistance and buried in the local cemetery.

One afternoon, almost with reluctance, I was driven to Heerde. The long flat road culminating in the entry to the town and the yew trees at the entrance to the graveyard contrasted sharply with the small burn and quiet hills which formed the landscape at Moffat. The village was about the same size as our home town with a similar sense of community. The graves were marked only by temporary wooden crosses, the pilot and four members of his crew alongside five young men from a Canadian plane. When later my mother was asked if she would like her son's grave transferred to one of the Imperial War Graves cemeteries she said 'No'; she liked the idea of his body lying in a small town graveyard. How right she turned out to be. That day, however, still finding it hard to accept that he was dead, I came back relieved that once again I could forget.

A Canadian officer was going over the German border one afternoon with an official despatch and asked me whether I would be interested to go with him. His objective was the town of Kleve, between the border and the Rhine. I went cheerfully – and was shattered. Nymegen was damaged, but Kleve and Elst (a small village that we passed on the way) were rubble and ruins. Nothing remained that resembled any building except the wall of half a tower. That people had once lived there, only the signboards gave notice.

I went back sobered. Acutely aware of a total failure of imagination, that all those years I had been a spectator, cushioned from the realities of life that others had had to face. If I had any strengths they were as yet untested. Taffy and I had enjoyed working in Nymegen, putting aside understanding of what had happened there before we arrived, yet despair was not the answer; rather an openness of mind to the validity of the experiences of others and an ability to accept them with humility.

In the beginning of February we began to think of Valentines. We thought that it would be fun to revive a forgotten art so we made a huge personal Valentine; a complicated affair of pink hearts, white muslin, tissue paper and pipe cleaner arrows. It was so beautiful we put it up on a notice board.

Next day Freddie came to us, red-faced and embarrassed, wondering if we could make a Valentine for his wife. He had only been married two years and most of that time he had been abroad. We said, 'Yes, we would try'. Then Frank arrived with a spokesman. He was too shy to ask for himself. The request was for a Valentine for his girl. '*The* girl', the spokesman emphasised. 'He's getting married on his next leave'. So again, we said, 'Yes'. After that it became an industry. I often wondered how they had been received when the postman dropped them on the doormat. Frank's verse read:

> The sea lies cold between us,
> The winter skies are grey,
> I send my heart for you to keep
> Till I return some day.
> You knew t'was yours already
> And only lent to me
> So now I send it back again
> Across the stormy sea.
> Be gentle with my heart, my love
> For it is pierced enough.
> I place its life in your fair hands
> With it I plight my troth.
> And surely I will come some day
> To end our parting's pain
> And when I come I'll take your heart
> And claim my own again.

When March 1946 came, after a winter in which the number of our customers had been steadily reduced and all our Canadians had gone back to Canada, rejoicing, those left behind became restless, counting the days until it would be their turn to go. The end was in sight. We knew that our stay, too, was likely to be short. We decided to give another party to celebrate Spring on March 21st. We put up a notice to this effect. The reply from the troops was instantaneous – 'Just the job'. With the Canadians gone, we faced the long grind of preparation alone. But this time we had experience and far fewer customers to cope with. We made a list of all the games we knew and all the novelty dances we could think of. Ben was gone but Ray said he would be Master of Ceremonies. We were determined to have a feature, like St Nicholas at the Christmas party – perhaps a Cupid dressed in a buttermuslin ballet skirt and Army boots, flowers in his hair, a silver bow and arrow in his hand. Sadly though, no man we approached was willing to appear in a ballet skirt. We dyed yards of material pale blue, green and pink, but still on the morning of the Party we had no Cupid.

It was Winks who said it first. 'If you'll do it I will'. I replied, 'All right. If you're in it too'.

So we did. We sewed white muslin skirts, with coloured bodices and overskirts. We borrowed a pram. At 9pm, when the guests were full of hilarity with games and dances and full of ham sandwiches and jellies, the M.C. threw open the hall door and down a pathway lined by troops as for a parade came Cupid transformed into Spring, clad in pale blue and green with pink azaleas in her poke bonnet. She sat in the pram clasping a biscuit tin from which she dispensed chewing gum. Pushing the pram was the nursemaid in pink with a borrowed apron. Cavorting around us was the conscripted messenger, Tommy, in pale green with yellow trumpet flowers, scattering the contents of a box of Canadian book matches.

It was our last extravaganza. Some time later I wrote my final notes: 'It was not just a case of tea and a bun as we had once thought when the war was very new. Now we knew better. We had known many thousands of men of all services, all types, all creeds, all nationalities. Soldiers, sailors, airmen; British, Canadian, American, Czech, Polish, French, Dutch. We had had our likes and dislikes, often been irritable and tired. Those men all needed one thing. Not tea and a bun. Not even entertainment or physical comfort. They needed reassurance. They needed our smile and friendship – the visible representation to them that there was still somewhere in the world love, joy and peace. It was a high standard to set and one hard to attain. Constantly, day after day, from early morning till late at night we represented to them their homes and their hopes. They expected us to be superhuman. We tried to be so. We smiled constantly; we told them, whatever our private views, that there was still hope for the world. We listened to tales of woe, stories of self-pity, accounts of happiness. It was a curious thing that the cheerfulness we regularly assumed to reassure them grew on us. We did believe that there was hope for the world because so many men, if they were treated decently, were decent. During all the years we did this work we never once had real trouble with any man. We had drunks, but always orderly ones; we had grumblers but they ended in smiling. We had faith in them. They knew it and repaid us a thousandfold. If an individual became too obstreperous his mates soon put him right.

I had a birthday in April by which time we too were beginning to think of home. Robert, my oldest brother, who had left for Tanganyika in 1938, would be back soon on his first leave since then – with a wife and baby daughter whom I had never seen. So too, Laurence returned from the Indian Army.

Hitler's birthday had been April 20th. For the last six years I had hesitated to acknowledge that it was also mine. I was in the canteen when a group of our long-term customers arrived outside. It was a beautiful day. A delegation came in and asked me to go into the courtyard with them. What became visible made my eyes water – an entire street stall of flowers blazing with colour in the sunshine. 'Happy Birthday' the men sang and handed over a note of appreciation. We ended up filling the bath with blossoms, after every utensil in the house had been used. It was a wonderful farewell. Their demob orders had come through. So had mine.

CHAPTER 9

Alec

Uganda (BOAR) 1945–46

For many who had played their part in it, the months after the end of the war were a time of unhappiness and indecision. The past was finally gone and with it the hopes and expectations that had once furnished the future. In some cases fresh paths had opened out of the war experience, others had closed. But the new ways were untried and still shrouded in uncertainty.

Alec Dickson was a man for whom decisions were never easy. He had a temperament which vibrated in response to his surroundings; his own personal longing to make some mark on his world; his sensitiveness to the impact of other human beings around him.

With the end of the war he began to be haunted by a feeling which was never to leave him – that he did not know whether or not he was a coward. Through no fault of his own for he had made many efforts to be engaged in scenes of conflict: Finland, to join the Commandos; to be posted back to North Africa; even the initial volunteering to East Africa with Abyssinia in mind. All such endeavours had been aborted. In some, his ways of advancing his own cause, battering on closed doors, ignoring proper channels of approach, appealing to higher authorities, had not made him friends.

He had been given a military MBE for his work with the Mobile Propaganda Unit and already there were approaches for a civil equivalent from two territories. But his heart was still with his Askaris and the Unit and his head knew, with foreboding, that he was unlikely ever again to have the chance of independent responsibility that he had enjoyed with the MPU.

He was exhausted and in indifferent health having had no real leave (which he might well have rejected anyway) since 1942. In the moments when he was at his lowest he just wanted to get home. Even there, there was sadness. With his father dying in 1944, his beautiful family home in Wimbledon had been sold and the mother to whom he was so much attached had moved to a flat in the centre of London.

Yet already correspondence (with copies to Capt A. G. Dickson) was going backwards and forwards between two Governors, Uganda and Gold Coast, who had seen the work of the MPU and were anxious to profit by what they had learnt from it in establishing Mass Education in their territories. Any future development they felt was dependent on the skills and personality of Alec Dickson.

In early July 1945 there was a letter from the Colonial Office Director of Recruitment about a possible appointment in Uganda: 'The Governor is anxious to discuss details of the proposed Department with you...his primary purpose is to establish an efficient service between the Government and the governed... This purpose it is hoped to achieve by means of Mobile Propaganda Units of trained African demonstrators... These units would not only disseminate news and Government propaganda of a political, educational, medical and agricultural nature, but would also be used as vehicles for the development of Village Welfare Services under the aegis of the Social Welfare Organisation...' The letter went on to speak of terms of employment and a three year contract, including a first year's probation. In the light of all this information did Alec Dickson wish to be considered for the post?

African hills

In September 1945 a letter from Sir Henry Gurney, now Governor of the Gold Coast, offered Alec Dickson, subject to the approval of the Colonial Office, a job as Education Officer in charge of Mass Education. This proposal was less tightly tied to a Government Department than that of Kampala and suggested that it would be a new post. Alec Dickson would have a reasonably free hand in the preparation of the scheme and for the leadership of the staff.

Over the next few months telegrams and despatches flew between the two Governors. In the meantime Alec Dickson was in Kampala assessing the situation from his point of view, becoming increasingly harrassed and unable to take any decisions. Major concerns were still with what was happening to his now demobilised Askari. His mind was in a turmoil, feeling that there were enormous possibilities for using the resourcefulness developed in these men by their experiences and aware that he now had no longer any contribution to make. He was lamenting his own loss of personal stature – that he was about to vanish into meaningless obscurity. In spite of the offers that had come in he was well aware of the quirks in his own nature and knew, now that he was engaged with the reality in Uganda, that any skills he possessed were not those that would make him acceptable to an orthodox Government Department. He was a man that needed a Patron, to be under the wing of someone older than himself, already established in his own way of life, who saw in Alec Dickson some promise – or some oddity – and was ready to protect him from the discouragement which overcame him when faced with committees or officials. In his Oxford years Alec Paterson, Prison Commissioner at the Home Office had played such a role. In Nairobi Sir Geoffrey Northcote had cast his mantle of protection over him when in 1942 he was arrested for what appeared to be treason and had been a major encourager at the birth of the Mobile Propaganda Unit.

The time in Uganda resulted in disillusion. When travelling with the MPU through the East African hinterland Alec Dickson had viewed the transfer of the Unit's work to civilian Mass Education in a visionary light. In Uganda he was faced with all the disappointments and difficulties. Among Colonial Administrative Officers and senior Africans there seemed to be an almost universal scepticism. Now the emphasis given the Mass Education Report appeared to have been reversed. 'Where education as a whole is backward, effort is most rewarded when it is directed to the Higher Levels'. He was coming to feel that he needed a sabbatical year away from Africa to recover any sense of perspective. Obligation, however had made him send a tentative acceptance of the Gold Coast offer.

By June 1946 the Governor of Uganda was trying to persuade Sir Henry Gurney in the Gold Coast that they needed to keep Alec Dickson until June 15th to open a Training School for Social Workers which they had set up and by which time staff from England would have arrived. However, by

Ugandan trainee

June 8th Alec Dickson, who had spent that day listening to the BBC broadcast from London of the Victory Parade in which some of the Askari he knew had taken part, was on his way home. He was emotionally exhausted and drained by the six months spent in Uganda and already having misgivings about the Gold Coast offer.

Back in London, increasingly fraught, so much so that his mother feared he might one morning be fished out of the Thames, Alec Dickson was beginning to feel again the attraction of Central Europe. When the possibility of a job with the Prisoners of War and Displaced Persons Division at the Headquarters of the Control Commission in Berlin was offered him, he accepted without any real enquiry into what would be involved. He immediately wrote to Christopher Cox, Educational Adviser to the Secretary of State at the Colonial Office, withdrawing his previous acceptance of the appointment to be Mass Education Officer in the Gold Coast.

Post-war Germany was very different from the Central Europe Alec Dickson had known after Oxford. He had hoped to be directly involved with the Displaced Persons but found himself an Assistant Director at Headquarters in Berlin. His colleagues had been in charge of Battalions, Brigades and Divisions moving into battle in their last years of active service. They were marvellously efficient. Alec Dickson liked them all. It was exhilarating to be with them. When preparing for a meeting with the Russians, the location alternating on each occasion, it was as though a set battle or the tactics of a football match final were being planned and enacted. But Alec Dickson was not a natural administrator nor was behind a desk his preferred habitat.

Very early he saw that he had made a mistake in withdrawing from the Gold Coast offer. He wrote to his older brother, Murray, himself back from the Army in the Far East to ask him to persuade the Colonial Office to disregard his letter of withdrawal.

Christopher Cox, himself an unorthodox character, gave Murray Dickson to understand that his brother's behaviour, his indecision, his 'instability' had caused a great deal of annoyance in the Colonial Office. Nevertheless, the job offer in the Gold Coast was renewed and a polite request made to Mr Dickson as to a date when he would return to Britain. It would be months before such a date was set.

The Control Commission required someone to fill Alec Dickson's place, and then a month's notice. During this time Alec Dickson managed to contact one of his early Sudetan German friends and made new lasting contacts, notably in the Control Commission of the French Zone, Leon de Rosen and the girl Leon was to marry, Olga, of Russian origin.

It was with Olga that Alec was at the Opera one evening when he collapsed with appalling internal pains and was taken immediately into hospital. It was some months before the Medical Officer would give him permission to travel home. In the meantime the Colonial Office, unable to get the date they wanted, behaved with great courtesy and restraint.

CHAPTER 10

Mora

1946–47

MOFFAT

For me the return to Moffat and home was difficult. In one sense not much had changed, in another everything was different. The perspective from which I now viewed my own place in the world, to which I had once been accustomed, was no longer one of acceptance, resignation to a future whose lines were already laid down. The horizon had moved and the earth with it. Now I was without contentment.

For my mother and Nannie life had altered too and contracted. The wartime privations had taken their toll of the house. With the men away Nannie now did the jobs of plumbing, carpentry, keeping the electricity going, as well as cooking. Without adequate heating, living accommodation had shrunk. Everywhere there was the remembrance of Alastair.

Not that all was gloom. After nine years Robert was returning from Africa with a wife and baby daughter. Their arrival was anticipated with delight – and perhaps some trepidation. Cupboards long shut were opened and household goods packed away were taken out, cleaned, dusted and hung out in the garden so that the house should once again take on its cheerful welcoming family face. The last of the blackout covering less used windows was stripped away. The prospect of a baby once again gave back to Nannie a primary purpose. Drawers were opened where long ago she had salted away, wrapped in tissue paper, the treasures she had made for me – little dresses, shawls, out of date underwear. My mother, with her first granddaughter about to arrive, was busy wondering about toys; was a pram still available, would the parents come provided with everything or not, how much could she offer her first daughter-in-law, how much hold back?

In the event she loved Kit, the daughter-in-law, from the moment she saw her. It was Robert, her son, who had become the stranger. Perhaps only Nannie, once more in the profession that was her first choice and with the baby's mother gladly welcoming her help, was the only member of the household to have found real peace.

Laurence was back from India and the Army. Silent and unhappy, he was disorientated by the enormous change to village life and a climate far different from the heat and sunshine to which he had become accustomed. None of us found it easy to speak of Alastair whose spirit haunted the house. Because we had all been separated in different parts of the world when he had been killed, we had never talked of his death at the time. Each of us had buried our sorrow and our love in our hearts and could not now resurrect them.

Like my brother, who had joined up and left for India after only a year studying engineering at Cambridge, I felt myself without any qualifications for a job. Whether I had any real talent as a painter after those years away I doubted and I sensed that my mother hoped I would stay at home and eventually settle down. That no longer seemed possible.

Until Robert's leave was over and the family went back to Africa, all went on quietly from day to day. Then Laurence found that Cambridge University was setting up a special one year course in Engineering for those whose study had been interrupted by the war. He applied and was accepted. When finished he emigrated to South Africa.

London

Meanwhile, remembering that when I left Edinburgh College of Art in the early years of the war there had been vague talk of a bursary to the Royal College in London, I told my mother that I wanted to go down there and find out whether such an award might remain open to me. If not I would still like to test myself as a painter. So I left for the South on a night train, seen off by my mother who, I guessed, thought that she had lost me.

Sharing a flat with a wartime friend I first went, nervously, to enquire at the Royal College if any openings had been kept for those who had pre-war awards. They were polite – not disdainful as I had feared – but said they were so overwhelmed by applications from potential students returning from war service that they had simply drawn a line under 1939. Perhaps seeing my dismay, they suggested a small Art School in Kensington called the Byam Shaw. Clutching my pre-war portfolio I went to see them. Having been closed for the last five years, this school, recruiting an entirely fresh intake, was glad to have me.

I went home in quite a new frame of mind to be with my mother until the autumn term started.

The first task was to find somewhere to live. Not having much money I was looking for student digs, a small studio, anywhere on my own to concentrate on painting. All the agencies I tried made no effort to scan their books. 'Hopeless' they said', 'Impossible' – there were so many people looking for lodgings, for accommodation of any kind.

The wartime friend had her own problems. I was aware of becoming a burden to her. My feet were sore, my spirit growing weary. I abandoned the usual agencies and began to try private, all-purpose services on the pattern of the Universal Aunts. Always the response was the same. They would meet a child off a train and help him or her to cross London to a station on another line; they would shop for the elderly or find caterers for a party – but accommodation – 'No'.

Then, as I was leaving the last one in despair, the lady who had interviewed me called out, 'Oh, by the way, we had an elderly lady in this morning looking for a paying guest (PG). She is a widow. All her children are overseas and she is lonely. You might try that'.

Appalled, I said, 'No! I'm a painter. I don't want to be a companion to an elderly lady. How could I paint in her spare bedroom?' 'Well, why not go and see her?' the interviewer replied. 'It's the only possibility we can suggest'. Tired and discouraged I agreed. The address I was given happened to be in the same area as the Art School. It might be possible to go for a month and give myself some breathing space. The interview was set up by the agency.

I approached the large apartment building behind Kensington High Street without much hope. The door was opened by a parlour maid in immaculate uniform. My hostess was clearly nervous and without experience of interviewing prospective PGs. She was wearing a very nice silk dress and sitting behind a silver tray with the best china laid out on it ready for coffee, which presently the parlour maid brought in. This was Mrs Anne Dickson. She told me that she had been widowed not long before and had been forced to leave a beautiful home in Wimbledon to move into this flat. Her four children, a daughter and three sons, were all overseas. She missed their company very much. That was the reason she was seeking a student or young person to live in.

I was shown the spare room. It was dark and overlooked a narrow alleyway. I knew without hesitation that this was not for me. We returned to the drawing room to discuss terms. She asked a reasonable sum. I suggested that we have a month's trial to see how the arrangement worked. Watching her I could see that she was relieved that, as yet, she was uncommitted. As she parted with me at her door another young woman, sent by the same agency, was making her way up the stairs. Much later Mrs Dickson was to tell me that she had liked this potential PG better and said to her, 'We're having a month's trial. Come back then and I'll be free to take you'. I was going out into the sunshine thinking, 'At least I've got a month to find somewhere else'.

Things did not turn out like that. This was a household full of warmth and hospitality. There was no question of my being treated like a stranger. Very quickly I became part of the family which, like my own, had a Scottish connection and a large extended kin. Our values were the same but the difference between rural and urban brought me to life again. In a capital city, where family relatives and children's friends were often passing through and where all knew – or suspected – that there was always a welcome when the door bell rang, daily life could bring unexpected interests. In Moffat, by comparison, days were slower and while our home was no less warm and hospitable the stranger arrived rarely and never without notice. My London hostess, who had a grandson at university, insisted from the beginning that I should call her 'Gran'. The dark spare room no longer seemed an insuperable obstacle.

Meanwhile, at Art school also, all had gone well. The size, thirty or forty students, suited me. A number had wartime experiences and we quickly made friends. The artists who ran the school, Patrick Phillips and Brian Thomas, supported and upheld by a devoted Manager Pamela Ovens, created an atmosphere not unlike a 17th century artist's studio. Once again I felt the excitement of painting pictures, delight in the smell of oil paint and its lusciously tactile feeling, the dreams of portraits akin to Rembrandt but signed by my own name.

Back in the Dickson home the month's trial had passed without anyone noticing – least of all myself. Gran and I had grown very fond of one another. She talked of her children: a daughter married and in Nyasaland (Malawi); the eldest son also married, a regular soldier with the Royal Scots; the second son who had worked pre-war in the Borstal Service, now transferring to the Far East in the Colonial Service; and her 'Benjamin', the youngest son, at present with the Control Commission in Germany.

Gran was open-hearted, ready always to answer any call for help, full of laughter, a wonderful hostess. She lived for letters from her family. The flat was pervaded by an atmosphere into which I found myself inextricably drawn. The Dickson kin became my kin; the Dickson friends my friends.

When I went home to Moffat for holidays it was at first hard to adjust to my own family life with my mother and Nannie. My mother was a woman accustomed to letting her sons and daughter go, setting no personal restraints in the way. On emotions which moved her deeply she was silent, though open and straightforward in all other matters. But I was close to her. I realised, and did not know how to counter, that once again – this time to an unknown family – she was afraid she had lost me.

During my next term in London, Murray, the second Dickson son, came home to make preparations for his journey to Sarawak. A quiet self-effacing man of sweet temper he was easy to make friends with. Sarawak, a small country on the northern coast of the island of Borneo, had been a fiefdom of White Rajahs. When the war ended Murray Dickson, whose regiment was stationed in India, had been posted there as a member of the War Crimes Commission, to inspect the civilian camps set up by the Japanese when they invaded the island. He had been enchanted by both country and people, especially the indigenous Dayaks. Now Sarawak was to become a British Colonial territory until the time came for Independence and, as soon as he had been demobbed, Murray Dickson applied to join the Colonial Service.

Knowing that his going so far away would distress his mother, he welcomed my presence in his home and, as she did, accepted me as part of the family. I too was glad to meet him. His mother's joy at his return and her efforts at entertaining relations and friends on his behalf (though not always to his taste), relieved me from some of the responsibility for companionship that I could not help feeling when we were alone. By the time he left for Sarawak Murray and I had become genuine friends.

A Dayak

I had come south to discover a purpose to fill the vacuum left by the end of the war. I had found the purpose and with it new horizons. To myself and to my mother I had set a limit to my searching, but now it seemed impossible to leave. Something hard to describe held me – a world of my own – a lotus eater's country where decisions could be indefinitely ignored. To exchange the community of the Art College for the discipline of working alone, the uncertain life of the freelance whose foundation would be my own talent, seemed at that moment unthinkable. There was also the knowledge, daily suppressed, that both families I now belonged to were without any tradition that would accept such a decision as legitimate. Or at least so I thought. Perhaps it was my own cowardice that held me back.

For five or six years now I had been independent, in Orkney, Shandon, and Nymegen. I wanted still to be independent. Sometimes I resented that my brothers had got away from our family responsibilities but I had grown up knowing that my role was a different one and I felt the disappointment would be profound if I did not fulfil it.

One morning Gran had a letter at breakfast. Her face mirrored her delight.

'My youngest son is coming home' she told me, 'He'll be here when you get back this evening'.

I was glad for her but absorbed in my own concerns. I had sold my first picture at the Ideal Home Exhibition, a landscape of the harbour at Kirkcudbright – a commission had come to the school from a hospital for a mural in their Children's Ward and I had been asked if it would interest me. In 1948 the Anglican Churches' first post-war Bishops' Conference was to be held in London. The painted ceiling of the main Reception Room in Lambeth Palace had been destroyed during the bombing of the capital: the commission for a temporary painted replacement had come to Brian Thomas. He in turn was indicating that he would need apprentices to help him.

I came back to Kensington Court Gardens in the late afternoon having quite forgotten about the arrival of the 'Lamb' – which was what Gran called her youngest son.

He was sitting in the drawing room with his mother. Though he stood up to greet me with a handshake it was clear he was not pleased to see me. He was shorter than I was, with receding red hair, quite unlike his older brother who was very dark. Gran filled the gap with family news and, mentally shrugging my shoulders, I went off to relax in my bedroom.

I was only superficially aware at that time of the post-war crisis Alec Dickson had been through. Nor did I realise that for him, differing from his detached older brother, the homecoming was fraught with sensitivities. In the circumstances I was merely an unfortunate extra annoyance. Home for Alec Dickson was – and always would remain – the safe haven, the refuge, the only place where the outside batterings of the world could be held at bay. The loss of the beloved home at Wimbledon after Norman Dickson's death was still an open wound. He had written to his mother from East Africa begging her to keep it but financial conditions had made that impossible. It was his mother who had always filled his home with love and welcome and, with a temperament very like his own, had given this youngest son an anchorage. Wherever he might be she was in contact with him, keeping all the family connections alive. To come home and face the reality that the companion she had taken in was already loved by her (almost without his permission) was more, at a time when he needed her utmost reassurance, than he could bear. As it happened, I was also inhabiting the room that had been his when, on his return from Africa, he had first lived in the flat as home.

I thought it a pity that we had started off so coldly but after all I was only a PG and had my own life to live.

The atmosphere changed when Alec Dickson came home. It became charged with a vital electricity. The household revolved round him, being prepared to go on errands, to take messages hither and thither, replacing the pillar box if it was preferable to have a letter hand delivered. The pulse beats of a larger world were now always on the doorstep. Fry, the parlour maid, who clearly adored Mr Alec, and his mother combined to enhance his comfort and tempt his taste buds with special dishes. His convenience was everything. Friends that I had never seen before began to frequent the flat. Gran's vitality, along with some anxiety, rose to meet her son's. I stepped quietly in the background, engaged with my own concerns.

As his health improved Alec began to talk to me and to show an interest in what I was doing. I got to know about his time in East Africa; the disappointments and difficulties that had gone with the return; his own indecision about the renewed offer of the post in the Gold Coast as Mass Education Officer. It was impossible to share the flat with him without becoming involved.

Then one morning to my great surprise, Alec Dickson said he had two tickets for 'Oklahoma' – would I go with him? We both enjoyed it. I felt accepted by the most difficult member of the Dickson family I had yet met.

Among the many friends who came to visit 8 Kensington Court Gardens at this time two were of German origin. One, Walter Wallich, had been the boy who, during Alec's first term at New College, Oxford, he had been asked to help and who later, during his time at Cambridge, had been arrested as an enemy alien. After a period interned on the Isle of Man, Walter had been shipped off, with thousands more, to the lumber camps in Canada.

Two years had passed before the British government concluded that, with the Russians now in the war, there was little likelihood of a German invasion of Britain. There was the realisation moreover that the majority of those interned were firmly anti-Nazi. A delegation from the Home Office had been sent over to the internment camps, deep in the Canadian forests, to screen the internees. Those who gave an undertaking to enlist in the British Army were eligible for immediate return to the United Kingdom.

First, however, was the screening, conducted by the most Senior Civil Servant who had been sent out for this purpose. Walter, when his name was called, had found himself facing Britain's Prison Commissioner and Alec Dickson's friend and patron – he had also been one of Walter Wallich's referees for British naturalisation.

Some weeks later, back in Britain, Walter had sought out his Cambridge landlady. She greeted him ecstatically.

'I have to report at barracks tomorrow at daybreak', Walter said after she had embraced him. 'Do you remember the papers I thrust into your hands just before the Cambridge police took me away? They were the thesis for my PhD degree. Could you please give them back?' The landlady smiled, 'I knew the police mustn't see them – I burnt them all that night!' For the first time since childhood in Germany, Walter Wallich wept.

He landed on the beaches of Normandy as a Captain in the Royal Engineers. Now he stood in Gran's drawing room with a good job in the BBC.

Another visitor who came one day to 8 KCG was Ekkehard Eickhoff. One day, looking after the cloakroom of the British Officers Mess in Berlin, Alec Dickson had encountered a 17-year-old German lad. Struck by his manners and the gauntness of his physique, Alec asked his name. He was an intelligent youngster. At the end of a short conversation the boy wondered if he were permitted to ask a question? Was Captain Dickson allowed to travel in the British Zone? The answer was 'Yes'. Was it possible that he ever got to Brunswick? That was where the boy's family lived. They would be anxious about him. Could the Captain visit them if he gave the address and tell them that their son was all right?

Alec Dickson did visit them. They were very grateful and a friendship was made. Soon after the war the British began to develop, in a stately home in the south of England, a centre of re-education for selected young Germans who might be the future intelligentsia of a reborn German nation. Among many others the young Ekkehard Eickhoff was recruited. Having Captain Dickson's home address, he at once made contact.

Gran welcomed him warmly, as she welcomed all her sons' friends. He was a tall, fair young man, very well educated, speaking excellent English, but still looking as if his later adolescent years had been lived near starvation. His clothes had a certain threadbare appearance, especially the shoes which were visibly worn through, though bravely polished. With his height he had very long feet. Nothing in the small Dickson family could possibly fit him.

It was Gran, determined that his need should be met, who turned to me saying, 'Mora, you're tall. Has your mother any of your brother's cast-off shoes?' I was taken aback, reminded inconsequentially that when in 1944 there had been a possibility for a few months that Alastair had been in a prisoner-of-war camp, the one thing that had worried my mother was the size of his feet and whether he had adequate shoes. Uncertain how she would receive such a request or, for that matter, not sure how I felt about asking her, I nevertheless wrote.

She sent a good pair of Alastair's old shoes by return of post with a note saying that she was glad to have a good use for them.

I later found that one of Gran's own relations had given her a hard time for entertaining a young German.

Ekke Eickhoff went on to rise to the top of his own country's Foreign Service and remained a lifelong friend.

I was in Scotland for Christmas when the preparations were finally over for Gran's youngest son to leave for West Africa, Alec Dickson's working tempo not being at ease with that of the Colonial Office – nor indeed vice versa.

CHAPTER 11

Alec

Ghana

In 1948 Alec Dickson arrived in Takoradi, the port of Accra, the capital of the Gold Coast (Ghana) on an Elder Dempster ship from Liverpool.

Very different from East Africa, this West African country had an Administration which felt itself to be the cream of the Colonial Service. This was indubitably the richest colony in Africa with revenue from cocoa, gold and tropical timber. Achimota, shortly to become the first university, renowned for its academic excellence, was at the apex of a pyramid of famous missionary schools.

However, two related occurrences had blotted this reputation and were to affect Alec Dickson's welcome in the territory. Earlier that year there had been riots in Accra. Returned ex-servicemen had immediately offered to help the Government maintain order. A major cause of unrest was the transfer of the new Governor, Sir Henry Gurney, to Palestine. The Administration was shocked as its perfectionist castle shook. A number of Europeans were wounded. In London there were also demands for the return of the late Governor and protests that they, the local Gold Coast population, were not 'communist pawns'.

Alec Dickson, arriving already filled with misgiving and barely recovered from a period of breakdown, was not encouraged by the news that Sir Henry Gurney,

A West African

whose personal observation of the work with the MFU in East Africa had led to the issue of the original invitation, no longer occupied the position of Governor. (Not so long afterwards, Sir Henry was to be assassinated in Nalaya.)

To arrive in a colonial territory as the blue-eyed protegé of a Governor who had just left was not a good beginning. The Director of Education, Alec Dickson's titular boss, let it be known that the education system required no modification from a new catch-phrase emanating from a London-based committee – mass education – least of all when entrusted to someone quite lacking in formal teaching experience, indeed without an academic record.

However, the open humour and robust self-confidence of West Africans restored Alec Dickson's own spirits. He was happy to be back on the African continent. Soon after landing, and probably to get rid of him as an embarrassment, he was given a car and a driver and sent to Ashanti and the Northern Territories on a trek round the country. He was impressed by those he met, both black and white, and began to make friends.

On his return to the South the situation was dramatically altered. Another new Governor had arrived, rather lacking in self-confidence *vis-a-vis* the highly assured top Colonial Administrators who in reality governed the Gold Coast. On that same day there landed too Kwame Nkrumah, a politician intent on supplanting the Nationalist leader, Dr Danquah, and making his own bid for power.

The crisis came on a Saturday afternoon. A game of cricket was in progress when across the pitch streamed a motley crowd of Africans fleeing from the police. At the order of a British police officer, a group of African ex-servicemen who were demonstrating were fired upon and one was killed.

That night there was rioting at the port of Takoradi and the revolution was on. The government imposed order rapidly but it had lost its nerve. In Accra, officers remained in their bungalows for the next two days; it was as though the government of the country had ceased to operate.

Alec Dickson received a telephone call – his first official communication since landing – asking him to go to the Labour Office and find work for the ex-servicemen. He enjoyed this. He found it satisfying once again to be dealing directly with the local people, whatever their grievances. The work was simply to go through the telephone book and one by one ring various companies.

'You'll know how dangerous things are now.' 'Yes, indeed.' 'Well, I'm sending you an admirable man as an additional watchnight' (night watchman). 'Of good physique, excellent war record. I'll be sending him to you in the next hour. What's that? You'd like two? Certainly.'

There was a double irony here. Some might think that dealing with aggrieved men who had just been involved in rioting – and finding work for

street child

the jobless – required an officer with several years' experience of the Gold Coast rather than someone just off the boat from England. But, in fact, very few of those men were Gold Coast citizens. Most came from Mali, Upper Volta and other far away French-speaking territories. It was these men, together with men from the Northern Territories, who manned the armed forces, filled the ranks of the police and undertook the manual tasks of the Gold Coast.

The work in the Labour Office was very temporary. No further suggestions were made as to how Alec Dickson should employ himself. Seeking to find a need that he could fulfil he covertly went through government files. There he discovered two entries which indicated that twice in the past an argument had been put forward that experience of some form of service to the community would give meaning to a common form of citizenship. With this information, Alec Dickson asked the Education Department whether a variation of the Mobile Unit that he had run in East Africa would be considered as a possible experiment. 'Provided it had nothing to do with the Army' was the reluctant reply.

No help in the work of putting such a proposal into practice was offered by government so Alec Dickson approached the missions. He retained the team model. The missions instantly grasped what the aim was and offered him the most outstanding Gold Coast teachers in their employ.

Kwame Nkrumah, who was at that moment in hiding from the police, referred with withering sarcasm to 'the school on wheels' which was being planned. Alec Dickson sought him out. He found him in his bath. Nkrumah was entertained at a young British officer actually wanting to reason with him and they talked for an hour. At the end of the discussion Nkrumah had no further word of criticism to offer.

In the vacuum that now surrounded him, Alec Dickson began to develop his plans with the support he had from the missions and the tacit approval of Kwame Nkrumah.

The area chosen for the first practical demonstration was Togoland, a narrow strip of the country to the east between the Gold Coast and Dahomey. Togo had once been a German colony. Now a UN Trusteeship Territory, like Cameroon to the east of Nigeria, it was administratively divided between Britain and France.

Togoland was chosen because it had a deeply rooted sense of independence and partly because of a tradition of village bands. The Ewe people also formed a strong homogeneous group inside Togoland.

The evening before they left Accra, Alec Dickson assembled the small team of ten and addressed them. He emphasised that if this endeavour were a failure the responsibility would be his. 'No', he was quietly admonished by Hosu Porbley, the number one teacher from the Methodist Mission, 'We agreed to work as a team – if we succeed we share in the success, if we fail we share the responsibility'.

This Gold Coast staff were not only intellectually gifted but they recognised the social issues in their country. They were aware of the political maelstrom that was coming and they also knew of the strained relationship between Alec Dickson and the government. This may well have added relish to their commitment to make this experiment succeed.

Among the team staff were Quainoo, a highly experienced Catholic Headmaster from Keta on the coast not far from Lome, the capital of French Togo; William Tsitsiwu, an Ewe, a teacher of singing from the Presbyterian Mission Amedzofe; Hosu Porblay, senior instructor at Kumasi College of Education; Matthew Adzaku, also Ewe speaking and familiar with the songs of Togoland, trumpeter from the Police Band and Kumasi Massena, a former sergeant in the Army and PT instructor. Briefly the team saw themselves as bringing a number of messages to the Togo people.

They were asking rural communities to invite the team to be their guests for two weeks or so. The team would operate from the local courthouse, a schoolroom or a church. They would impart to young teachers a dozen ways of making new ideas acceptable to adults and especially attractive to women. Together with the local young people they would offer to construct something which the villages valued – a water point, a miniature dam, an extension to their school. For this they would pledge their efforts to enlist the cooperation of the Public Works Dept, even of the well-disposed private contractors. Finally their efforts would be linked to mount a local adult education campaign, with the hope that a Literacy Bureau might be set up in Accra to support these endeavours.

The last two elements in the 'package deal' represented risks. At that time Alec Dickson had no authority to pledge the loan of a tractor or two bags of cement and the idea of a Literacy Bureau, dear to the heart of several missions, was as yet a vision only. It seemed important that whilst the emphasis must be self-help, the scheme had a right to claim a modicum of support from the government.

The most vital ingredient was the role foreseen for the local teachers. The team was setting out to motivate them to bring joy to their schools.

Once in Togoland, independent and out of reach of the government, Alec Dickson had regained his own joy, working closely with colleagues he respected and who, in turn, were committed to a partnership under his leadership, their contributions respected and valued.

Confident as time went on that the programme was worth sharing, Alec Dickson wrote a private letter to the Governor of French Togoland, resident 10 miles across the frontier in Lome. Two days later, a large beflagged car drove into the school compound where the team's show was based and out stepped, in full uniform, the Governor of French Togoland. He was shown round all the activities that were going on and kept repeating 'Mais c'est une ville en fete'. At the same time the questions he asked were penetrating, concerning the possibilities of reproducing this situation. He greeted each of the African staff and shook them by the hand. When he stepped back into his beflagged car the Governor said that this was the most enjoyable day he had spent since coming to Africa.

A week later a letter arrived at Government House, Accra, from Lome – as from one Governor to another, felicitating Sir Gerald Creasy, the British Governor on what he, the French Governor, had seen – a unique example of 'rural animation'. He had a suggestion to make. Let the two governments form a combined team to tour the Northern part of Togoland – because the people there were a great deal less sophisticated, their need for this kind of mass education was all the more evident. He would make available two young staff recently arrived from France and would be happy to offer the fullest cooperation.

Pressure was coming too from London with messages from the Colonial Office asking what measures the Gold Coast government was taking to promote mass education in conformity with Westminster policy. Suddenly there was capitulation.

All this activity did nothing to raise Alec Dickson's value in the corridors of power in Accra. He had committed an unforgivable sin in communicating with the Governor of another country without going through the British Secretariat. He came within an ace of being dismissed the Service. He had placed the Governor of the Gold Coast in such a position that the suggestion of a joint tour had to be accepted. Alec decided to leave, waiting until he got back to Britain to negotiate his resignation directly with the Colonial Office.

When, with Independence, the Gold Coast became Ghana, Kwame Nkrumah became Prime Minister and £1 million was voted to establish a Department of Mass Education and Social Welfare.

PART II
COMING TOGETHER

CHAPTER 12

Nigeria and British Cameroon

1948–50

Life went on quietly as usual in 8 KCG: I belonged to the family now. Murray Dickson wrote to me regularly from Sarawak. When he was close to it he found the emotional climate in his home vaguely upsetting but, removed by distance and the difference in my background and, though he was not aware of this, by my wartime experience, he could write to me freely. Over those years I had cultivated an instinctive understanding of men.

By this time my mother had been down from Scotland for visits to my second home and for an exhibition in which I had several pictures hung. The knowledge that the family into which her daughter had been absorbed was one which she liked and trusted eased the situation. She met also my Art School friends and teachers. With her own quiet talent for being open with her children's friends and herself belonging to a large kin, my mother found it easy to make contact with all ages.

This was a happy time for me. The temporary ceiling for Lambeth Palace was created in sections on the floor of the Art School's largest studio. It was of classical design, a space open to the sky representing the trajectory where the bomb had travelled but filled with putty, flying above or peering over the ruined surround in innocent curiosity about the ceremonial figures being entertained below. The ruins enclosing this scene had symbols of the hardships and resurrections endured during the war. Each of Brian Thomas' apprentices had a special appointed task. Mine was to paint the rosebay willow herb, a handsome wild flower that had sprung up in profusion wherever the destructive carnage had taken place.

The installing of the separate panels within the Palace drawing room was a time of great excitement. So far we had only seen them on the floor. While working, the four helpers and Brian Thomas had been welded into a close team. The final vision of our work done above us was, for an instant, a triumph of our painterly ambitions.

Meantime I, too, had joined the Dickson caravan. Alec Nyasulu, Captain Dickson's Sergeant in the Mobile Propaganda Unit in East Africa, had been sent to Edinburgh University to take an Education Course. Alec Dickson had asked me if I would invite him to Moffat for a weekend. Such requests were impossible to refuse. His conviction that any challenge would be accepted was absolute. So I did, though I had never met the other Alec, and neither Moffat nor my mother or Nannie had ever seen an African.

The invitation was accepted gratefully. It was the other Alec who put us at ease when we met him off the train and who assured Nannie that his skin would not leave a stain on the sheets as she had feared. Walking down to church on Sunday a small galaxy of local children, to my embarrassment, began to follow us along the road. But Alec Nyasulu, who had no doubt met the same curiosity in Edinburgh, had no hesitation in stretching out an arm and inviting the children to touch him. Giggling and shy they did.

Although from the 8 KCG perspective, things seemed to be going reasonably well in the Gold Coast with her youngest son, his mother was anxious about official reports in the press of serious unrest in the territory. Alec was now writing about both friends and foes, for and against, with few in between. With the temperament that was close to his own, Anne Dickson understood this. What she feared was that he might get positively involved in any uprising, on one side or the other. I had been on a bus with her one day when, feeling that the conductor was browbeating an elderly customer, she had marched down the aisle and accosted him. To my shame I tried to look as though I were not travelling with her!

Then we heard of the success in Togo. The spell of Africa had again taken over.

A month or two later the news came that Alec was hoping for a transfer to Nigeria and could be expected home quite soon. There was rejoicing and trepidation in 8 KCG. When he arrived, cheerful, anticipating immediate action from the Colonial Office, the London flat was instantly full of a large amount of baggage – Gold Coast cloths and artifacts forming the major part of it – and of round-the-clock activity. The normal ambience of the flat rose by several degrees.

The Colonial Office, however, remained silent, resistant to the idea that a young man 'on temporary appointment' could get himself transferred from one territory to another when it suited him. Any original appointment had been for a specific country – and that for the rest of the applicant's career. In addition, Alec Dickson had not only caused displeasure to the Government of the Gold Coast, he had actually entered into correspondence with officials back in London. Moreover, how had it happened that several Members of Parliament had directed well-informed letters of enquiry to the Secretary of State asking to know what was being achieved in mass education in West Africa – unless Mr Dickson himself had started the ball rolling?

A personal visit to the Colonial Office made it clear that, at any rate for the moment, Alec Dickson was *persona non grata*. In fact, a life pattern was developing and the hiatus between employment opportunities was to be much longer than anticipated.

During this period, while 8 KCG was his base and when he was there between visits to friends, attending conferences, speaking at meetings, writing professional articles, and interviewing influential persons in his field, we began to get to know each other well. I became deeply interested both in what he had already done but, even more, in his ideas and visions about future development. Flatteringly, he was also interested in my world. He came to a talk by Stanley Spencer at the Art School and we went to galleries and exhibitions. I reciprocated, hiding my ignorance, by accompanying him to concerts and, as time went on, sometimes sitting up till 2 am to listen to his large collection of records. Neither of us moved from our primary personal ambitions but it lit up life for each of us to have a sympathetic friend.

Gran was in her element entertaining, for tea or a meal, a string of interesting guests with African connections coming to discuss the situation in various territories. One was Peter Canhem, administrator, devoted to the Gold Coast, trying to persuade Alec Dickson to return. Later the friendship was to prove very valuable. I accompanied Alec to a meeting with the Rev. Michael Scott who had been pleading the cause of the Hereros of South West Africa before the Trusteeship Council of the United Nations.

There was a stimulating, heady, atmosphere as one friend after another tried out his or her ideas – all concerned with the future of Africa, not the past. Then there were periods of depression when it seemed to the Dickson household that the door to being part of that future might have been permanently closed.

Help, however, was on its way. After months of uncertainty the Colonial Office received a letter, formal and specific, on Nigerian Government notepaper, asking that Alec Dickson be attached to their Government to undertake development work. Alec Dickson himself was asked to go for an interview to the Colonial Office and offered a transfer to Nigeria.

The initiative behind this approach had come from a Senior Resident, a highly respected official in the Nigerian Government, E. R. Chadwick. E. R. Chadwick was internationally known as having put community development on the map. Articles were now appearing and conferences being held to define community development and mass education (called by UNESCO Fundamental Education).

Alec Dickson had contacted E. R. Chadwick while in West Africa and got on well with him. Knowing his situation in the Gold Coast, Chadwick had indicated interest in possibilities of a transfer but made no promises. Now, in a letter to Alec, he wrote of a development project being started in Nigeria which might suit his talents, stressing that it was still only in Chadwick's own mind and giving no information of any actual plan. E. R. Chadwick was to become a patron and sponsor, a generous friend of Alec Dickson.

Meanwhile, I could no longer delay the end to my course in London and returned to Scotland with the intention of launching myself as a painter still uppermost in my mind. For the convenience of her family, my mother had decided to leave Moffat and move to Edinburgh. The year I came home I had two pictures accepted by the Royal Scottish Academy.

When the transfer to Nigeria went through and Alec's departure date was set, Gran invited me back to 8 KCG for the two weeks before he left, to bring some calm common sense to the hectic atmosphere that was building up in the flat. Murray Dickson was also there on leave. It was while I was visiting that Alec suggested that I tour West Africa with my pencil and brushes, making my way exercising my talents, with contacts that he could suggest. While he talked I listened, appalled, my confidence in my own abilities rapidly slipping away. As he expanded on possibilities – get in touch with the Elder Dempster Shipping Line, would they take murals? sketches? portraits? Contact the United Africa Company, Unilever House, suggest commissions, landscape, decoration, African portraits. What about the Church of Scotland? illustrations of their mission stations? staff portraits? flora and fauna? school sketches? scenes of African life? Material for an exhibition when I came home, a contribution to both Art and Africa . . . ? – I began to find belief growing in me. This was the first time someone had taken my painting seriously and had confidence in my abilities. Why not? By the time I had seen him off to Nigeria I was committed to an immediate future whose practical application was a total mystery to me.

The first thing to be done, with considerable apprehension, was to tell my mother. To my surprise she was quietly pleased. It did not occur to me then that she might be thinking further ahead. I had known, because Gran – a very different character – had told me openly, that she wanted me as a wife for one of her sons. This I disregarded. I knew Murray to be uninterested and Alec had other things on his mind. As indeed had I.

Now committed to the reality of going to Africa, I needed to make some money. Stimulated by the confidence recently shown in my ability to sell pictures and realising that being well known in the small town of Moffat I had a possible market, I began to hawk my wares about. The despised flower paintings would sell; watercolours of people's houses; postcards for hotels;

the occasional portrait. It was a humbling experience but also a valuable one. Later, when the time came to seek possible commissions from some of the companies connected with the African trade, I learned from a contact the verdict of one of them – and recognised the truth of it. 'A beautiful draughtswoman, with no commercial sense!'

Fortunately there was time and slowly a few hundred pounds began to accumulate. The news from Nigeria, communicated directly to me by Alec (partly because Gran had gone with Murray to Nyasaland to visit her daughter and the London home was empty) was once again uncertain. The arrival in Lagos had not been met with any great welcome. E. R. Chadwick was stationed in Enugu, Eastern Region, hundreds of miles away; the anticipated Community Development plan seemed no nearer reality. Alec Dickson's address was 'c/o The Manager, Church Missionary Society Bookshop, Lagos.'

Already he was having doubts about his own Nigerian transfer and regretting his suggestion to me that I should come out on a painting tour starting in the Gold Coast. As always he was very self critical.

I wrote a reply to him directly: '... having once viewed you with extremely detached eyes I have no illusions about your monstrous egoisms and other failings. But who is there among us who is not at times despicable and which of us has not known even his best actions to be sometimes underlaid by the meanest motives? But it seems to me you have been given great gifts on the credit side as well as enormous faults. We, your friends, are none of us blind to the bad in you but we continue to love you with quite astonishing devotion. You cannot persuade me that this is delusion on our part . . . the important thing is that you undoubtedly have a fairly large proportion of the divine fire inside you. Suppose you were to abandon a job which was of infinite good to other people simply to do something more flashy in the eyes of the world. I should think it regrettable but it doesn't cancel out or alter the spark that made you originally do the first job and do it well. You are like a surrealist painting with a deluded sense of values about yourself and a curiously good one about the things in living.'

Whatever his feelings were, I was coming to Nigeria anyway.

'Please, just to please me, be a little patient and a little restrained just at first. I don't want to arrive in Nigeria and be a) ostracised because I know you b) suspected of being a revolutionary c) friend of a corpse d) friendless altogether.'

The letter was written in April 1950: I planned to go out in October.

However, first of all my mother had to sell her Moffat House and find a suitable replacement in Edinburgh. Fortunately my brother Robert, with a son now as well as a daughter, was again on leave in Britain and able to be of help when the right house came on the market.

It amazed me how easily things connected with my travels were falling into place. Gran, now back from Africa, was constantly communicating with me and asking for visits. The Church of Scotland had made enquiries and given me the freedom of all their missions and transport if needed. The Editor of 'Corona', the Journal of His Majesty's Overseas Service, had commissioned some drawings and there was an interview fixed with the United Africa Company. I had also been given a great many introductions.

William Tsitsiwu, studying music, and Hosu Porblay, political economy, the two senior members of the staff of the Togo Mass Education Unit were now at university in Glasgow. I went one day to visit them and introduced them to my aunts, whom they charmed. They took me to their hostel and Tsitsiwu offered to sit for a portrait in his Ghana robes.

There had been a letter from Brian Thomas, my teacher at the Art School, saying that sooner or later I would be tempted by the devil with virtue, with the desire to serve. He entreated me to resist and to remember that nowadays so many people served but that the artist's was the higher function – to adore the Holy Spirit. He touched a struggle in my spirit.

British Cameroon

In July Alec was posted to the Cameroons – like Togo a UN Trusteeship Territory divided between Britain and France, the French part being much larger. The British section was administered by Nigeria.

Alec had had nearly five months in the wilderness. The surprise was that he had survived it. He had not moped in Lagos but made the best possible use of his time, finding friends and getting to know as much of Nigeria as he could. One of the friends, Kareem Animashaun, a clerk in the Government Secretariat, proved to be a mine of information on the workings of Government and the character of each local region, East, West and North. A quiet man with a consuming interest in facts, he remained a lifelong friend.

When E. R. Chadwick came back from leave (where he had visited Anne Dickson) and the instructions to move to the Cameroons came through, Alec discovered that arrangements had been made for him to have the company of another young officer, Charles Swaisland, a specialist in social welfare. There was an instant rapport between the two men. Charles Swaisland was a Quaker, a quiet intelligent man with a sense of humour. Chadwick had seen very early that Alec Dickson, if allowed to go his own way with a congenial companion, himself a man of stability ready to give support, Cameroon, like Togo, was far enough away from the seat of Government to avoid interference in the early stages of any potential development. It was Chadwick's imagination and vision that brought these two men together.

It was the rainy season in Cameroon, the second wettest place in the world. The house given to Alec Dickson in Buea, the small capital, halfway up 13,000 ft Mt Cameroon, was damp and the home of rats. The Community Development project, through no fault of Chadwick, was a non-starter. The local Bakweri tribe of Southern Cameroon had appealed to the United Nations to have the land back which the Germans when in charge had converted into large banana plantations. This was embarrassing for the British for whom the plantations now formed the CDC (Cameroon Development Company). Any alternative scheme was judged out of the question.

Alec Dickson and Charles Swaisland, sitting with steady rain thundering on the aluminium roof, were faced with a dilemma. Chadwick was engaged in Eastern Nigeria. With the collapse of the Bakweri project the two officers had to be seen to be doing something of value – or senior Government officials would become impatient and separate them, posting each one where they thought best.

In the five months interval while languishing in Lagos waiting for constructive action, Alec Dickson had visited the Community Development project, UDI in the Eastern Region, for which E. R. Chadwick had become internationally famous. Fostering self-help was the heart of this concept. There, in Udi, before his very eyes, Alec had seen young Ibo farmers clad only in loin cloths, struggling to fell trees so that their village could be linked with a feeder road. He was inspired by this sight. While he was watching, a group of schoolboys passed on their way home. For a few moments they looked on as the illiterate village youths strove to lift the felled trees into position. Then the schoolboys broke into laughter. One used a word to denote naked men as being contemptible. Riled, Alec Dickson asked them why they were not joining in. 'We, Sir?' they asked in surprise. 'Yes you'. Alec replied. 'But Sir, we are educated.' Then one of them added, 'We can't be forced to work!'

This roadside conversation had made a great impression on Alec Dickson. Education was expanding all over Nigeria and with this the numbers of those completing primary school would be increasing too. If they were growing up convinced that manual labour was not for them, that they had no obligations towards illiterate villagers, then community development would be doomed. An illegitimate elite would rise to the top, untrained and unwilling to give leadership in their own communities. Chadwick's idea of villagers cooperating to further their own development would be betrayed by those youngsters.

Through a day and a night in Alec Dickson's bungalow on the slopes of Mount Cameroon, he and Charles Swaisland discussed the implications of the negative impact that schooling appeared to be having on the local culture. More significantly, they discussed what they themselves could do to bring about a change in attitude. They realised that in Chadwick's absence very cogent and convincing arguments had to be presented if sceptical senior administrative officers were to be persuaded that attitudes could be changed. Generalisations would get them nowhere – recommendations of what action could be taken immediately and within the Cameroons had to be advanced.

Charles Swaisland had recently returned from leave in Britain where he had helped in the running of courses in Aberdovey, the new Outward Bound School inspired by Kurt Hahn, the Headmaster of Gordonstoun School. It was valuable to have a model which could be quoted.

Unshaven and exhausted, Alec Dickson typed out the results of their night's work. Then, in pyjamas, he rushed to the local Post Office where the postmaster was just closing the sack for the airmail service to Enugu, the provincial capital and seat of administrative power. The postmaster was amazed to see a British Officer in pyjamas asking him to open His Majesty's mailbag. 'I'm wearing my Yoruba dress this morning', Alec joked, referring to the major tribe in Western Nigeria. The postmaster cut the knot and inserted the envelope.

At this precise time central government in Lagos was being pressed in the UN about the Bakweri Question. The report that they received from the Cameroons might give them breathing space. It was forwarded to the British UN Representative and a copy sent to Doyle Shute the Senior Resident in the Cameroons. He sent for Alec Dickson and Charles Swaisland and told them what had been happening, being himself a man interested in ideas. Alec Dickson said, 'Well, if Lagos has sent our report to New York, now they can give us the money to start the programme'. So the Citizenship and Leadership Centre, known for a special reason as Man O' War Bay, was born.

CHAPTER 13

Man O' War Bay visit

1950 – Man O' War Bay

On December 6th 1950 I stood on the platform of the Caledonian Station, Edinburgh, with my mother and an uncle waiting to board the night train to Liverpool. The baggage surrounding us consisted to a large extent of painter's tools; paints, brushes, canvas, small easel, paper, sketch books etc. etc., all done up in so far as my secondhand knowledge went to withstand the West African climate.

It had taken much longer than expected to make the travel arrangements on an Elder & Fyffes banana boat; to overcome the difficulty of having no papers as an accredited agent; to have finally in my bag an immigration permit from the Nigerian Police; to say 'Goodbye' to both our mothers who, in the last week, had developed uneasy qualms.

As the train drew out of Edinburgh I was immensely relieved to be gone. At midnight, however, standing on the platform of Carstairs Station, waiting for the change to the through train from Glasgow to Liverpool, I was assailed by doubts. Alone in the darkness this enterprise seemed madness. I knew the elaborate programme to paint my way round Nigeria to be spurious. That the Brian Thomas prophecy that I might lose the struggle between Art and what in his view was the Devil would be fulfilled if I went on. The truth was that I wanted Alec Dickson and to meet him in the habitat which, if uncomfortable, was natural to him. I was also well aware that he needed me but feared being a rival commitment to his all-consuming visions and that he might never be able to take the decision to risk it.

In this final uncertainty two more of Brian Thomas' words came into my mind, 'Always carry a sketch book' and 'Never forget the great work'. As the enormous railway engine, with a tremendous noise of power and steam, came to a halt in the dark alongside Carstairs platform I had my sketchbook out and scribbled a hasty drawing. Then I climbed on board.

MV *Reventazon* left Liverpool docks next morning for Tiko, the banana port in the British Cameroons. It could accommodate twelve passengers but was not full. On board was a very distinguished one, Brigadier Gibbons, High Commissioner of the UN Trusteeship Territory of British Cameroon.

Four months earlier, when I knew that permission for the community development project had come through and that Alec had moved to a house in Buea halfway up Mount Cameroon infested by rats, I had written to him: 'I can't bear the sound of rats. Do something about them before I burst through the undergrowth crying "Mr Dickson I presume!" I hate them and had quite enough of them in the war. Actually I'm frightened of so many things I sometimes wonder why I'm coming at all. Snakes and spiders and all sorts of creepies – the only things I feel at all capable of dealing with are people'. Looking back at the Liver Tower rising from the urban coastline as the ship left the harbour I knew that this was the time to start.

It was a wonderful ocean voyage – my first. Without sight of land, except for the turquoise blue Canary Islands on the horizon, until we came through the Bight of Benin – where it used to be said 'few came out though many went in' – to wake on a misty morning slipping past the triangular Small Cameroon Mountain in the dawn.

I had drawn and painted the Captain, the High Commissioner, the Chief Officer Mr Harvey, the Stewardess, the sailors painting lifeboats in the tropics, scrubbing decks, preparing the empty ship for the loading of its returning cargo of bananas. In the two weeks hastening to its destination my confidence had been restored.

Because of our distinguished passenger, MV *Reventazon* came to anchor in the bay beside the little town of Victoria. In a rolling sea we climbed down a rope ladder into a small boat. I could see Alec on the quayside with Charles Swaisland and his wife Cecillie. The *Reventazon* blew a foghorn salute and drew up the anchor to sail round the headland to Tiko, the banana port. It had given me a happy introduction to the great adventure.

Once the baggage had been stared at by Immigration and I had been vouched for by

The Captain

Mr Dickson we all got into the Studebaker and drove to Buea, 3,000 ft up the mountain. Victoria was the administrative centre but Buea, in a much more temperate climate, was where the Germans had set up their senior residents' dwellings when they had been the colonial owners of Cameroon. It was here that the High Commissioner, my travelling companion, lived in what was still known as The Schloss.

We unloaded at Alec's small bachelor bungalow. I was introduced to his staff – Andrew, the elderly cook and David his nephew who did all the difficult chores in a tiny detached kitchen shack with an ancient wood-burning stove and very little else in the way of shelves and cupboards. The steward was Ali, not very intelligent but faithful and fearless. It was Ali who burdened himself with my luggage and took it up to the small room belonging to the Basel Mission which I was to inhabit for the next few months. And it was Ali who, every morning at 6.30 am, knocked on my door with a cup of tea and a jug of warm water, sometimes accompanied by Mongu the household little black and white terrier.

Charles and Cecillie had some lunch ready, then I prepared to make myself acquainted with Africa and Alec Dickson.

It was clear that Alec was in very good spirits because the project was going well. Chadwick had given the go-ahead and Dickson and Swaisland were accepted into the small British community. I had returned to the kind of Dickson menage that I had grown accustomed to in London – in other words a life filled with energy and activity of which I was expected to be a natural part. Even Mongu had the look of being perpetually on his toes. When not needed for the Man O' War Bay affair I had the advantage of turning into a self-sufficient and independent painter.

Before I arrived official permission had come through to look for a suitable site for the new training centre. It had been a happy time for Alec Dickson. There came a day when, emerging from acres of banana plantation, he found himself looking at a secluded bay, a jetty and an old, apparently abandoned, plantation manager's house perched on the cliff edge. Geographically this was where the great bend of West Africa swept round to the South. The east-west coasts were flat sand and mangrove swamps; this was the only sea shore in what was then Nigeria with cliffs. At one end of the bay stood a lighthouse called Cape Nachtigal after the German Consul who had staked the claim for this territory in the 1880s. Out at sea was the conical volcano of Fernando Po: inland loomed the vast whaleback of Mount Cameroon, at 13,000 ft the tallest mountain in West Africa. The view was breathtaking and had every criterion for this kind of training centre as part of it.

'What do you call this place?' Alec Dickson had asked an African after they had exchanged greetings. 'Manowabay' he replied. Could he really be saying

'Man O' War Bay?' Looking at the local chart in the Marine Office in Victoria it was found to be the truth. The bay was so named because round about 1820, when Britain was endeavouring to suppress the shipment of slaves from West Africa, this was the spot where the naval vessel engaged on anti-slavery patrol used to shelter and then sally forth when intelligence was received of slaves being taken aboard at Douala round the corner to be transferred to a large ship standing off the coast.

'You'd better get some stationery printed', Chadwick said. 'The Community Development Leadership Training Centre?' Alec asked. 'No, no, call it simply Man O' War Bay' Chadwick replied.

Very soon after my arrival I was taken down to see Man O' War Bay. Of course there was a sketchbook in my bag. The site lay four miles east of Victoria on the coast. It was along a jeep track through the bush and then a CDC banana plantation. The old German manager's house stood on cliffs which plunged straight down into the Atlantic Ocean. To the west the nearest shore was South America. To the south the ocean went on to Cape Town and then Antarctica. We were not very far north of the Equator.

The house, which was very large, still showed the results of 40 years desertion. It was intended eventually to hold the students. As yet there were no staff quarters and a great deal of work needed to be done to clear the overgrown site, repair the jetty and redefine paths. That was only the physical work.

Students were to come from all over Nigeria, seconded by firms, missions, organisations, Government departments – all of whom had to be contacted and persuaded that this new kind of training would be of positive value. On the Outward Bound model, courses would last only a month. Staff would be seconded for one course or two from among the young District Officers in Nigeria and African staff from the Army or Police. The entire business of housekeeping, travel, use of the sea or mountain as physical exercises on a site whose access was not easy had still to be thought of. It was December. March was the date set for the first course but all this work was as yet at the planning stage. Any idea that my role should be that of a 'tourist', whose existence was hardly known in Africa in 1950, was instantly banished.

Anyway, I was still a painter and, while acknowledging that this fact could not take precedence over involvement in what was for everybody else the excitement of a creation – the heat and sweat, ups and downs, bringing into living action a new community development centre – I was not going to let my painting languish. But clearly adaptations were needed. Oil painting was impractical. The heat affected the paints. It was impossible for me to sit in front of an easel in a village without being overwhelmed by children. On the other hand they loved being drawn. I got used to a constant audience as time went on. I drew repeatedly – using watercolour, pens, ink, chalks, any sort of

African faces

multimedia that happened to be there – or could be invented. African faces fascinated and enchanted me. Ali and Andrew went into the sketchbook; African police, who liked to be painted in tribal clothes; the prisoners in their beige shirts and shorts who worked in gangs cleaning up the streets, building, resting, talking with their guard. Babies carried on backs, loads on heads, colour, cloths. Life everywhere was relaxed and cheerful. Any ideas of needing a 'commercial sense' disappeared. I made pictures for fun and gave them away or kept them for the great work as seemed appropriate.

No programme had been arranged for me. If time was free I put my materials on my back and went out to look at Africa and its people. If Alec was going somewhere on the job I went too with my painting kit; to Tiko to see the bananas being loaded; to a Scout Meeting; to a Baptist Mission Convention; to the small domestic science and cooking group in Victoria. But at weekends there were fun things. We went with the Swaislands on a picnic to a crater lake at Kumba some miles up the road that led eventually into Nigeria. The lake on top of the extinct volcano was beautiful and the water very cold. No one had told me that there was an intention to swim (an activity which I had disliked since learning from an ex-army swimming instructor at North Berwick), and I was quite unprepared. But the challenge had to be faced so I took off my cotton dress and leapt in in my underwear!

Seaward of the Cameroon Mountain was the Small Cameroon, a Hans Anderson illustration triangular peak rising from sea level. Elizabeth O' Kelly, from the Country Women of the World Organization was in Victoria on a professional visit. Alec had got to know her and we liked her very much. Before she left Africa she was determined to get to the 3,000 ft top of this spectacular mountain. Alec also wanted to go – would I do the same? Thinking of my rolling home hills, comparing the Small Cameroon's perpendicular sides covered with forest with quiet walks up Hartfell on a Sunday afternoon, I was not so sure. But, like the decision about swimming, I could see no way of refusing this challenge.

Very early in the morning the house was a-bustle. Ali woke me with tea and hot water about 5 am. Andrew and David were making sandwiches, packing drinks, getting climbing sticks ready for 'Madam'. Ali, who was coming with us, was contriving headloads out of extra jerseys and numerous possible necessaries and comforts in case we got stranded or had to spend the night on the top. John, an aspiring policeman whom Alec had met on the street and offered temporary employment to, was joining the group. Elizabeth provided her own stewardboy.

The whole climb proved easier than we had feared. The companionship among the party, black and white, was relaxed and close. At one point when a largish animal burst through the bush in front of us and rustled away behind us I thought I would exercise my 'pidgin', the lingua franca of the Cameroons. 'He make good chop?' I asked John who was behind me. 'Yes Madam', he replied, 'it's edible'. The joke was on me – the animal was a porcupine.

The next encounter with a mountain was a very different affair.

One Sunday morning a French aeroplane from Douala, the capital of French Cameroon, crashed on the mountain behind us. It was a regular service to Paris carrying families home on leave. It was also carrying gold. The police heard that the aeroplane was missing and the bush telegraph from the mountain itself began to talk of fires in the night, corpses and catastrophe.

Alec went down to the police station to find out if there was any more news. I heard a car coming back up the hill in great haste. 'It's on the mountain', he said. 'A hunter brought news this morning of a great fire. A small party of police are going up but they're all African. I hate to think of women, perhaps badly hurt, and there being no one to speak to them in their own language. We must go at once. It's a climb of 7,000 ft. The police have left already, so we'll hope to catch up with them.'

We went into the kitchen and told Andrew to stop cooking the Sunday lunch and get ready to come up the mountain with us. That went for David and Ali too. To their great credit they at once began to prepare. We stripped blankets off the beds and made up three headloads, taking water, some food, bread and bananas, warm jerseys, a bottle of whisky, a torch and what inadequate medicines we had in the house. They were pitifully small – a pot of vaseline, some elastoplast, an old sheet for tearing into bandages and some aspirin. I had on one of my nicer cotton frocks and a pair of light shoes. Somehow in the urgency of getting away there seemed to be no time to go back to my own room and change.

The plane had crashed on a far shoulder of the mountain away from any of the recognised routes up. We had to have a guide who could only be found in a village called Bonakanda, home village of the hunter who had reported the crash, about one and a half hours walk along the foot of the mountain and then four hours climb. But first we must go to the Chief of the area, ask his advice about guides and tell him what we were doing. His house was a mile away and we could leave the car there.

Chief Endelli opened the door himself and ushered us into his sitting room. Here we had some luck. In this house, at this very moment, was the Bakweri hunter who had come down with news of the crash. Chief Endelli instructed him to go back up the mountain with us to lead us to the plane. Even while we were speaking to the Chief there was a terrific crash and an unseasonable tornado burst over the mountain. It delayed us for an hour. As soon as the sun came out Andrew, David and Ali put their loads on their heads, the guide went off in front at a fast walk and we straggled out behind him in a long line.

We made Bonakanda in an hour, already late to be starting a mountain climb when tropical dark fell at 6.30 pm. Andrew was already showing signs of wear and tear. David had become very nervous of sleeping on the mountain which was haunted by ghosts and bogies. Only Ali plodded on fresh and undisturbed.

At Bonakanda we found the police. They too were getting nervous and by some oversight had forgotten to bring any lamp. A small crowd of visitors were reassuring them with all the tales of mountain ghosts they knew. Knowing us to be immune from ghosts they tried to dissuade us from going further by assuring us that a herd of elephants had been seen across the path we would be taking. However, when the police saw that we were not to be deterred and that I, a woman, intended to go on they were shamed into borrowing some hurricane lamps and preparing to come too.

Now it was real jungle. We climbed straight up from the village through dripping tangled bushes and trees. The path was narrow and slippery with decaying vegetation. We could see only a few feet in front or behind. It would have been quite possible to walk into an elephant. Alec and I climbed in silence, reserving all our strength. The Africans sang and shouted to keep off the ghosts. When I slipped, which I did very often for my Sunday shoes had not been made for this work, a voice behind me would say, 'Sorry too much' and the faithful Ali put out a helping hand. Up and up and up. The undergrowth cleared and the great forest trees took over, towering up and shutting out the sky. Even the police were silent and overawed.

After an hour we sat down to rest and have some food. Here we discovered that Andrew was not with us – neither was his headload which had contained most of the food. Still, we had bananas and water and all the medical supplies.

On and on and on. Now the trees gave way to open savannah interspersed with volcanic rock. Here we were joined by Bakweri hunters, fierce wild men who roamed the mountain. The cold began to strike. David had not been seen for a long time and it was David who carried our warm jerseys and extra socks. A policeman told us he had turned back some hours before. Ali, resourceful in such emergencies, borrowed a cloak from another policeman who gave it up cheerfully and wrapped me in its thick serge folds.

It was about now, with dark creeping on and the mountain becoming wilder and rockier, that we began to face the implications of the climb. What were we going to do when we, perhaps, found ourselves faced with dead and dying and desperately wounded men and women? In sobbing breaths we started to whisper over and over the Lord's Prayer – in French.

It was quite dark when we reached the spot. The ground flattened out and the borrowed lamps glimmered and flickered on high outcrops of lava rock. It was not difficult to find the aeroplane though in normal times it would not have been recognisable as such. A huge circle of earth had been burnt completely black. Bits of metal, engine, luggage and clothing lay scattered in a radius of many yards about it. In the centre a small heap of twisted metal, all that remained of the body of the aircraft. It must have hit the outcrop of rock beside which it lay with tremendous force and exploded into flames.

At first we could not see any bodies. Everything looked inanimate, black and burned. Then we saw that the dark brown figures that lay in grotesque attitudes among the burnt grass had once been human. Colour, race, sex could no longer be distinguished. There were twenty-nine of them – all dead.

Close by was a little grass hut built by the hunters for shelter. It was already overcrowded with seven hunters and a dog crouching round the fire in the middle of the floor. We bent double at the low entrance and squeezed in. When the last policeman was sitting with his back to the door there were sixteen of us in this precarious shelter. By the light of the flames the hunters looked wilder than ever. They ignored us and talked loudly to each other in an unknown tongue, casting glances at me, now and then bursting into maniacal laughter. All our food, our warm clothes and our toilet articles were with the errant Andrew and David; Ali's load contained medicine, bananas, a bottle of water and the whisky. We dared not produce the latter for fear of the effect it might have on the hunters.

Outside the wind rose and thunder began to roll and crack among the rocks. It was indeed a night for ghosts. Gradually, one after another, the hunters wrapped themselves in blankets and stretched head to tail around the dying fire. I shivered in my cotton dress and the one blanket that had survived the climb. The policeman had regained his serge cloak. It was no moment for squeamishness or prudery; stretched out between Alec and Ali I took off my shoes and thankfully rested my sore, chilled feet on the warm black thigh of the nearest hunter. There was barely room for us all and as the night crept on and the unearthly cold of the small hours penetrated the hut we imperceptibly drew closer and closer, black and white alike, conscious of the need for warmth and reassurance.

It was not a bad night; better in many ways than the long succession of nights to come when I was to wake sweating from exaggerated nightmares. The dawn, bleak and early, was heartily welcome. We breakfasted on the last bananas and combed our hair with our fingers. I looked sadly at the remains of my shoes and the resourceful Ali produced a piece of rag in an attempt to keep body and sole together. We walked across to the wreckage and those inhuman roasted bodies. I was conscious neither of shock nor revulsion, only a complete detachment. The police appeared entirely unaffected.

We staggered off the mountain at 3 pm on Monday. The last few miles had seemed an endless penance. As we passed through the villages the people called 'No man alive?' and Alec replied 'No man alive'. The car was where we left it. Buea looked the same, jacarandas and poinsettias still blooming vividly, though the welcome was not exactly warm – except from Andrew and David, excited to see that the ghosts had not got us. Doyle Shute, the Senior Resident, who had been having his siesta when we left on Sunday afternoon, was clearly angered. 'Madness. Madness. Of course we knew they were all dead.'

'Did you see the gold?' asked an eager junior officer who had been playing tennis when we left.

The senior police officer who had given Alec permission to go with his men obviously regretted it. There was a feeling around that it had been a quixotic thing to do. Only Alec Dickson who was not a genuine member of the Colonial Service but was setting up that new-fangled experiment at Man O' War Bay would have got away with it.

A message came down from the Schloss that a French group would be coming over from Douala the next day. Would Mr Dickson come up to the High Commissioner's Residence and describe the situation on the mountain as he had seen it. Alec went up and returned upset about the credit the British had taken for having been so quick to send a potential rescue group to the site. It was unlikely any mention was made of me. Not for the first time I was thankful to be in Africa without any sort of pressure from relatives.

It had already been arranged that a day or two later we were to visit northern Cameroon. Still exhausted, we were both glad to go. Bamenda was nearly two hundred miles north-west of Buea. The small station of the American Baptist Mission lay in the most beautiful country I had yet seen. Compared to the heavy rain forests of the south, the clarity and colour of this landscape was ravishing – blue and mauve ranges of mountains decorated the horizons of the plateau. Near at hand the strange shapes of single trees were silhouetted against a radiance of light.

We stayed with the energetic and enthusiastic Pastor of the Mission who was interested in the potential of Man O' War Bay, ready to give introductions and spread the news.

I revelled in the sights and sounds of this strange country. The people and their customs were very different from the coast. Tribal Chiefs called 'Fons' lived in villages of round thatched huts surrounded by a multitude of wives. Nomadic Fulani women, tall and light-skinned, walked the roads with striking dignity, babies on their hips and orange calabashes holding baggage on their black plaited hair. I painted the village brassmaker, his head wrapped in a towering white turban, topped by a small round red cap: the church and its open Drum Hut under a thick circular thatched roof from which the Drum was beaten on the Sabbath to summon a far flung congregation. I painted the Public Works Dept., carpenters and joiners hard at work in a deep black shade against a brilliant light. For Alec too the visit went well; the openness of the landscape reflected on open acceptance for and interest in his activities and ideas. Gradually the nightmares went away.

When after ten days we returned to Man O' War Bay the pace had quickened and the resurrection of the site was going well. There was bustle and work everywhere and talk of starting courses before the rainy season. Alec Dickson was on the point of leaving Buea and moving to a tented staff encampment on the site. Communications between Enugu, capital of the Eastern Region and other centres in Nigeria, were flowing reciprocally tapping resources of every kind, human as well as material. Chadwick was pleased and instantly Alec was totally absorbed.

I was only too well aware that I ought to be leaving. Already three months had been spent in the Cameroons. There were other commitments to fulfil, with the Church of Scotland Mission in Calabar, Eastern Nigeria, and visits had been promised to my brothers in Capetown and Tanganyika. I was living in a vacuum, with painting no longer the central focus of my life.

So a passage was booked on the *Warri*, plying from Victoria to Calabar. Alec drove me down to the hospital where Audrey, the nurse, was going to give me a meal before I went on board at 8 pm. He handed me a letter and rushed back up to Buea to deal with the official mail which lay almost ankle deep on his sitting room floor.

Audrey let me have a bath. I lay in it weeping over the letter of goodbye.

CHAPTER 14

Mora

Calabar, Itu, Uburu

It was a clear starry night when we weighed anchor from Victoria Bay. Cape Nachtigal, overlooking Man O' War Bay, sent two cheerful winks every 8 seconds. On the well-deck beneath a slung tent the Nigerian passengers lay among their goods and children, a heterogeneous collection of limbs and garments. The *Warri* was in no hurry; not expected to be in Calabar before dawn.

The jetty at Calabar, up the mouth of the Cross River, differed greatly from the languor of Victoria. With much noise and shouting the gangway was precariously slung over the side. A seething mass of boxes, bundles, umbrellas, sacks, baggage of every description, each item on the head of its owner, struggled to gain a place on the narrow plank. Among it all, women with babies tied on their backs and small children hanging round their skirts, pushed forward as best they could.

The Principal of Hope Waddell School for Boys, Norman Macrae, was there to meet me and drive me up the hill on the brow of which the school stood. His wife Claire had a welcome and breakfast ready. They had heard about Man O' War Bay and what was happening there which interested them. Wherever I was to go in Eastern Nigeria someone was to be found who recognised the name of E. R. Chadwick and now Alec Dickson. It was good to know that the connection was not broken.

This was Mary Slessor country. A remarkable Scottish missionary from Dundee, she had lived among the villagers on the other side of the river and become respected and revered by them. For two weeks I was to be the guest of the school, putting life on mission history.

This meant me taking unsuccessful drawing classes, making portraits of staff, sitting drawing in the printing shop and the carpenter's shop, watching boys washing under the pump, making ready school meals, playing games, being taken round primary schools where one teacher said he 'hoped to see the drawings when they were much improved – alas they never were! and

view from Hope Waddell School

sitting in with the Principal at village meetings. The reality of Africa very different here from any preceding imagination.

A programme had been laid out before my arrival in Calabar. It was to go 200 miles upriver to visit the leprosy work of the mission. There were two different models – Itu, a long-established colony under the direction of Dr and Mrs Macdonald, where built up by self-help on a large and beautiful area of land, some thousands of people lived a self-sufficient life – the only distinguishing feature being that everyone suffered from what is now known as Hansen's Disease, then called leprosy. The second model, Uburu, was leper villages, often set up quite near to normal villages, with a central clinic whose Doctor travelled round bringing a weekly surgery to each affected village. The province to which I would go, Ogoja, had a incidence of the disease as high as 10 per cent. Itu took in, Uburu went out.

My first reaction when told of these arrangements was apprehension but everyone around me seemed to regard the idea as so ordinary that pride forbade me to reveal my doubts.

The embarkation from the shipyard below the school was exhilarating. The yard was crowded. Our car nearly ran down an inefficient policeman and pushed preoccupied crowds out of the way with the mudguards to the accompaniment of chattering, whistling, hooting, and cursing. Men dragged carts loaded with stink fish (imported from Norway) shouting 'Give chance there, Give chance!' I picked my way over pulleys and ropes, up slippery planks and over two or three lighters on to the launch. I was the only non-African passenger. When the launch hooted and extricated itself it was still attached to one lighter on each side, loaded with fish and passengers.

Canoes slid in and out of secret waterways among the mangrove swamps, full of produce and fat women or carrying fishermen intent upon their catch. Later on when the banks became firm, the launch stopped several times at villages, was hauled into the side by ropes tied round a tree trunk and a terrific meeting took place between friends on board and those on land. Small boys leapt into the water to bargain loudly with other small boys for handfuls of nuts or peppers. Relatives were seen off by their entire clan with great emotion and much advice. It was hard to realise, travelling in comfort on a comparatively up-to-date launch,

Hope Waddell teacher

the banks thronged with brightly clad women, that in some of these places whole missionary families had died of fever.

Towards evening we came round a bend in the river and saw Itu in front of us. Scattered roofs, shining or red-painted corrugated iron, known locally as 'pan', glimmering through the palm trees on the hill. Dr Macdonald met me at the jetty. We drove up the hill and through a grand red mud gate with a lintel across the top into a lovely garden and a community life in the full and usual sense. Everybody worked – it was compulsory until the disease actually prevented it – schoolchildren, teachers, police force, nurses, court officials, brass band in white with pink sashes. Every building had been built by the community, every function was undertaken by patients. The only sign was when I stretched out a hand to the children with an instinct to touch and they recoiled, shocked that I had forgotten.

I had gone upriver inwardly afraid for myself and of what I would see and found there was no place in this colony for fear of any sort.

It was another long journey to Uburu and the Ogoja Leprosy Scheme. Dr Jessie Ridge with her colleague, the young temporary doctor in charge of the tiny hospital there, had driven to Itu to pick me up. We spent a night at Umuahia where there was a concert in the evening. It was near here at Uzoakali that the development of the new drug D.A.D.P.S. (Di-amino diphenl

Sulphone) had taken place. For the first time in centuries a breakthrough had occurred, not a cure yet but bringing a marked and encouraging improvement to the condition of certain patients.

Then, on the next day, to Uburu, the centre of Dr Ridge's work. She was delighted that I had come clearly feeling that most visitors were taken to Itu and few, if any, came further. Dr Jessie dealt with ten widely spread clinics and an estimated 22,000 suffering from Hansen's Disease within the area of the scheme. The mission land was flat and sunbaked, at first sight barren. In a wood just behind the mission station there was a juju shrine of stones topped with withered palm branches and a few dirty hen's feathers. The people believed that both witchcraft and Christian medicine could help them. This was the most powerful juju of the Uburu clan, consulted by the same people who came to the hospital for treatment.

Every morning except Sunday, Dr Jessie got ready her medical bag and the D.A.D.P.S. tablets. I filled my painting bag with sketchbooks, pencils and brushes, a small bottle with water, paints and a folding stool. We set off early when it was still cool to visit two, perhaps three, far flung clinics. It would be a long hot day.

The first clinic at Apojo dealt with two clans. Originally they themselves had come requesting treatment from the doctor. They had been told it was impossible unless they built the segregated village themselves and lived in it. To the doctor's surprise, they had done so, E. R. Chadwick having offered a gift of roofing material. Through this contact, in this remote place Dr Jessie (who had previously worked in Nyasaland and heard rumours about the MPU) knew the name of Alec Dickson and Man O' War Bay.

When we arrived the open treatment centre with a mud and mat roof was surrounded by men, women and children. All were naked except for a loincloth so that when they stood in front of the doctor she could clearly see the condition of their skin, whether bearing the signs of leprosy or, because of the new treatment, beginning to show the shine of returning health.

Before the treatment started there were prayers, the men on the right hand, women on the left, children in between. There could be nearly one hundred. Prayers over, patients at once fell into a queue, children first, then women, last the men. Each carried their own temperature charts with a record of temperatures night and morning since the doctor's last visit. This was done under the supervision of one or two patient clerks in each village.

I sat quietly behind Dr Jessie on my folding stool watching fascinated as each patient passed before her, catching quick sketches when I could. It might have been a pathetic scene but it was not. Humour was never far away, especially in the independent women, and there was a scattering of cheeky children to make jokes both with us and about us in vibrant Nigerian English.

Each patient as they passed the doctor said his/her number – 'Ma, thirty one'... This ritual triggered hilarity especially among the older women who had no English and for whom memorising their numbers had been a very difficult feat. Sometimes they forgot and would stand giggling helplessly. 'Ma, sickety sicks' always produced a chuckle from the queue or a whisper from a tiny child which was translated by a neighbour little bigger than himself. They filed past the doctor, were examined, got their pill and passed out of the clinic. There they handed over their charts to a fellow patient and received a dose of iron. This was poured down their throats and mouths were inspected to insure that no pill had been saved for the black market. Such magic medicine could be sold at a good price.

Not only medical problems but a wide variety of social problems were brought before the doctor on this parade. There was the woman who begged

leper patient

to be protected from her husband. Further enquiry illicited as much from the queue as from the woman herself, that she had fallen in love with another man and left her husband for him! The doctor was prepared to be evangelist, nurse, farmer, builder, architect, surveyor, lawyer and councillor, all rolled into one.

There was a bad case with no toes left and fearfully twisted limbs, who flung down his tablets in a sudden rage and cried that he would rather go back to his juju. But there were successes too. Aja Okoro was eight years old. He had lost several of his toes and had very swollen legs. He had been found suffering from starvation and neglect. His hair had been the pale copper colour of undernourishment. He had first been given large quantities of vitamins, then the D.A.D.P.S. treatment started. Four months later he could walk and play singing games with the other children, stamping his feet and laughing. His hair was beginning to grow back black and curly.

Having finished this very large clinic, there was still another one to visit in the heat of the afternoon. In the evening we would arrive home exhausted and have a shower in the outside hut with a bucket of water suspended above manipulated by pulling a rope. Then young Alastair MacDonald, doctor in charge of the Uburu Hospital, would come in for supper with us and we would sit talking and relaxing while the insects battered themselves to death against the Tilly lamp. Dr Jessie would speak of the work to which, in spite of all its difficulties, she was devoted. I came to admire her spirit and energy, her patience with intractable problems and her constant good humour. We became friends and have remained so.

I showed the drawings that had been done during the day to a sympathetic audience and told them about Man O' War Bay.

With the return to Calabar at the end of April, my mind was already made up. I would fly to Lagos, stay for a day or two with friends of Alec, then leave for Capetown by Elder Dempster boat. From Enugu to Lagos was to be my first flight in an aeroplane.

When the launch tied up by the jetty at Calabar I was handed a letter from Alec Dickson: news of the first course, 65 students; difficult white staff; a lifeboat had arrived from John Holt. I left Lagos for Capetown and then the desolation set in. While in Nigeria there had been still many links and I had come to love the country and its people. Now I was truly cut off. However, desolation could not survive in Capetown. Laurence and Mary, my brother and his wife, had a house in Somerset West, behind Table Mountain on the coast and facing the spectacular Hottentots Holland mountain range. Even better than the view was my second nephew Alastair, named after our brother, a few months old and enchanting. His parents asked me to paint a mural on his bedroom wall. Refusal was impossible so I did. When, some years later, as the family increased and they sold the house, the buyers paid extra for the mural!

There was also a letter from Alec Dickson – factual, but with the news that he would have leave when the Cameroons rainy season started, putting a temporary end to courses. This meant that he would be in London for two months, meeting people, visiting the Colonial Office, seeing the Outward Bound School in North Wales and generally gathering information that would be helpful to the programme at Man O' War Bay. A message was sent to Robert in Tanganyika. My sister-in-law managed to get me a berth on a Union Castle Line to Southampton.

I had been in Africa nearly six months when the liner steamed up the Bay of Biscay. Walking the deck in hot sunshine with the pleasant woman who shared my cabin a message was brought me from the bridge. It just said 'Will meet you when you land. Dickson'. I turned to my cabin mate and said: 'Got him!!'.

PARTNERSHIP

Man O' War Bay 1950

Ahead of me lay four of the fullest most creative years of my life. The time had come for support. So I married – and Mora, my wife, enriched my happiness, deepened my judgement, and sustained me in frequent depressions. Henceforth she would partner me in every enterprise.

Autobiographical note by Alec Dickson, 1933

PART III
TEAM WORK

CHAPTER 15

Marriage

Moffat – August 1951

The first visit to the Cameroons had been for both of us a decision-making time. I went out to be a painter and came back to be a partner. Brian Thomas' words 'the great work' were not forgotten, simply changed in nature.

Alec Dickson had always found it hard to make decisions. He was aware himself of this constriction in his temperament. He preferred to leave his options open. There might always be a better way. He needed to decide if I would cramp his style or supply the missing elements. It was only when I left Buea that the balance was tipped. I recognised this at once when the cable on the ship was opened. After that no proposal was necessary for either of us. He simply said, 'You'll come back with me?' I said 'Yes'.

It was a home-made wedding – tailor-made to the bridegroom.

In October 1950, not long before I left for the British Cameroons, my mother had sold the house in Moffat and moved into Edinburgh but close family friends in Moffat had offered their house and grounds for the reception. The wedding would be in the church which I had known since childhood, by the minister who had served as a wartime chaplain with General Slim in Burma. The local baker made the cake, Nannie made my dress, as she had created all my clothes since I was small. I asked my mother to give me away (brothers on both sides were overseas) and lend her car for the occasion. A cousin was my bridesmaid.

In late July one vital component was missing – a date. Alec Dickson in London, preoccupied with his return to Man O' War Bay in early September, had no time to be concerned with wedding arrangements. On July 25th he received a letter from me explaining that I would gladly elope with him but that such an action would be hard on our respective mothers and scandalise my relations. A decision about a date in late August was needed urgently – and, by the way, it was important that before then he come up for a weekend to meet my mother who had never seen him.

Galvanised, an answer came back by return of post agreeing to August 30th.

Ten days before the wedding Alec came to Edinburgh for a weekend. The visit was a complete success. My mother, who must have been very nervous, was charmed – and so was Nannie. It was taken for granted that anything arranged by my family would be the right thing to do.

But what about a honeymoon? Alec Dickson hardly recognised what the word 'holiday' meant. Certainly he was not thinking about it. Then, as so often, ready-made inspiration descended on me: the Lake District – a beautiful place. A few months before a new Outward Bound Mountain School had been established there. So a week at the Woolpack Inn in Keswick was booked and all that remained was to get everyone to the ceremony.

Among the guests, on a day when the sun shone, were Hosu Porblay and William Tsitsiwu of the Gold Coast Mass Education Team. At the reception they startled my mother by formally handing to her a present for the bride. It was only when the customs of their homeland were explained to her that she realised the ritual nature of such a presentation.

For my own relations formality had been disgracefully disregarded when I came out of the vestry practically running after we had signed the register, forgetting that my bridesmaid was recovering from polio and using a stick. My explanation that my only coherent thoughts were with the fulfilment of a long search was thought frivolous. As we climbed into my mother's car, hidden on a back road, my mother was saying to Nannie, 'She's gone'. She did not know how wrong she was – once again.

Man O' War Bay

Alec Dickson, Principal of Man O' War Bay Training Centre, arrived in Lagos on September 26th. It was a very different landing from his first. Man O' War Bay had run two experimental courses before the rainy season and was already an accepted institution, not only in Nigeria but in London.

Meantime, at the mercy of the Colonial Office to arrange my passage and left with a long list of things to be done including endorsements on my new passport for French, Spanish and Portuguese possessions (a visa for one visit only) and obtaining an International Driving Licence, my time was divided between my two homes, London and Edinburgh.

At 8KCG Gran was almost regretting that I had married her son because it was going to take me away to Africa. In the basement of the block of flats a portable canoe done up in an enormous bundle required very difficult arrangements be made to move it on to whatever ship would eventually give me a passage from Liverpool.

A tin trunk was bought and stored with all the Dickson possessions and papers left behind in the care of his mother. Replacing the canoe in the basement, the tin trunk was heavy enough to contain a body. A secretary, who at the last moment had taken down in shorthand clearing up letters, delivered them the day after Alec Dickson sailed. They had to be checked and sent off. In my best hat I prepared to dun the Passages Department of the Colonial Office while wishing I was free to make my own travel arrangements.

Meanwhile every post brought literature about Community Development from friends and officials who had hoped to reach Alec before he left and the prospect of my own luggage grew steadily heavier. There were people to see and offices to visit. In one of the latter the receptionist of the Africa Bureau asked for my address. She then said, 'Mr A. G. Dickson? That couldn't be Alec Dickson could it?' Not yet accustomed to my new designation I blushed and said 'Yes'. 'My dear, how did you do it?' to which my stock answer had become, 'Love your mother-in-law before you love her son'. This was reassuring. I was beginning to end my letters to my new husband '. . . after all you haven't seen me for so long and may be wondering if it was a good thing to have a wife!' I sometimes felt myself that the whole thing was a dream.

Eventually however, a visit to the Colonial Office proved productive – after it had been established that I did not come under A–C. A nice young man who dealt with Ds said 'Oh yes, Mrs Dickson, you're down for October 10th' and then went on to prevaricate, 'But it might be October 15th'. All that seemed to be lacking was permission to bring me into Nigeria – nothing was said about the collapsible canoe.

Packing up in Edinburgh, after a 'Thank you' and 'Goodbye' visit to Moffat and the purchase of a ship in a bottle, the Colonial Office rang me on October 2nd to say there was a booking confirmed; Elders and Fyffes MV *Nicoya* on October 10th. My mother was beginning to feel that she had been wrong about her post-wedding remark to Nannie but both of them remained admirably cool surrounded by the pandemonium necessary to get me to the Liverpool train in time.

This second journey to the British Cameroons allowed me a night in a respectable hotel in the city before embarking in the early morning to be greeted by the news that the canoe and everything else was safely on board. Gladly I left behind not only my families but, I suspected, a plethora of belated invitations, letters, relevant or unwanted literature and headed for the open seas.

ship's Captain

This voyage had a very dissimilar atmosphere to the year before. The ship had its full quota of twelve passengers, some Colonial wives among them. I was an object of curiosity and conscious of being assessed as not belonging. Nor did I want to. I was glad that Man O' War Bay was four miles from Victoria, the small capital, along a rude track through a banana plantation – not inviting for coffee mornings or polite visits.

Two days before we were due to dock, a ship's telegram arrived from Alec. He had been summoned to Ibadan, the University city in the Western Province of Nigeria – nearly a thousand miles from Victoria – to address a meeting about Man O' War Bay, now becoming of wide interest. Peter Wallis the site builder would meet me and arrange everything. Charles Swaisland had been posted back to Nigeria.

I replied, 'Unsurprised, Good luck. Much love.'

Peter Wallis was on the quay to meet me and very efficient about all the arrangements. A room was booked in the Victoria Resthouse. On the verandah was Fineboy, Andrew's replacement in the Dickson kitchen. A tall middle-aged man, with a cicatriced face, he greeted me formally. It was clear that he took his orders to look after Madam seriously. Lurking behind him was the devoted Ali.

The next day all three of us drove out to Man O' War Bay where, along with the staff quarters, Peter Wallis was overseeing the building of a small Principal's house. On return to the Resthouse a telegram was sent off to Alec at a Czech friend's address in Lagos: 'House still invisible. Suggest diffidently a decent sized mirror and cushions'. It was to be an unanswered request.

My arrival however re-animated work on the house. When a week had passed by with no sign of my absent husband I told Fineboy and Ali that we were going to move in. The Studebaker, thoroughly overhauled, was collected from the garage and loaded with all the Dickson baggage from Buea, my own from the Resthouse, even the canoe. Fineboy sat beside me as I drove down the banana plantation track. Ali kept an eye on the loads behind.

The bungalow was still a shell, with neither doors nor windows, but it had a tin roof and adequate walls and floors. We arrived about an hour before the fleeting tropical sunset, at 6.30 pm. While Fineboy cooked a supper of eggs and sausages on the ancient wood-consuming stove in the tiny detached kitchen, Ali put up my camp bed in an empty room and arranged the mosquito net over it. He lit a Tilly lamp and balanced it on a bedside crate. From a small bag I took out my overnight possessions which included my father's tiny Bible. When the meal was done and I was sitting on a tin trunk as dark descended Fineboy came through the doorspace and asked solemnly if Madam would like him to sleep on the floor at the end of the bed? Madam, already full of nervous tension, refused as firmly and politely as she could. He left – no doubt to sleep on the verandah across the doorspace. I put on my nightdress, said a prayer, extinguished the lamp and climbed under the mosquito net pulling a sheet over my head prepared for a sleepless night.

The next thing I knew was Ali beside me with a cup of tea held on the palm of one hand. The sun was shining. From now on I felt at home in West Africa.

When Alec came back from Nigeria our life together truly began. It was not to be easy. I took the car to Tiko Airport and drove him and his constantly accumulating baggage back to Man O' War Bay. Already his mind was concentrated on every detail concerned with the next course which was to be the first all-Nigeria one. It was clear that the one sitting/dining room in our small house was also going to accommodate an office.

In March/April 1951 after I had left the Cameroons for Calabar the first experimental course had taken place, followed by a second one in April/May before the start of the rainy season. No time had been lost since the memorandum suggesting such a training course had been submitted to the authorities in October 1950 five months before.

Alec Dickson, once decisions were made – with the imaginative backing of E. R. Chadwick – drove himself and those who worked with him towards the practical realisation of the vision, regardless of difficulties or risks on the way.

In the beginning the site had no accommodation for Principal or other seconded instructors. Quarters for the African staff were just being built. So while Alec Dickson and the six young Britons, District Officers and from the Basel Mission, had all lived in a tent near the jetty, the senior African staff shared

Elizabeth Omoyoju, Lagos secretary

Almond Tree Sea school

the same dormitories as the students in the plantation house. Thirty-six students came on this first course, twenty-eight of them Cameroonians, the rest Nigerian. On the second course forty from the Cameroons and twenty-four Eastern Nigerians nearly overwhelmed the staff. Yet they were good days – everyone involved felt themselves to be pioneers.

Like the instructors, all the students were seconded by their employers: Government or company clerks, teachers from missions or native authorities, policemen, coalminers, forestry assistants, nurses, dispensers. Behind Alec Dickson's thinking lay two important concepts which were to prove seminal. Already the date of Nigerian Independence was known – October 1st 1960. The foundation of each course was to prepare students to be able to take responsibility in their own community. At Man O' War Bay they could discover that this was possible and also ways of doing so while testing out their own individual potential.

Here two profound problems had to be faced: the Colonial Government was viewed as the Universal Provider and the educated Nigerian should never undertake manual labour. (No white man in Nigeria thus degraded himself. Students travelling overseas suffered a major shock on discovering that every kind of work in Britain was done by local people). Man O' War Bay was not attempting to change character but to arouse in responsive students an awareness of opportunities, needs and duties which after Independence would devolve on them and to promote unity in a country put together by Lord Lugard out of a host of tribal backgrounds.

This time I was the only wife on the compound which created for me a different and unaccustomed atmosphere. Alec, the husband, took it for granted that I was an integral part of the whole operation. From the start of our marriage he had accepted my capabilities and admired my talent. He expected me to exercise both at my own discretion. He was sure that I would help in the solving of his problems. It never occurred to him that I would have problems of my own. Support then was not mutual.

The young seconded instructors had a different concept of the place of a wife. It took time for them to accept that the Principal discussed policy and official quandaries with his wife and valued her advice – sometimes over their own. Not for the first time I found myself holding a balance which Alec was often not aware existed: this was during the hectic period of preparation for the third course in January 1952.

The entire establishment, black and white, instructors, business manager, staff, cooks, servants and all manner of essential workers, lived at close quarters on a relatively small compound, isolated from Victoria by a road which, though only four miles long, represented separation in its atrocious uncared for state. There were no staff eating arrangements except in our house. Lucas, now our cook, was young and enterprising, master of the art of shopping in the Victoria market, but his new 'Madam' had no idea how to cater for meals for a group of hard working young men with the kind of provisions that a rural Cameroon market supplied. Nor had she any notion of the economics of such a situation. Alec, accustomed to a bachelor menage, which Andrew, once instructed in the list of foods his Master would not eat, ran independently – and satisfactorily – on a £1 a week, had no time or interest in those domestic concerns. There were complaints.

I felt like taking the next banana boat back to Liverpool.

Personal problems with both time and space were also very hard for me to deal with. The initial visit to Buea had been as an independent painter, regarded as such and free to use what time and talent I had as I pleased. But being a wife changed everything. It had been clear to me since the baggage that must be stored on the ship at Liverpool had begun to accumulate that materials for painting in oils had to be abandoned in favour of bundles like collapsible canoes. But now, among the tensions common to everyone on the site, I needed to clear my mind to use again my own talent. Brian Thomas' words still rang in my ears: 'Always carry a sketchbook', 'Never forget the great work'.

sketch of a typical Nigerian woman

I began to assess the element of time in a different way – a way which was to develop over the years into a discipline and a valuable working method. It started with the reversal of a common statement into a serious question. Instead of 'I have no time!' with all the frustrations that caused, I began to ask myself 'What time have I got'? The sketchbooks and tubes of watercolour to which my artistic baggage had been reduced were taken out and put always at hand. Surprisingly, the changes involved in this mental redirection were unconsciously helped by Alec. Domestically he was without concern but he was proud of being married to an artist and was always urging me to make pictures – birthday cards, posters, etc. – which my fine art training felt to be beneath me. That too required mental readjustment.

The question of space was physically insoluble, needing on my side a major alteration of attitude. Both husbands and artists squander space: both like to leave materials, whether paints and brushes, documents or papers, lying about. At least in our case this was true. The house, when finished, had two rooms only. A bedroom, in which bathing in a tin tub, shaving, dressing, and general toilet all took place and a sitting/dining room usually knee-deep in papers – on the floor as well as on the table where we ate.

The house and its verandah were open to all. No doors were ever locked, even when we were away on tour. We lived in a communal West African ambience. Privacy, except under the mosquito net, was unknown. Alec Dickson liked to work at home. He found the orderliness of offices unacceptable. He also preferred to have me in the room with him so that he could discuss whatever he was doing.

By nature I was a loner, especially when working. A lack of self-confidence in me, which even wartime experiences had not eroded, had escaped my husband's notice. He liked to challenge me, often in the form of a joke, but I grew aware that he always expected me to succeed. He was a born teacher with a talent to inspire the hidden potential in those from whom he could be making extraordinary demands. In a letter sent to him not long before

waiting for mum

our wedding I had written: 'You give me myself... something in your spirit provides the elixir of life in mine'. I was not the only one.

Now we would work one at each end of our dining table, my husband typing, myself drawing. Every now and then he would wander round and say cheerfully, 'You know that man's head is too big' or 'She didn't look like that!' Sometimes I could have hit him. It was like having a diary read or being caught unawares in a state of undress.

But along with my wedding vows there was one unspoken. In no way would I try to change this man, nor start to build barriers by concealing my work. Drawings, however tentative, eventually hope to have a public. One day the thought came suddenly that at the other end of the table, why there he was – 'the man in the street or in the train' – interested, ready to encourage as well as to criticise, but returning immediately to his own consuming concerns as I would to mine.

Then in January, late one night, the students arrived and for all of us the whole focus of life changed.

The two lorries on which they had embarked from the railhead at Enugu, capital of the Eastern Region of Nigeria 400 miles away, were mechanically almost at their last gasp when at midnight they chugged through the final banana trees on to the compound. We were all waiting for them. Every paraffin lamp was lit. Ali went round shouting 'Studie done come!'

The passengers were tired, amazed, disgruntled young men, disguised by the red dust of the laterite road so that it was at first hard to distinguish the new instructors among them. Some of the students had travelled for as much as two weeks to reach the collecting point at Enugu, on foot, in canoes, on horseback or on wheels, to an unknown goal and an unimaginable experience. For all of them the Cameroons was a foreign country, a neutral base.

Then the cooks appeared on a brilliantly lit stretch of grass staggering under large bowls of food. The Principal shouted a welcome. It became known that beds were also ready in the house. Suddenly the nerve-wrecking arrival assumed normality. Here and there the darkness was cut by a flash of brilliant teeth. One or two of the more ebullient southerners responded to Alec Dickson's welcome with a warmth of personal contact. The new staff began to make themselves known. For them too food and beds were ready. For everyone a long lie-in was promised in the morning. The course had begun.

On that first morning, coming early out of our house, I saw standing by himself on the cliff edge and gazing out to sea, a young man in the long white gown of a Northerner.

Nigerian schoolboy

I said, 'Good morning. What is your name?'

'Good morning, Madam. I am Ibrahim'.

Then he raised his chin towards the water. 'What is that Madam?'

'That is the sea'.

'The sea', he repeated, 'The sea. Last night in my sleep I hear always a strange noise. This makes me afraid. When it is light I get up to look. All this water! Now I will surprise my children when I go home!'

As long as it lasted, our whole domestic life was oriented to the course. By now the staff/instructors had their own eating arrangements but casual or official visitors were my responsibility. The three members of the Dickson domestic staff, Lucas the cook, Ebenezer the steward (by nature an elderly independent Nannie) and the faithful Ali, were the rocks upon which the household was founded. Absolutely reliable and able to face crises with enterprise, I would have been lost without them.

The first afternoon, after a parade in front of the big house, during which each student was issued with a pair of shorts and a coloured singlet (their course uniform denoting membership of a particular team), they were interviewed individually by the Principal and two of his staff and given a name label to wear at least for the next few days. This took place in our house.

schoolgirl washing floor

There was nowhere else private enough. Not all the young Colonial Service instructors agreed with this arrangement. While each group sat on the verandah I was able to begin the task of identifying them.

Great importance was attached to names being known to staff within at least a week, preferably within five days. This was something that Alec Dickson felt to be essential. He always remembered that when he left his own school the Headmaster had not known his first name. Alec Dickson did not have orthodox views of institutional practice. Personal relations mattered. Giving students a regained identity after a disorienting journey and the first stirrings of 'belonging' were vital ingredients in a course which was to last only a month and to make great demands on them. It was a way of dealing with men that I had experienced and understood.

The programme deliberately engendered an atmosphere of urgency and adventure, a word which has no equivalent in any African language, shaking the students out of any accustomed regime and forcing them to make decisions for themselves. Every morning began early with physical training under the leadership of either Lance Corporal Ekechuku of the Nigeria Police or Sergeant Major Riga Addingi from the Nigerian Army. Both were excellent men, with all the West African characteristics of ebullience, out-going warmth and a penchant for jokes. Like every other activity, PT was not orthodox. Indeed it owed a great deal to Alec Dickson's experience with the Mobile Propaganda Unit. For obvious reasons no normal apparatus was employed (it was unknown anyway in most Nigerian schools). Man O' War Bay used exercises with logs, pyramid building, tumbling, games played with implements made from palm leaves or bamboo.

For most of the students – teachers, clerks in government or with the big companies and so on – strenuous exercise had been left behind at school. For Alec Dickson, who usually took part, and for a number of the students, it was an unpleasant shock! The thinking was always that whatever was learnt on a Man O' War Bay course could be adapted or transferred when the student returned to his own village or community.

Everyone had to enter the sea and learn to swim. Those from the coast or close to big rivers, the Niger or the Benue, were expected to help the Northerners, many naturally afraid, who had never before seen any large stretch of water and certainly not the sea.

The West African seaboard – delta or mangrove swamp – ran for hundreds of miles but here, where the Cameroon coast turned south in a great bend, were cliffs. A real adventure for all was when the students were expected to work their way, clinging to small protuberances along the submerged base of the cliffs, until they reached an enclosed grotto. It was truly frightening. Only Alec Dickson would have risked such an undertaking: only Alec Dickson could have brought it to a successful conclusion. As always, afterwards there was a lesson to be reinforced. 'When you were afraid did you ask the man next to you whether he was Ibo or Hausa, Christian or Moslem before you would accept his help?'

There were exercises, called Civil Crisis, which took place in the evenings during a discussion or a singsong when groups from different areas taught each other their songs. Suddenly an interruption would surprise us all – though the staff had worked hard beforehand preparing the scenario. The dispenser on the labour lines of the plantation would arrive distraught to report an outbreak of typhoid fever and a desperate need for help; an explosion on the lower slopes of the mountain followed by fire – an aeroplane crash; an urgent message from the Commissioner of the Cameroons saying that an outbreak of cattle disease in the north prevented meat coming south and would mean a food shortage – could Man O' War Bay provide information that would help to expand the fishing industry; numbers of coastal fishermen, where did they get their canoes etc. etc.

The training centre, though only 4 miles from Victoria was isolated. We received no papers or letters; the closeness of Mt Cameroon meant that wireless was useless; the telephone line was often down. Our students took it for granted the Centre was the nearest place to ask for help.

Because I was the only involved staff wife on the compound the students found me interesting, as I did them. It was to me they brought all the extra-mural problems with a touching faith in my ability to produce solutions – or to influence the Principal. It was a good thing to keep in with 'Ma'. I became accustomed to being asked for an interview, listening to complaints or requests or apologies, sometimes disguised, sometimes openly and ending with 'if you will tell the Principal he will listen.' Naturally, being a discreet wife, I discriminated between what could be passed on and what was an attempt to steal a march on others.

There were, too, problems of genuine importance and trouble. A young Moslem teacher was concerned about the diet of his only infant son. He had been struck by the difference in height between the Europeans he met in the Centre and the rather small men of his own tribe and had come to the conclusion that the root of the matter lay in feeding. So he wanted a diet sheet for his son which would induce him to grow. We worked it out together. Some foods could be got in his district which the child would normally never be given. Eggs, for instance, rarely eaten – chickens being preferred – certain vegetables, even fresh milk. But the core of the problem went deeper. At last we arrived at it. 'But Madam', he said, looking very troubled. 'The real difficulty is my wife. She is not educated. She does not understand these new ideas. She will not agree to change her way with the child. How can I convince her?' I urged him, when he went home, to introduce new ideas gradually so that his wife might get accustomed to them. He hesitated. 'Do you think I should beat her, Madam?' I must have looked very startled for he added hastily, 'I have not done it yet. I thought I would ask you first.'

A question often asked was 'What did the Principal pay for you Madam?' They lived in a country where bride price was of vital topical interest and had no conception that it might not be universal. The answer 'nothing' was met with astonishment and exclamations about the good bargain he had got!

mother with child

cooking class

In discussion I would tell them about the custom of dowries. The idea that a bride might not cost you anything but might even bring money with her to her husband seemed to them highly commendable.

Although educated, some of them speaking excellent English, I was probably the first European woman they had ever had any real contact with. They found it hard however to relate what I did to what their own women could do. Every course we devoted one evening to the problems of women. A talk was given by an excellent African woman teacher, mother of seven and wife of a political leader. She knew better than we did and spoke moderately, asking for nothing more than a fair deal for their wives and a chance for their girl children to go to school. As she went on, the indignation of her audience rose. Gone were the fine ideas of equality for all when Nigeria got her independence with no discrimination. It was often the most intelligent and highly educated who fell on the speaker in a fury of refutation when her talk ended. It was the only time I gave way to anger when, worsted in argument, they resorted to Scripture asking in triumph 'How can a rib be anything but a servant to the whole?'

In the courses that followed the first one, Alec Dickson began to consider fresh concepts. One of these was the introduction of a craft. To most of the students the idea that a man could produce something with his hands was old-fashioned. They had achieved freedom from manual labour by being educated. We wanted to show them that a craft can be exacting and skilled, requiring also cleverness and intelligence. In days focussed on hard physical work it seemed important that somewhere there should be time, however short, for peaceful concentration and a delicate touch.

So Eric Order, an Efik from Eastern Nigeria, arrived with his footloom. He was a professional weaver from a district where only women wove so he had had a hard struggle with his mother and sisters before he managed to get training. The craft of weaving was widespread in Nigeria. Each district had its own patterns, human as well as in cloth. In some only the women wove, in others only the men: more rarely both men and women.

a weaver

Unfortunately Eric was not by nature a teacher and his own experience as a man learning a woman's craft made him uncertain about teaching a class of outspoken boisterous males who had no intention of learning. I had learned weaving as my craft at the College of Art in Edinburgh. When the course ended with Eric in despair and the students rebellious, Alec asked me if I would take over the teaching while Eric was the demonstrator. I did not think I could but then it was a challenge. So I said 'Yes'.

There were obvious lessons to be learned. Each member of the class had to be occupied. It was useless to have one large professional footloom. My own beginning had been with a warp on a small rectangular wooden frame. We were surrounded by bamboo and other kinds of woods. Each man could make his own frame.

When the first lesson in weaving on the next course was due, I used shock tactics learnt from my husband and his colleagues. There was one great advantage over the students. I was a woman. So they were prepared to find me interesting and treat me with an innate courtesy. They had been told to bring their machetes and before they knew where they were, accompanied by L/Cpl Ekechuku who had been acting as my bodyguard and by Eric, every student was out in the surrounding bush cutting wood for a simple frame and learning to put it together.

The results of the weaving class in terms of cloth were small. One student announced that he was making a football jersey. He was an Ibo, an enterprising people from East Nigeria. Two or three managed a belt or a tie. But the real value of those periods wrestling with the intricacies of fine cotton thread, while Eric's footloom hummed peacefully in the background, was that they enabled us to get to know each other. Many problems and personal difficulties were put before me while I corrected the tangles in a warp which I might otherwise have known nothing about. It was important for me too. I became an accepted member of the staff.

The next challenge, when the courses had been in action some months, was the teaching of First Aid. Up until now a qualified member of staff had done this but a time came when there was no one. Asked by Alec if I would take the class, I agreed.

The lessons, on the verandah of the big house in the afternoon, started in the traditional way, following the pattern of the Red Cross manual. The sea glittered and sparkled. As the setting of a broken bone was described heads began to nod and attention wander. A practical exercise in how to put on a splint was greeted with jokes and laughter but no conception that a human being was also involved behind the injured limb. At the end of that course, after a test in which my students could answer questions in fine resounding words, but whose response to dealing with a simulated casualty suffering from pain and shock was pitiful, I consulted Alec in despair. As always he was constructive and encouraging, ready to consider alternatives. We discussed the reasons for our inability to bring home to the students the human as well as the technical side of First Aid. This led to my determination to try a totally different approach on the next course.

outdoor class

The lesson began in the usual way. It was suddenly interrupted by a piercing scream and a crashing, tearing sound just out of sight round the corner of the house. The atmosphere became electric.

'Something's happened', I called out. 'Come on, we'd better see what it is.'

In a flash every student was on his feet, down the steps and round the corner. Lying on the grass, clutching a leg in which there was a large gash oozing blood was Sam, one of the junior staff. His eyes were rolled up in his head. He indicated with moans and sighs that he had been climbing the tree and fallen off. Nigerians are natural actors. In London I had attended a Casualties Union course. Surrounded by the First Aid class, none of whom were doing anything to help and deafened by the arguments which had quickly developed, Sam put up a convincing performance.

'Come on', I said briskly. 'What are we going to do?'

The more alert young men began to pull themselves together. One ran off for a basin of water. Gabriel tried to manipulate the injured limb in a way that would rapidly have compounded any fracture. Ekpo and Eugene went for a blanket to make a stretcher. One of the more observant suddenly realised that the red liquid was not blood at all. Relief all round, except for Sam who was enjoying the limelight. Now beside him, under a tree, the lesson was continued – but with a great difference.

The class was thoroughly stirred up, ready to talk and argue and listen with interest. There was an object lesson at hand. Every one had seen Gabriel pull the leg about while Sam screamed. They recognised the justice of the observation about humanity when dealing with a patient – this was not just a limb but a limb attached to a man. Suggestions started to come from the group. The Principal should have been told of the accident, so should Sam's wife. She would have made a terrible fuss. Might she have been given something to do such as boiling some water? In the face of an actual victim lying on the ground the reality of what I was trying to teach them took over. The African staff, who gallantly agreed to act as any kind of body, would give a vivid account from the patient's point of view. Especially Sergeant Major Riga Addingi.

'What you think I am? You think I a piece of meat? Or perhaps you think I already dead so it no go matter how you carry me? Pah, You U.S. Useless'.

I too began to get an insight into the conditions in which many of these young men might have to deal with genuine accidents when they returned home. There would be no neat triangular bandages or ready-made splints in a bush village. The familiar injunction in the West to tear up a petticoat for a bandage did not apply when both patient and rescuer might be wearing the minimum. Many large forest leaves could fulfil useful purposes and local remedies were not to be despised.

So we became closer, respecting and learning from each other. And from my husband I learnt a valuable lesson – never discard in despair, seek always an alternative.

The first two weeks of every course took place in the Cameroons. When dealing with exercises, adventures or situations where decisions had to be made or plans immediately conceived, each individual student was encouraged to discover their own potential, often hidden until they faced the pressures of Man O' War Bay.

For the second two weeks the whole student body, varying between 45 and 60, as well as staff, moved into Eastern Nigeria where a tradition of rural self-help still flourished, strongly supported by E. R. Chadwick. Man O' War Bay would spend the next fortnight working with a village, assisting them in building culverts on a feeder road, constructing a bridge, adding a room to the primary school.

This was hard manual labour of a kind which our young men would previously have despised. It was undertaken by both staff and students. Now aware that they were being judged by different values and having found in the weeks before a communal spirit of pride in themselves and what they could do, the teams were prepared for anything – at least this was true of the majority. Those less convinced recognised that opposition was not acceptable. Sergeant Major's motto 'Making the Impossible Possible' accompanied by full-throated singing or chanting created an atmosphere hard to resist.

On the day of the move the whole compound was up at dawn. There was an exhausting difficult journey to be faced. One hundred miles to Mamfe at the Nigerian border, the last fifty being one-way on every alternate day. It was

building a new market

vital that the transport reach the single traffic limit before midnight, any later and we would be halted on the upward road for a night and next day. The road was unmade-up red laterite, liable to ambush heavily laden lorries, in which all the passengers had to be unloaded to supply human pushing power. Rivers had a ferry or were forded; traffic bridges were non-existent.

By 8 am when the last lorry had sorted out its troubles, both mechanical and with its driver and groaned off among the banana trees, it was time for our breakfast. The compound was quiet and peaceful, occupied only by the office staff, carpenters, canoe repairers and other workers. Our Studebaker was standing beside the house, already packed by Lucas and Ebenezer who were coming with us, and all the camping equipment, food, lamps, kerosene, jerry cans of petrol and whatever else would be needed for fourteen days in the bush. Ali would remain in charge of the house. When he cleared the table I said to Alec 'Are we ready?'

It was a forlorn hope. I had seen him come down from the big house, his arms full of papers. Now in front of the empty table he sat down, spread out all his official documents and began to work on the accumulated paperwork of two breathless weeks.

It was his nature to participate in every activity; to deal personally with every crisis; to know individually, in so far as was possible, the name and temper of each of the human beings surrounding him. Dealing with the recalcitrant as well as the enthusiastic, the mediocre and the quick-witted, both Nigerian and British, was exhausting now that the moments of calm had come. Those few hours before the next plunge into hyperactivity were immensely valuable. But for me, car packed, decisions made, anxious about the hazards of the road ahead, this stasis was almost unbearable.

At 11am I made coffee and put it beside Alec with a gesture of irritation. At 12pm I went out of the house to inspect once more the arrangements for leaving and found Ebenezer sitting upright in the car clad in his best spotless white uniform. It was not then clear to me that he had reason for this smartness. My own problems foremost, I told him off. He said nothing and continued to sit stubbornly unmoving. It was only much later that I knew that for him travel over the border into a strange country whose people he did not understand demanded that he showed them that he, Ebenezer, had a status of his own.

At 1pm, wishing that Victoria had a solicitor and I could sue for divorce, I unpacked the picnic lunch and handed it out. All this time Alec sat busily at peace. It was only at 4pm, when I had given up, that he suddenly began to pack away the papers and cheerfully call out, 'Well, who are we waiting for?' And as we went out to the car said to me 'You drive'.

By the time we left the banana plantation behind he was fast asleep.

During the dark run up the Mamfe road, through the rain forest and fearful of juju appearing at any moment in our confined brilliant headlights, my mood changed. Beside me Alec slumbered peacefully, Ebenezer sat behind, upright, wide awake, still in his best uniform. Lucas, in his working outfit, snored fitfully. In each case their confidence in me was absolute. Soon Alec would wake and take over the wheel.

Next morning in the Mamfe Resthouse the breakfast was excellent and we had caught up with some of the staff. There was a feeling of holiday – though it was not a word that Alec recognised. Manipulating the Cross River on a primitive ferry, we were in the open rolling country of Eastern Nigeria facing the next hundred miles to Awgu.

There were crises enough when established in the village in which the students were going to work. We woke on the first morning to be told by Ebenezer that the cook belonging to the staff mess could not find tea, milk or sugar in their baggage. It had been left behind. The young instructors, mostly British, were difficult about their food. Because I was the only woman on the camp complaints always came to me although it was no longer my business. One showery day a student from the North asked to see the Director and then told him that students of his calibre did not work in the rain. He did – and went on later to a statesman's career.

But for me those days were leisurely and pleasurable. Waking under the mosquito net with Alec already gone, I would listen to the students singing as they marched out with headpans, spades and hoes to whatever project was being undertaken. Sketchbooks had been the important part of my baggage. I sat on a bank or under a bush drawing our students, watching how they reacted to hard physical work.

For both of us the evenings were the real relaxation. By the light of hurricane lamps we met in the school or centre where the students slept. By then most of the staff preferred their own company but Alec loved party games and so did our Africans. It was a method of communication easily understood. We played charades, made lists of objects beginning with the same letter and with the help of the local market Kim's game was reinvented. The students sang or taught us universal West African games. We had Hat Nights. Sitting in a circle passing round a hat, when the blindfold person in the centre shouted, the owner of the hat at that moment had to stand up and deliver an impromptu speech, subject unknown until that instant. Being unselfconscious Nigerians the result was brilliant. Through family games together a family feeling grew. The enjoyment was mutual.

When the rainy season arrived in Cameroon, said to be the second wettest place in the world after Assam, it was impossible to conduct courses in the continuous downpour that lasted through July, August and September so

student accommodation Shere Hills

Alec and I travelled round Nigeria to visit our students. On the last evening at Man O' War Bay each one had been asked to stand up during discussion on the verandah and say publicly what they would do to help their communities when they got home. It was often a moving two hours. At the end the Principal would announce that when the rains came he and Madam would drive into Nigeria to see what was happening. It might be an unexpected visit. They might be given warning. Either way they must be prepared.

When we travelled in the rainy season in the early 1950s it was still the era when white men from Government travelled alone – if wives were with them it was ceremonial. They did not sleep in donkey sheds or wade over rivers in the dark.

Those were happy days driving from North to South, East to West, to towns and small villages, where a policeman might have started a football club or a rural Emir in the North was discovered, his robes girt up around him, stamping a bare foot in a pool of wet concrete.

Nigeria was a huge country with a population close to 100,000 million. It had a wide diversity of cultures and of religion; in the south, Christian or animist, in the north, Muslim or pagan. Even in the early days we had students from every area, the number gradually growing and spreading as Man O' War Bay became better known. Self-sufficient in the manner in which we travelled, Ali now having joined Lucas and Ebenezer in what had become the Chevrolet station wagon, we were prepared to camp anywhere our students, now the hosts, had ready for us. Once in the north when we arrived without forewarning, we spent the night in one small room in an open space of trodden mud, with three inhabited mud huts and a donkey which made the night hideous. It was Lucas, Ebenezer and Ali who went for a short while on strike because of the insult to our dignity – and by transference to theirs.

In Kano, capital of the Northern Region, an old walled city where we had a group of students, one was kin to the Emir. By his arrangement we spent one night in a beautiful resthouse within the walls opposite the Emir's palace. The Emir was travelling but his son assured us all was well. Built of red earth with a containing wall, overshadowed by a spreading tree, we were supremely happy. In the cool of the evening, sitting on the flat roof, our students came to visit us. Alas, next morning, an abrupt message from the British District Commissioner informed us that it was forbidden for any but the Faithful to sleep within the city walls. There was no reprieve and to the shock of our students we were unceremoniously evicted.

student with transport

Driving into Oyo in Yoruba land we were late. On the road we met the search party and with flapping robes and cries of greeting the car was stopped. Oyo, the centre of a large population, had given us many students. As we drove round the town to reach the Town Hall where a reception was laid out Franklin, who had climbed into the back of the Chevrolet with Lucas, Ebenezer and Ali, had his head stuck out the window like some air-hungry puppy and was shouting as we passed 'This is my Principal! This is my

Northern village

Yoruba girl

Principal!' At the fine porticoed Town Hall the rest of our students and one or two local notables were on the steps to greet us, dignified and formal in their flowing gowns or immaculate European suits. Refreshment was provided, beer and fruit juice (they had remembered that we did not drink alcohol) and sweet sticky cakes. Speeches were made and we were given presents of local craft items. Unprepared for anything so handsome I was emotionally overcome and just hoped that our Nigerians, themselves emotional, recognised that it was gratitude that made my lips stumble. Alec, never at a loss for words and with a reputation to sustain, made up for my hesitations.

Europeans were apt to take their customs and their household goods with them when they travelled. To be ready to accept what was provided in the different situations in which our students lived and to enjoy the simple hospitality of a family home was the first step to genuine friendship. A friendship which did not depend on place or circumstance but which could be relied upon regardless of material or national differences. For a considerable time many of those students kept in touch with us. Once we received a present based on a family joke. 'Sir, this is a mat for your only wife made by my second wife!' Personal correspondence was always answered. This was my job. Gradually the individual report that was sent out to each student's sponsor at the end of his course became my work too.

In 1953 both Alec Dickson's beloved mother and my much loved Gran died. The loss to Alec was very great. Since he had first gone to school his mother had been at every turn his most loyal and active supporter. We were in London when she died. I knew that she was satisfied to have handed him over to me and felt I had not failed her. Man O' War Bay was beginning to be recognised in Britain as well as Nigeria and his mother, who had brought her son through many unhappy periods of his life, knew that, at this moment, he was creatively engaged in work that consumed him.

For me, my Gran's death at a time when she had become stricken and in pain, left a vacuum. But it was one which, in her own different way, my mother was ready to fill. She had come to love her son-in-law and, in a sense, she would have her daughter back. The years in Africa had given me a self-confidence in my own way of life which might have been eroded had I been in day-to-day contact with my two families – both more orthodox certainly than Alec and now than myself. I had sometimes wondered how, when the time came, the stress involved in the double maternal presence could be resolved. Now it was.

Mount Cameroon

Man O' War Bay lay in the shadow of the great whaleback of Cameroon Mountain, 13,300 ft high. For the courses too, the Mountain came to have a significance beyond its physical size. Mountains themselves in this country were a source of myths and stories, perhaps to be overcome but also to be much feared. Mount Cameroon, according to the local people, was haunted by a Half Man. Brooding, enormous, often swathed in cloud, Mount Cameroon could be unseen but always felt.

There was a recognized route up the mountain with three huts where rest could be taken or a night spent. While arduous, the climb held few physical dangers and many people, usually Europeans, had climbed it. Mary Kingsley went up wearing her brother's trousers. Richard Burton was the first man to reach the top.

The first experimental courses had not planned to attempt the mountain but in 1952 the final challenge called out to be met.

For the students the knowledge that this endeavour lay between them and their return home often cast a shadow. None of them would ever have actually attempted such an enormous ascent. For even the most courageous and sophisticated there was an apprehension that there might be encounters with spirits to be overcome and, if the spirits were not of their own tribe or community, they were still to be respected and feared. The mountain climb became the climax of a Man O' War Bay course. The students were divided into groups, each group going separately over two days. With each group were members of both European and African staff. They left very quietly in the early morning travelling by lorry as far as Buea. We were up to see them off, to joke and encourage and to respond to the waving pink palms fluttering from the back of the lorry as they disappeared through the banana trees.

The next evening after dark, all of us, including Ebenezer, Lucas and Ali, were on the alert – however much we pretended to be engrossed in normal chores – waiting for the rumble of the lorries and for signs of the success or failure of the expedition. What came first was the faint, faraway sound of singing which, as it drew nearer, turned into a jubilant full-throated roar indicating that the human spirit had triumphed once again. Sometimes this was accompanied by the trumpet belonging to one of the police instructors.

When he returned home one of the students, a young teacher, wrote: 'The first thing I discovered is what I have been teaching in school for years without ever believing it myself. It is true it's colder the higher you get even though it is nearer the sun. You have made me daring like the Great Francis Drake'.

There were disasters as well as triumphs. E. R. Chadwick contracted sleeping sickness and had to leave the Nigerian Service. He was greatly missed. Gradually the calamities were overcome and the successes showed the way to fresh endeavours. For all those engaged in the day-to-day running of the courses the work continued, strenuous and unremitting. Slowly however, we began to get visits from Nigerian politicians and from those then in power.

In 1954 there was a request from the major Secondary Schools in all three Regions for a course to be run for their senior boys. On the part of the staff, including the Principal, there was some hesitation. The courses were planned for and aimed at adult men. It was felt that certain aspects could not be tackled by boys – and the schools could only give us three weeks. So the Community Development experience was left out and extra activities at Man O' War Bay substituted.

The decision was made not to climb Mount Cameroon.

When the seventy young students arrived however, they made it plain that they had boasted to their friends left behind about their courage in outfacing the Mountain – and no doubt told exaggerated tales about the dangers to be met in doing so.

Their deep disappointment won the day and the usual arrangements for the climb were made. Twenty-nine of the first party reached the summit and returned triumphant heroes in the dark of the second evening.

On Thursday May 5th the whole campus was up early to prepare for a very important visit. Chief Awolowo, Prime Minister of the Western Region, and nine of his Action Group leaders were arriving at Man O' War Bay for lunch; the first time a Nigerian politician of his status had come to see the Training Centre for himself.

Shortly after dawn news reached us that two of the schoolboys of the second group, Henry Obineche and Eugene Labinjo, had been lost on the mountain. Immediately every able-bodied member of staff was alerted. Two search teams were made up, one led by a visiting Chief Inspector of Education, the other by Alec Dickson. At the last moment before they left my husband told me that, with an elderly European administrator, I must be responsible for the Prime Minister and his lunch party.

Later in the morning the second group of boys, who had spent the night in one of the mountain huts, arrived back. It was a very different homecoming. Frightened, silent, but glad to see their companions from the first group, those of the African staff who returned with them did their best to raise morale and instil hope before, at midday, the guests arrived. Meanwhile, Lucas and the cooks belonging to the Centre worked on the lunch. Chief Awolowo and two of his aides would have it in our house; the rest of his entourage with the students.

It was only too plain that this disaster, once known to the Nigerian press, might spell the end of Man O' War Bay.

At twelve noon, resplendent in flowing Yoruba robes, Chief Awolowo and his accompanying colleagues stepped from a fleet of cars. They had been told in Victoria what had happened on the mountain and knew the reason for the lack of an obstreperous welcome on the campus. My own experience of Nigerians had so often been of courtesy and resourcefulness in a crisis that it was immediately clear to me that the Chief was in command of the situation.

The lunch that had been dreaded was not short of laughter and anticipation of a cheerful outcome. When, after it, we walked up to the Centre for the Chief to speak to the students, I sensed that far from criticising or condemning the ethos of Man O' War Bay, Chief Awolowo was prepared to encourage the young Nigerians before him for their readiness to encounter the challenges of the training. He told them to look towards independence when their country would need young men like themselves of valour and enterprise.

When the guests climbed into the limousines, wrapping their robes around them, the send off – unlike the welcome – was rousing. Then, with no news from the search parties, gloom descended.

The next days passed in unmitigated despair. The search parties returned without success, only with news that the weather had worsened on the mountain. Telegrams had to be despatched to the families, the schools, the Government, both Regional and Central, sponsors, supporters. As the hours went by hope was gradually lost. It began to be assumed that the boys were dead. Our main feeling was not for the catastrophe overtaking Man O' War Bay but one of personal grief for the boys. Only one small incident lightened the darkness.

One day Ebenezer indicated that he had something to say to us. He found it hard to begin. 'Master in very bad trouble . . . because Mountain trouble . . . and Mountain no like juju . . .'. He, Ebenezer and one of the drivers together had paid 10/- to a local juju man for a spell to bring the boys back. We wept. For a moment I became a pagan and prayed that the spell would work. Its value lay not in the large sum of money collected but in the affection for us shown by Ebenezer and the others.

On Saturday May 8th the Course was dispersed except for four senior boys who, on police instructions, were detained as witnesses for an inquest.

Alec Dickson sent in his resignation to the Nigerian Government.

A week passed.

On the 8th day since the boys disappeared the telephone in our house rang. I answered it. A voice said that a wireless message had been picked up from Idenau, the remotest plantation 40 miles on the farther side of the Mountain. It read simply 'Two boys found. Please send transport'.

Alec was down on the jetty pretending to inspect the seaworthiness of the canoes. I rushed down waving and shouting to him. Clutching each other I stammered out, 'They're found!' With tears streaming down his face, he asked 'Alive or dead?'

We did not know. The message had not said and it would be another twelve hours before the radio link was again open.

Taking Sgt Major Addingi with him, the Principal climbed into the Land Rover and left immediately. In driving rain they splattered along the coast road to Debunsha where it was said to rain every day of the year. Then there was a ferry across the river and finally a trek on foot.

In the plantation dispensary there was a light on. Two small figures in black macintosh capes got up from their chairs. Henry Obineche and Eugene Labinjo were alive.

It was a remarkable story.

They came from different regions of Nigeria: Henry Obineche from the East, Eugene Labinjo from the West. Henry was small with a badly disfigured face. When a child he had fallen into his mother's cooking fire. Nevertheless, he was a leader with a good brain, ready to seek out knowledge not just to accept it. His subjects were Botany and Natural History. He had promised to bring back rocks and plants from the summit of Mount Cameroon for the school museum. He was a Catholic.

Henry Obineche

Eugene, whose father belonged to the Salvation Army, was a quiet follower. His hobby was photography and he had brought his camera with him and was determined to take home a photograph of himself on top of the Mountain.

When the second group had reached Hut 3 it was clear that the weather was worsening. By this time Sergeant Major Addingi was in charge. The two Europeans in the group had found the climb too much and returned to base from Hut 2, leaving the African staff and John Lukom the guide. As the mist thickened, Sergeant Major wanted to turn back from Hut 3. The boys were indignant. The previous group had reached the top and put their names on a piece of paper into a bottle buried there for climbers – to leave evidence of their success. Group 2 were not going to be jeered at by their colleagues when they returned to the Centre. They must go on.

The summit was only a short distance from Hut 3. With some reluctance Sergeant Major Addingi agreed but on condition that the group kept together and turned back as soon as their names were in the bottle. All unnecessary baggage was to be left in the hut. Everything appeared to go as arranged until, back in the hut, it was discovered that two boys were missing.

Addingi and John Lukom immediately went back to shout and search. Heavy clouds were gathering: there was no sign of the lost boys. The priority now was to get the rest of the group safely back to Man O' War Bay.

Meanwhile, on the summit, Henry and Eugene had disobeyed orders. They hid behind a rock and started to gather specimens and to take photographs with Eugene's camera. These absorbing activities took more time than they realised. Suddenly, in the gathering mist, they noticed that the group had disappeared. They shouted but voices were muffled by cloud. They ran about looking for a path, only putting more distance between themselves and the searchers. Realising what had happened and that panic would not help, Henry took the lead. They sat down and considered; then, Catholic and Salvation Army, they prayed and sang a hymn.

It was bitterly cold. This was no proper summit, only a huge, desolate, moonlike surface of lava rock, now wrapped in cloud. The boys assessed their possessions. They were few. Extras had been left behind at the Hut – macintosh capes with hoods, jerseys, canvas boots. Henry had a stick, cut earlier to help him climb, and his specimens; Eugene a packet of biscuits.

While they sat considering, the clouds cleared for an instant and far below they glimpsed the sea. We'll go down there, they decided. Once arrived at the coast it would be simple to walk back to Man O' War Bay along it. Unfortunately it was the wrong side of the Mountain. The first night they spent on the summit huddled together for warmth. Bewildered and afraid they prayed again before they slept.

On Day 2, still in intense cold, without food or water, the canvas boots torn off their feet by the hard lava, they wandered up and down rocky humps. Then Henry, taking the lead, told Eugene that this was a crisis. At Man O' War

Bay they had been trained to deal with crisis and to use their minds to find solutions. Afterwards he said to us, 'We were often disappointed but we never despaired'.

On the third day they reached the rain forest. There was moisture enough to wet their throats and from now on they ate grass. Once they saw a little stream. Henry knew that all streams went into the sea, but not this one – this one returned back into the mountain. They hoped to climb a tree to find a lookout point but rain forest trees were 200 feet high. On the 4th day, as they got lower, elephant tracks and the chattering of monkeys often deceived them. The former were followed hoping that they might lead to a banana plantation; many times the latter sounded like a village but was not.

Lost on Wednesday, they calculated that the 5th day was Sunday. By mutual consent it was decided that this should be a day of rest so they sat down, prayed, sang hymns and told stories – and maybe saved their lives. On the Monday, refreshed, they went on. On Tuesday Henry flung away his specimens which he had continued to carry. The next morning, the 8th day since they had been lost, they heard the sound of chopping and found in a clearing an old man cutting wood. He took them to the plantation manager whose radio message alerted Man O' War Bay. So remote was Idenau that he did not know anything about boys being lost or the fears at the Training Centre that they were dead.

There was a small service of thanksgiving at the Centre, led by the Cameroonian Postmaster from Victoria. Eugene asked if he could send a telegram to his parents. The message read, 'Luke. Chap 15 v.6. Rejoice with me. Safely back at Man O' War Bay.'

For some weeks the boys suffered physically. Their legs swelled. Their stomachs had difficulty digesting a diet that was not grass. Otherwise the trauma was worse for the staff. Henry and Eugene had never doubted that they would get back.

Once again everyone had to be informed. Telegrams flew hither and thither. Both the Nigerian Government and the Colonial Office asked Alec Dickson to rescind his resignation – but we were in a state of almost terminal exhaustion. It had been four years on a rollercoaster, meeting near disaster as well as triumphant success.

Working, as Alec Dickson did, starting new endeavours with all that that entailed, meant a surge of energy, mental, physical, conceptual. Every ounce was summoned. No exhaustion was recognised, no other precept permitted to interfere. This was not a measured work pattern: no other aspect of life was recognised while the creating of the vision was in progress. But of course the time came when collapse set in – often triggered by crisis, by criticism or the disbelief of others. Man O' War Bay would survive without us – and did – to become the Citizenship and Leadership Training Centre, moving into Nigeria when independence came. The resignation was not withdrawn.

We travelled home on a banana boat from Tiko. As it passed the entrance to Man O' War Bay there was a canoe full of our African staff waving 'Goodbye'. Our Captain had the courtesy to blow the foghorn in reply. At first our emotions were refrigerated like the unripe banana cargo but the long quiet days out of sight of land worked a gradual cure. And we had our therapy with us. Since the courses began and we had taken up our rainy season tours, many students had written to us describing what they had undertaken since arriving home: recollecting incidents, frights, celebrations; boasting sometimes that they were 'Better Men' – Riga Addingi's clarion call.

We had brought all those letters with us. Now we sat down to devise a booklet describing the Man O' War Bay experience, illustrated by Alec Dickson's excellent photographs 1951–1954. It was to be printed in Edinburgh when we got there and would have a wide distribution.

CHAPTER 16

Interim One

11 Morningside Place

This was the moment when my mother's steadfastness and reticence was to be of great value to us both. She hardly knew her son-in-law. For him this was his first return to Britain without a personal home to welcome him. All his siblings were living or working overseas – in Malaya, Sarawak, Nyasaland. His own mother had been dead only a year and he had found no family name to call mine.

Perhaps fortunately, my two brothers were also in Africa so the Edinburgh home we arrived at was unshared. Fortunately, too, my mother had a large garage and only a small car so the Dickson luggage, legendary in London, could be disposed of reasonably.

There was the Man O' War Bay booklet to be printed and many contacts to be revived. Alec was fairly confident that he would get offers of work. He went to see the Permanent Secretary at the Scottish Education Department, described his West African experiences and expounded his belief that the nature of Scottish scenery offered marvellous opportunities to combine schooling with adventurous service. The Permanent Secretary observed drily, 'Here in Scotland the education system is thirled to the certificated teacher'. When he had looked the word up, Alec Dickson discovered that the Chambers Dictionary related it to 'bondage', 'servitude'.

He made another approach to the Moderator of the Church of Scotland. This time his argument, based on the Rev. Tom Allan's campaign 'Tell Scotland' was the need for an inspirational awakening among young people. When the meeting took place the Moderator asked whether Mr Dickson had considered teacher training? It did not seem the moment to talk about how to make young hearts burn. At home, life was more difficult. My mother and Nannie had a routine which included fussing over me. They enjoyed and spoilt Alec while he charmed them both. He was content to live anywhere as long as the household went on smoothly around him. I was not. I had lost my own independence.

When we had settled in, I suggested one day to Alec that he might write a proper book about the Man O' War Bay experience and make use of my sketches. He laughed and told me that I had another think coming. He was a deadline man with many other things to do, articles to write, audiences to speak to, jobs to seek.

It was a blow. In this vacuum I felt the need of some work of my own nor did I believe it would be easy for my husband to find another job. A visit to the Colonial Office in London had made it plain that he had never been more than a non-pensionable, temporary Colonial Servant. I was aware now of the suspicion, even if sometimes tinged with admiration, with which he was regarded by more orthodox potential employers. Indeed, I knew him well enough by now to recognize that at heart his desire was to be self-employed within the mainstream of vital social change.

Quietly, in odd corners and at odd times, I began to test out my own ability to write a book. Meanwhile Alec was beginning to brood on what was becoming obvious. There was no job because he had no profession – all he had were ideas.

Then news came that Sergeant Major Addingi was being sent by the Nigerian Army on a Physical Training Course at Aldershot. This was followed by a telephone call from Sergeant Major himself, already in England nearly a month early due to a mistake in dates. A Tiv from Gboko in the Nigerian Middle Belt, he was a man of simple background, great character, humour, vitality and warmth of heart. Joining the Army he had had to learn Hausa, the lingua franca of the Muslim North, and later he had taught himself English.

It took Alec a very short time to persuade my mother to have Riga as a visitor for two weeks. Arrangements were made that he be put on a night bus from London to Edinburgh. Two days later, in the very early morning, we went down to Queen Street to meet him. In those days each long-distance bus had a stewardess, in this case named Jeannie. She had been told that her Nigerian passenger spoke only simple English. Not far out of London Jeannie went round her bus, chatting to passengers, asking if they were comfortable, if they wanted a rug? She passed Riga without a word. Sometime later she brought round cardboard sandwich boxes. Still she said nothing. When the boxes were collected the next delivery was rugs. Aroused when she silently handed one to him, Sergeant Major put on his parade ground voice and shouted down the aisle, 'Why you no go talk to me? You think speak I French? You think I speak German? You talk to all these people – why you no go talk to me?' After that the whole bus talked to him and when he climbed down the steps in Edinburgh balancing his kitbag on his head he and Jeannie were firm friends.

He had started from his barracks in Northern Nigeria with 96 eggs and a bag of ground nuts for me. Unfortunately in the excitement and confusion at Kano Airport the bag with the eggs had been thrown on to a lorry with disastrous results. On arrival it was only the nuts, by now transferred to a large OHMS envelope, that survived for a presentation to my mother.

Both she and Nannie greeted him as though they were well accustomed to such a visitor. Tall and handsome with a cicatriced face, wearing over his full uniform the scarlet of his Sergeant Major's sash, his courtesy and warmth entranced them but it was not until the next morning that the relationship of guest and hostess changed.

When he came downstairs and my mother asked him if he had slept well, he replied, clutching his stomach, 'My belly done go away since I come for this country. Belly palaver. It give me deep humbug, Ma'.

Once my mother and Nannie had been given a translation the whole atmosphere altered. This was a man in distress, needing help. He disliked meat and 'leaves'; living on buns and tea upset his bowels. Then Nannie suggested porridge. When she had made him a bowl and he had discovered that it closely resembled 'Kamu', a Nigerian dish, this problem was solved, at least while he was in Scotland.

There was one other difficulty equally easily answered. Though he would not admit during the day that he was cold, Riga had found sleeping in barracks very chilly. Automatically my mother had put a hot water bottle in his bed and when he finished his bowl of porridge he exclaimed, 'This ting put fire for my bed, I no be cold at all, Ma!'.

In the short time Riga had been in the house, Alec had at last found a name for his mother-in-law. Almost without realising what he was saying he had begun to call her Ma and she, though she would not have been pleased if I had used it, recognising the African connection and the personal affection 'Ma' carried from her son-in-law, accepted the title gladly.

We had made an arrangement to borrow the family car and take Sergeant Major, who had never been in Britain before, round Scotland. Next morning as we left, Ma handed him a hot water bottle of his own and told him to leave it on his hotel bed when it would be filled for him. After the first night he rejected this advice saying, 'I go fill it myself from that pump (tap)', adding, when one night he found himself with two, 'These things for my bed they no be up to standard at all!' It was to be a journey full of incident, a revelation to Riga Addingi, and indeed a revelation to us seeing our country through his eyes.

In Kingussie we had the good fortune to find the band of the 1st Battalion the Queen's Own Cameron Highlanders (which had been Alec Dickson's Regiment in 1939), beating Retreat before departure for Korea. At first there was some confusion in Sergeant Major's mind between Cameron and

Cameroon. Having recently been at Man O'War Bay, also a mountainous country, he imagined for a short time that he was seeing the Cameroon Highlanders.

The pipes and pipers entranced him. An obliging red-haired Corporal allowed his kilt and accoutrements to be acutely examined and answered many questions. Why did they have holes in their boots? What did he call this dress which was like women's underwear? How long did it take to play these four flutes so finely dressed in native cloth? Did the village pay for their entertainment and feed the officers free? It suddenly seemed shaming to say that all they probably received were some bottles of beer.

As the band swung by Addingi watched thrilled, unaware that he was stealing some of their thunder. For the small boys of Kingussie a pipe band was commonplace beside a black soldier wearing over his uniform the scarlet of his Sergeant Major's sash. They spent their time with backs to the spectacle gazing up at Riga's shining face.

After the performance the Colonel of the Battalion came up to us. He had served in Nigeria and spoke to Riga about his own experiences there. As he left he shook Sergeant Major by the hand, and in doing so, left an indelible impression. 'This ting never happen to me before. A Colonel shake my hand,' Riga kept repeating. It was not for us to point out that Colonels in Britain do not habitually shake their own Sergeant Majors by the hand any more than they do in West Africa. 'I shall tell my people. A Colonel shake my hand'.

At Kyle of Lochalsh it was a very beautiful evening. We watched some boys playing shinty on the tough ground below the town. Eventually we strolled down to have a closer look, trailed by another little group too dumbstruck to answer the Sergeant Major's cheerful questions. Alec and I left him beside the shinty game while we wandered on. Five minutes later, looking back, we saw an astonishing sight. Small Scots boys were practicing forward rolls and handsprings on the boggy highland turf at the command and encouragement of an African soldier. When we got near the sound was even more surprising than the sight. A few big boys stood round scornfully, hands in pockets, while the younger ones performed. 'Make I show you,' commanded Sergeant Major, stripping off coat and beret and turning a perfectly controlled handspring. 'Now you, and you, and you, Toms. Well done. Better.' Then: 'You big boys. Why you no go do 'em? You be no good, useless, lazy, you just stand there and drink tea!' While we held our breath, expecting a rude answer, the big boys took their hands out of their pockets and sheepishly began to turn somersaults.

One evening in Wester Ross we walked together beside a loch. Riga was telling us that his own people would long be in bed and asleep. Here the sky was pale pink with the lingering light of a Scottish summer sunset. We met three sheep trundling amiably along together. Suddenly we looked at each other and laughed. There were two blackfaced sheep and one white; we were two whitefaced humans and one black. It was the resemblance, not the difference that mattered – they were all sheep, we all human.

We came back through Glencoe. As we entered the valley in lowering weather, Alec told Riga the story of the massacre of the MacDonalds by the Campbells in the 18th century. Being a Tiv, from a small tribe, Sergeant Major understood it immediately.

'You see, we have to be careful,' Alec said, 'My wife is a Campbell' (through my paternal grandmother). I was in the back seat. Electrified by this news, Riga turned round and, with real seriousness, insisted that I get down on the car floor while he put a rug over my head. So I drove through Glencoe in stuffy darkness while Riga Addingi kept a sharp look out for vengeful MacDonalds. Neither of us explained that such violence would not now be tolerated. He came from a country where tribal rivalry still lay very near the surface and we no longer felt like turning his misunderstanding into a joke.

Back at home in Edinburgh we showed him round 'Ma's' house, knowing that we would have to answer many questions about the way we lived. The gas stove was explained to him; my mother demonstrated the making of butter pats. As each new wonder unfolded he shook his head and murmured 'Baturi. Baturi'. 'You Europeans'. In the end, as a sign of her real affection for him, my mother took him into her little private 'snug' and showed him the photographs of her three sons and seven grandchildren. He examined them all, then turned to her. 'Kai, Ma', he said, 'You done try too much'.

Once Sergeant Major Riga Addingi left 11 Morningside Place it was to be another few months before relief came. The very quietness of my mother's house began to tell on us both. Ironically, in the calm I found it more difficult to settle to the manuscript I was attempting than it would have been in the bustle of Man O' War Bay. In Edinburgh a portion of my mind was constantly aware of the effect of our presence on the other members of the household – and indeed myself. Not for the first or last time I resented being pig-in-the middle.

Iraq 1955–56

On several visits to London, Alec had put out feelers among his network of friends, both personal and professional. One day in Spring 1955, when he would have accepted almost any job, a message came from the UNESCO office in London where one of his network contacts was on the staff. Would Mr Dickson present himself in the South for an interview about a possible appointment as Chief of UNESCO's Technical Assistance Mission in Iraq, heading a Fundamental Education Team. He took the next train and came back having accepted the job. He felt humiliated because he had had no other choice and this had resulted in a lack on his part of sufficiently rigorous questioning. Mass Education, Community Development, Fundamental Education – what matter they all meant the same thing. For me it was at least a job – incidentally the best paid one we were ever to have.

In June Alec Dickson flew to France for a briefing with UNESCO. He returned five days later having had an experience which confirmed his growing fears. It was a madhouse in Paris. At first he had been told that he was not wanted. Then that he was. It transpired that through a mistiming he had arrived while his predecessor was still in the building. This vexed the UNESCO staff. It was policy that incoming and outgoing Chiefs of Staff should not meet in corridors. Of course they did.

Mr Trowbridge was a sincere and charming American and the two men liked each other immediately. Over lunch it became clear that he was returning to Virginia a saddened man. UNESCO had negotiated with the Ministry of Education in Baghdad an agreement that a team of international experts would bring literacy and enlightenment to a particular village in the desert 29 kilometres south of the city. There was very little support for projects and it was impossible to get funds. Mr Trowbridge had liked the people and the team included two excellent Mexican sisters, experts in rural health and home economics. On practical matters he was helpful. Where did we stay in Baghdad? Well, we could rent a house for a year or there was Weekes Boarding House or the YMCA.

When Alec arrived back it sounded to me like Operation Frustration but there was one successful battle won. UNESCO had laid down that the expert travelled out on his own, with his wife following when he was established. This Alec refused to do so when we landed in Baghdad on July 11th we were together.

Having lived in West Africa, we had not given much thought to temperature, nor realised that midsummer was the worst time to arrive. We came out of the aeroplane door and walked across the tarmac feeling as if we were in a hot oven. Alec, originally red-haired and with a sensitive skin, would gladly have turned round and left at once for Edinburgh. When we passed through Customs the Mexican sisters, Enriquetta and Maria Lopez Peralta, met us and took us in a taxi to the hotel Zia. Very welcoming, they were clearly glad to have a new Chief of Mission. It was plain that little remained of the former team or of its endeavours. The Literacy and Crafts experts had departed and not yet been replaced and Enriquetta, the senior sister, was not finding it easy to retain any official presence in a country where women were little regarded. With small experience of the kind of professional world into which we were now to be plunged, we felt ourselves personally at a loss – though officially it was essential to show a knowledgeable public face. I was also aware that my status presented a problem for the Mexican sisters who had expected to have the new Chief of Mission on his own during their introductory talks.

Later in the evening, when the air conditioning was making us feel shivery, the Baghdadi junior elements of the Fundamental Education Team came to greet us: the driver Mustapha, at the moment without a car; a group of seconded young teachers; two senior middle-aged men, Mansour and Khalif, and two young women in the traditional black 'abas'. Talking to them, our spirits rose. Very smartly dressed, they were charming, courteous, anxious to be helpful and hospitable.

During the vacancy the office seemed to have disappeared but the local portion of the team had found suitable premises in which to meet. Next morning while the new Chief of Mission was at the first gathering of the remnants, I set off in a taxi to inspect Weekes Boarding House.

With the address in my hand, translated into Arabic, we started off with a flourish. Then, in a fine broad boulevard, we came to an abrupt halt. The taxi driver waved his arms, indicating a row of houses. I showed him the number and then discovered two important facts – houses in Baghdad did not have numbers and there was no charge for telephone calls.

The taxi driver drove to a taxi office and more or less placed me in front of their telephone. Mrs Weekes said, 'Opposite the fish market'. The taxi driver failed to find the fish market and his charges were exorbitant when I got out to walk. Fortunately a very small onlooker knew the name Weekes and took me there. Mrs Weekes answered the door. Though no doubt kindly and providing a valuable service, her establishment was clearly not for us so we ended up in the YMCA.

Run by Mr and Mrs Robertson, it provided self-contained flats for married couples as well as ordinary YM accommodation, meals included. Our unannounced arrival meant that we were fortunate enough to end up in a good sized *en suite* room with an adequate air conditioner. Even so, in summer when the night temperature fell about 30 per cent and the generator was off, everyone took their beds and mosquito nets up to the flat roof and slept there. After an initial embarrassment we joined the mass exit and found it an entertaining and fascinating experience. Each morning, with the pink predawn and already the threat of rapidly rising temperatures, we all decamped down below again.

The gradual addition of attractive materials, bought in the huge covered market or suq, gave our room a Dickson character, added to by pictures as I became caught up in the wonderful visual opportunities for sketching. Free

Christian village Iraq

of all household chores or family obligations I even began to think about a Baghdad book.

The YMCA lived behind high stone walls with iron gates securely locked at night. Within the large compound was a working garage, a tennis court (on which Alec disported himself) and facilities for rest and recreation. The staff were Armenians who had a feudal loyalty to the British from the days when RAF bases in Mesopotamia had been guarded by them. They were an ancient people, almost the original Christians. The YM suited us admirably though as we got to know the International Community I occasionally felt that we received appraising looks. As a residence the YMCA was not what was expected of a Chief of Mission.

Most of the other inhabitants were unobtrusive, ordinary young Britons. They maintained the buses, trained the Army, carried out electrical contracts, and were the backbone of the public services. A first impression was that they were admirable ambassadors, contributing more to Iraq than the superior international agencies.

It was in the YMCA that my husband, a de-tribalised Scot, first learned to dance Highland reels. There were regular, well attended evenings of Scottish dancing to which Iraqi brothers were allowed to bring their sisters – being non-contact. The fathers had never seen the elan with which Alec Dickson

Baghdad street

cavorted, whirling his partners round with complete abandon. Sometimes chaperones came too and sat outside the hall peering through a window, assessing partners. No complaint was ever made.

One of the disadvantages of arriving in Baghdad in July was that everybody who was of importance was out of the city for health reasons – in London with family, in the United States, in Vienna. This was the season to escape the heat.

Each member of the Fundamental Education Team had an Iraqi counterpart, an essential element in UNESCO philosophy. Bassam, formerly of the London School of Economics, now Assistant Secretary at the Ministry of Education, was attached to the Chief of Mission. The two missing experts were Victor Slee, British, specialist in Crafts who would not come until January and Dr Lutfi from Ein Shems University, Egypt, Professor of Mass Literacy who was expected to arrive very soon. Alone of the team he spoke Arabic as his mother tongue.

We met him off the plane. A very pleasant, immediately accessible man, who had not been much out of Egypt. He was excited by the opportunity of working in Iraq and gently pleased when he discovered that he was the only Arabic speaker the team had. He was proud that classical Arabic could be spoken and understood all over the countries of the Middle East. That was until, having settled in to his temporary accommodation, he went out alone in the afternoon to explore the city. When later he came to have supper with us, he was shattered by the destruction of one of his cherished beliefs. Though he could still read the papers, spoken Iraqi Arabic was a mystery to him: Iraq, as in every other Arab country, having developed an idiomatic common language for its people.

The first visit to the Ministry of Education took place not long after Dr Lutfi arrived. To him this ceremony must have been familiar; to Alec Dickson, Chief of Mission, while courteous and welcoming, it was like no other office introduction he had ever encountered.

Offices in Baghdad were not meant for work but for the building and maintaining of personal relationships which were essential if a man were to preserve his position to do any work. Now in modern surroundings, this was how, traditionally in the desert tent, the Sheikh had conducted his affairs. Until he realised this fact the baffled Westerner hovered for months on the brink of a nervous breakdown. When we began to meet our fellow international experts we discovered we were not alone.

A farrash, or office messenger, would show the visitor in round a screen with, behind it, a large door. At the end of the room was the official's desk. Ranged round the walls were suites of plush sofas and chairs, many of them occupied by men drinking tea and carrying on animated conversations with each other and the official who rose with a smile of welcome to greet the new applicant.

'Delighted to meet you. Have a seat. What will you have? Tea, coffee, hammuth (a lemon drink)?' Introduced to all his neighbours, encumbered by a cup of tea, the latest visitor sank into a chair. The previous conversation then closed up again round him.

At the next gap the foreigner took a deep breath. Clutching his papers, attempting to stand up, he says, 'About this Report, Sir'.

The telephone rings. The official picks it up. The conversation, composed mainly of courtesies, seems to go on a very long time. When it finishes the foreigner then tries again. 'About this Report, Sir'. The door opens. Two more men are shown in. Greetings and introductions take place. 'Tea? Coffee? Hammuth?'

Eventually, Alec Dickson recognised defeat. Courteously, in despair, saying 'Perhaps it would be better when the Minister himself returns from Europe,' he took his leave.

In smaller offices this was also how junior officials conducted their affairs. Returning to the room that the Fundamental Education team had recently acquired, the Head of Mission found that the local young teachers attached to the team felt free to wander in and out with friends, and friends of friends, coming in too. The telephone was more or less public. Conversation flowed freely. There was welcoming courtesy and refreshment – but work had to be done elsewhere. In our case, if really urgent, in the flat in the YMCA.

Professionally the undertaking was doomed before our arrival. Mr Trowbridge had left in despair, followed by his admirable Deputy. One or two small projects had been set up in villages near the capital. Enriquetta and Maria, the Mexican sisters, had two sewing classes; there was a Literacy class in Abu Ghraib village, a Games Club in Washash village run by the Iraqi teachers. There was also a Mobile Cinema which had a regular round but the former Chief had failed to get support or any funding for such projects.

There was also the original community development at Dujailah in the Province of Kut, 29 kilometres from Baghdad, which had already been condemned before we arrived. Attempts to revive some of the ancient Mesopotamian irrigation plans had had the disastrous effect of bringing up underlying layers of salt until the soil, desert sand, now looked as though snow had fallen on it. Dr Bassam had never visited there.

That the programme's whole emphasis – and budget – should have been spent on paying a diminutively small team of expensive foreign experts, working in one single remote village in the desert so far from Baghdad that no Iraqi official ever visited it, seemed to Alec Dickson a strategy drastically misconceived. When the Minister of Education returned to the country two months later, this view was reinforced. By this time Alec Dickson was advocating radical change.

Even then I think we knew that when our year's contract ran out we should not stay. We had arrived in Baghdad not only in the burning hot summer but at a time of holidays, of some of the great festivals, of universal hospitality. Those who could leave the city had gone, those who had to stay, relaxed. Gradually we learned the rhythms of a society quite new to us. Now there was a hiatus. Long afternoon siestas took the place of days at the office: after dark, life returned and went on far into a cooling darkness. Nothing could be done until, in September, government returned to again be active.

We began to understand customs and culture, to be cautious in expressing admiration for people or things. On looking at the financial accounts it seemed the team owned a horse. What was this? My predecessor, Mrs Trowbridge, before lunching one day with an Arab sheikh, had warmly praised a horse which she had been shown. After the meal, richly caparisoned, there stood the horse. Etiquette demanded that she be given it and that she accept it! It was consequently delivered to the office in Baghdad. Alec called it Unesco which the Iraqi staff thought disrespectful.

Servants must never be excluded from parties even though they had to eat last. Mustapha, our driver, went on strike one day. Unknowingly, we had offended him by not inviting him to one of our social gatherings. During this time of laxness we had invitations from the Iraqi staff and found beautiful gardens in hidden courtyards lit by the moon. I explored the covered suq and began to make pictures. Though expressed admiration was banned neither children nor adults minded being drawn.

With the Mexican sisters I was invited to a 'masquf' party by one of the young women on our staff. Clad in my nicest dress and best shoes I went only to find that it was a picnic on the mud flats of the Tigris river, eating fish speared on sticks and cooked before a blazing fire. In the darkness it was easier to be relaxed. I took off my shoes and sat round the fire on a rug with great *sang froi*. The Mexican sisters did not find it so simple.

It was an all-female party. We were rowed over to the mud flats by brothers who then cooked the fish and sang to us from the outer darkness keeping their distance. Quite successfully I ate the delicious fish with my fingers. After we were finished all debris was flung into the night during which exercise, to the great enjoyment of the females, one of the brothers fell into the river. As the party left votive candles were lit and sent adrift on the water as thanks for gifts received.

As we became more familiar with the city we grew aware of the fascinating make-up of Iraq's citizens. The international community was large and various but without roots. There was a small refugee Russian community and an

desert village Iraq

uneasy Jewish remnant. The country spanned the dividing line of the Muslim population, between Sunni and Shia. There were Kurds from the north and Marsh Arabs in the south, Assyrian and Armenian groups and the Yezedis far out in the north-east desert.

Alec was desperate to get out of the city, to explore the rural areas which were potentially the ultimate target of Fundamental Education and were precisely the areas he was strongly discouraged from visiting. At this moment, when a surfeit of welcoming entertainments were beginning to encourage his frustration, an invitation arrived from a European acquaintance in a northern town, Shaqlawa. It was the Id holiday. We did not yet have a car so one was hired with driver and we left at 6 am next morning.

We drove over the Baghdad wall into true desert which we had not yet seen. There was no road and the car navigated on any of three or four tracks. Other cars approached heralded by moving clouds of dust sailing over the plain. There was only tarmac about ten miles before Shaqlawa, a long way to the north. Until then it was a terrible drive. We failed to understand how the driver found any direction in the desolation of sand and red hot air.

Every now and again a small booth selling iced Pepsi Cola would appear, a miracle of survival – or a plodding string of camels. After some hours I began to pick out scattered villages of flat sand houses. To our eyes, vegetation there was none though we heard later that for about three weeks in the Spring a miraculous blooming sprang up in this desolate landscape and as rapidly disappeared.

Erbil was passed, said to be the oldest town in the world, round and walled, rising high out of the plain on a mound of accumulated refuse and the ruins of thousands of years ancestry. Not until we were past the city did the ground begin to rise. Scrubby trees on little hills appeared and we started to see wild groups of Kurds with their women unveiled unlike those in the south.

We arrived in Shaqlawa in the late afternoon to a great welcome. This was a resort for both Europeans and Baghdadi escaping from the city to the cool mountain air. The gardens were filled not only with flowers but with sleeping visitors.

There was a group of young Americans belonging to IVS (International Voluntary Service). They were fair-haired, clean, hard-working and very depressed. They had come to work with the local people on a farm project, but the reality was a great shock. As from the verandah we watched women winnowing with the traditional implements, Don could not help explaining his group's frustrations. 'Man, they are backward. They live like Bible times.' Not far from the threshing floor lay an up-to-date machine, a gift from the USA, in a sad state of repair. 'Waal, at least they see the threshing machine is better than the old donkey', Don added without conviction. The answer to that was 'the boy with the bicycle sees the Cadillac is better but that doesn't help if he has no means of buying one or keeping it in repair' but we did not say that to him.

Having at last left the city behind, Alec was determined to leave what was a sophisticated resort and see more of village life. We paid our ceremonial calls in Shaqlawa and on the second day hired two mules and a guide to visit a village. All went well until the path began to go downhill into a lovely valley. Unacquainted with mules I was disconcerted when my saddle began to slip forward over the beast's neck, needing constant readjustment from the muleteer. Eventually, when it became clear that the saddle was in a state of permanent disrepair, I had to climb on behind Alec for the rest of the journey with great damage to the base of my spine.

Arriving at last we were greeted by a cheerful and lively old Chief and his village elders. We sat on rugs in the courtyard of a modest stone house with the young men of the family leaning over a balcony, much intrigued. One of them who spoke English was brought down to act as interpreter for his seniors. Round the fringes of the courtyard some Kurdish men with guns lying casually on their laps looked on with some bewilderment.

There was chit chat. The Chief complained that all the Americans bring in artificial insemination adding, 'What use is that – after all we have a bull'. Tea arrived, made in a samovar. We attempted to leave but food was ready, a huge round tray with bread, eggs, watermelon and glasses of buttermilk. Then we left on saddles tied up with rope while the Romeos on the balcony eyed my mounting technique very critically. With a badly sunburned husband we were back in Shaqlawa an hour later. No one there was interested in our expedition.

We arrived back in Baghdad on Monday, after another long hot journey, the appetite for further exploration whetted. Already ideas of a touring course as the only way to take Fundamental Education to the villages had begun to crystallise in Alec Dickson's mind.

So far the newly constituted team had not been to Dujailah, UNESCO's original community development project. As yet there was no official car but the Mexican sisters were anxious that we should see the only work that had actually been attempted by our predecessors so we all went in taxis. It was a hot, very fast, drive over waste land thick with camels and sheep. After $3\frac{1}{2}$ hours we arrived in Kut, a small town on the Tigris. It was a desolate little town – and very friendly indeed. Tributes were paid to the Mexican sisters by two local doctors. The Mutasarif and the authorities welcomed us warmly and supplied refreshments. We drove over the Kut barrage, an immense waterworks, to Dujailah.

Dujailah was not as bad as we had feared. The flat land, on which there were some trees, was laid out in huge squares known as Shakhas, with the small family house in one corner of each square. There were no communal buildings or social centre. For people who lived naturally in close villages such a layout seemed in itself a disaster. So far only a few of these lone houses were inhabited. The land, showing scattered patches of a sticky green, was already salting, white crusted areas outlining certain boundaries.

The few women in residence clustered round the sisters with a genuine warmth of welcome though the evidence of actual achievement was pitiful – two empty schools and a quantity of derelict equipment. While the Head of Mission talked with officials who had accompanied us from Kut, I went with Maria to visit two families. The women, whom I was to come to greatly admire, were full of personality and spirit; the embroidery and weaving which they showed us was quite lacking in any local patterns or traditional stamp. Fresh from West Africa there was a scarcity and poverty which we had not seen before.

Driving round to Shakha 8, Dr Lutfi asked for a newly literate youth to demonstrate his skills. A boy of about 12 years old was produced. He wrote something down but only Dr Lutfi knew its merit. Then it was suggested that I ascribe my name though it seemed an unfair test. To our great astonishment he read out MORA DICKSON correctly!

After glasses of chai and squash we climbed back into the taxis to return to Baghdad. Alec was determined that a place so remote, so lacking in communication, which had never had a visit from any Iraqi politician who wielded influence in the capital – not even the counterpart of the Chief of Mission – would not be wished on the Fundamental Education Team as a centre – out of sight out of mind.

At the end of August when we had been in Iraq for six weeks, an official car was at last granted to the team, the Minister of Finance having refused a request for two cars. Our own Minister was not yet back on seat, indeed we had been warned that it might be another month before he arrived. Frustration began to build up again. It was hard to persuade Alec's colleagues or the teachers working with the team that a few small projects in surrounding villages was what International Fundamental Education was all about.

Taking Mustapha, delighted to have a real job as a driver, Alec Dickson decided to have another expedition beyond the peripheral villages. It was on return from this weekend that I made a decision. As always the visit had gone well and we had been welcomed courteously with interest and curiosity. The usual delicious and refreshing soft drinks were produced. Then the Sheikh, in whose house we were being entertained, asked my husband if I would agree to see his wives. My husband asked me. I said 'Yes'.

Conducted rather nervously into the back quarters by a young man who left me at a curtained aperture, I was received by an older woman. The room, furnished with curtains, cloths and cushions, was full of women and children. Greeted by sibilant whispers and interested looks, it seemed clear that not many Western women had been entertained by them. I was taken to a raised dais and seated beside my guide, the older woman. From her air of authority I now thought her to be the Sheikh's senior wife. Fresh drinks were brought while the women sat and stared and whispered. Some of the children ventured near me, some even stretched out a hand to touch. On both sides there was bafflement that we had no common language. My lips became weary of smiling but in a ceremonial society it would have been discourteous to offend by leaving too soon.

Returning to the male world the first thing I said to my husband was, 'If it's the last thing I do, I must learn Arabic.' Next morning a Lebanese teacher in Baghdad accepted me as a student, to learn simple spoken, not classical, Arabic.

For me Baghdad had become a delight. With no housekeeping to occupy me and as I gradually acquired some language, starting with the long ceremonious greetings and responses, the streets and the suq became welcoming places full of colour – quilt makers working on the pavements, sellers of fruit and spices, Kurdish porters carrying huge loads on their backs, women wrapped in black abas with enchanting children, little boys until they were five years old disguised as girls to keep off the evil eye. Unlike their village sisters, the mothers did not slap me on the stomach with a questioning look. A more sophisticated city generation walked along with proud faces flaunting their Western clothes. Being a foreign woman none of the taboos applied to me. I could wander among the cloth stalls, the silver and jewellery booths,

desert designs, from the Iraq museum

the food displays, the shops for exotic plants, the adornments for camels and horses, the carpets and a thousand other oriental delights under the enormous market's roof. Small boys in red caps rushed about with trays of tea and stallkeepers sat amid luxurious fabrics offering to prospective customers tiny cups of coffee. The sketchbook and the prospect of another manuscript were always with me.

For Alec it was a different story. He would come back to the YMCA, depressed from a conference with Dr Lufti and his counterpart Dr Bassam and some of the Ministry staff. There was to be no cooperation, virtually no help. Dr Lutfi, a gentle kindly soul with no experience of the wider world of international officialdom, was losing hope. It seemed there was to be no blooming in the desert for Fundamental Education. It was mid-September and the temperature in our flat remained still at 108°F. Alec Dickson suffered greatly from this heat.

The Minister at last returned from Finland to his desk. Alec Dickson put on his nicest tie and went hopefully with Dr Lutfi to this first interview. He had made notes of suggestions for the team to work on that had arisen from travel outside the city during the fallow season since our arrival: the possibilities of work in the larger rural areas, the Liwas; talks with some of the Mutsarifs, the senior village councillors; reactions from one or two sheikhs. The interim Report had been on the Minister's desk in time for his return, beginning with expressions of greeting and going on to lay before him what had happened or not happened in the two months since the new Chief of Mission had arrived in Iraq.

The Minister was not pleased. He made his displeasure plain. This was no way to write to a Minister. He was not going to listen to any complaints or speeches. Then he simply dismissed the two 'experts' whom he himself had requested from UNESCO – Dr Lutfi remarked, in some distress, 'as only a king can do'.

When Alec Dickson got back to the office the junior Iraqi staff were twittering like lost birds. The Minister had sent a directive for a meeting three days later. He would have his Advisers with him. 'A kind of Grand Jury', muttered Mansour the senior member of the Iraqi staff.

Three days passed. The cold war continued. The United Nations Representative had been consulted – he was sympathetic but powerless. The Iraqi staff and Dr Lutfi were preparing for appeasement and the Mexican sisters were very unhappy.

After seven days, a go-between with Ministry connections brought news of a three hour talk with the Minister. Some concessions had been made; access to schools would be granted, training would be in Baquba, north of Baghdad – of what kind was not clear. Mr Dickson must understand that plans were for discussion and the Minister himself had the final say. This time Alec Dickson had a boss who had nothing of the 'patron' in him and the Minister had received a UNESCO 'expert' entirely focussed on actively doing a job – and one who was determined to develop his own ideas.

The next day Alec Dickson and Dr Lutfi were sent for by the Minister's office where they were lectured for half an hour before the Minister left abruptly for lunch with the Prime Minister.

Two days later Dr Lutfi and Alec Dickson left for the north to see what the situation really was at Baquba.

Somewhat belatedly it was becoming plain to us all that having a UNESCO team was a matter of prestige on both sides. There was no urgent call for rural improvement and some fears on the Iraqi side about what it might lead to. For UNESCO the work was secondary to the importance of access to a country so far unclaimed. The host government was always right. Experts were replaceable. Later, when a visit from the UNESCO Director General was announced, we were to see the establishment of a National UNESCO Committee, the evening before his plane flew in, only to have the Committee dissolved almost as his aeroplane left the runway two days later.

Alec and Dr Lutfi returned after an adventurous journey to Baquba which had proved to be a very agreeable place with a charming Principal of the Institution which was to be our host. He was adamant, however, that they had no room at all for any extra trainees or staff. On the way back the driver had taken the wrong road and in a wild remote spot the car got stuck in a river bed. Then, from behind some rocks, appeared two Kurds armed to the teeth. Poor Dr Lutfi thought that his last hour had come. However, his Chief of Mission made the strangers push the vehicle which, laying down their guns, they did in a very detached fashion and then just sloped off. The driver eventually found his way home.

After this journey a more optimistic attitude developed in the team, because their Chief, Alec Dickson, in spite of a rebuff at Baquba, was not without hope that some good might still come to pass. He greatly enjoyed getting away from Baghdad with its bickering and politics into the rural areas and villages where they were welcomed and the team's good intentions not questioned. We suspected that this was because the villagers themselves were accustomed to visitors coming and leaving while their own life continued in the old traditional way. Meanwhile the welcome was warm and the courtesies equally polite.

Each fresh expedition strengthened the thinking in Alec Dickson's mind that middle-aged professional experts were not adequate for the task. Very highly paid and sophisticatedly educated in good universities and colleges, they lacked any conception of rural life or what elements in it might be built upon and had often lost the ability to adapt. He wrote to UNESCO – one of the letters which the junior Headquarters Staff in Paris later told him they greatly looked forward to – suggesting the use of much younger, more flexible youth groups. To those higher up the idea was received with incomprehension.

Another uncomfortable meeting then took place in the Ministry. There was a determination to confine any work to the two small centres just outside the city already set up by our predecessor and to Dujailah the disaster in the desert. When told that the Mexican sisters were on leave and our Crafts expert not yet arrived, the Minister again lost his temper and blamed UNESCO for breaking their contract.

A Land Conference had taken place in Kut to which the Fundamental Education Chief of Mission had been invited to speak. He got on well with the Americans who were there. The state of the land at Dujailah came under discussion. It was being abandoned by the settlers and was pronounced as hopeless by the delegates so Fundamental Education was now confined to the group of small villages within easy distance of Baghdad.

The Mexican sisters returned from leave in good spirits. Our young Iraqis were prepared to get down to work in the villages. One night we hastily had to remove our beds from rain on the roof – the hot season was passing. Although what was actually happening was minimal, we were heartened to discover that it was possible for a team of International experts to work together in complete accord and with devotion in difficult circumstances. There was too, still permission to talk in rural schools. Though we missed the ebullience and spontaneity of West Africa and found it harder to make friends, there was much in the society of the ordinary people to respond to and to enjoy. Always, when we arrived anywhere, there was interest and a welcome.

With official permission to talk to schools, the team had taken advantage of this and in both the city and among the rural population visits had gone well. It was more likely that the teachers were delighted to have someone of importance taking notice of them than that they or the pupils understood the Dickson message, but for both sides it brought distraction and interest to the days. A contact was kept up with Dujailah, not the original FE plan, but with the town of Kut from which the first settlers had come. The school there, with lively staff and youngsters ready to respond, had begun to take up some very simple suggestions for community action in their own neighbourhood.

Then the blow fell. In early December the Minister, who must have been kept aware of what was going on, refused to let the team train the Kut boys and a few girls and thereby in Alec's eyes dealt a death blow to the work he had hoped to develop.

A few days later an International Delegation with an interest in Fundamental Education arrived from UNESCO. There were six of them led by a Briton we knew and had had contact with in earlier days, John Bowers. That evening, UNESCO, in the persons of our team, put on a dinner for them in a first class hotel. It was very successful and we hoped they had absorbed our difficulties and would help to make the Minister ready to compromise. The next evening Alec and I entertained John Bowers and the Lopez sisters. In the meantime John Bowers had had a meeting with the Minister and Dr Bassam. It was a shock to us when he said how charming he thought the latter and that his delegation had quite seen the Minister's point of view! A suggestion was made that Alec Dickson and John Bowers go together to see the Minister and that he, John, would apologise for the Chief of Mission's over-enthusiasm.

At that point a rare occurrence came over me. Shaking with indignation I lost my temper and told him that even the worst organisations backed their employees in public or sacked them. With soothing courtesy, which did nothing to abate my anger, he then gave us some advice: to advise the Minister only – it was not our job to work; to take a month's holiday and go to Persia; to do nothing to annoy the Minister; not to cooperate with anyone. What he meant by the latter was not plain to any of us.

We decided to resign but all the same had to have lunch with the Delegation next day. Before that, Alec asked me to go down with him to the Fundamental Education office. Everyone there was sunk in gloom. I had been rehearsing speeches of protest all morning. Dr Lutfi sat in a huddle like a hibernating bear. He had been very hurt by the Delegation's rejection of a book which he had written.

When we got to the lunch however, at 3pm the situation had changed. At a second meeting with the Minister the Delegation had begun to understand how the team felt. It had been impossible for any discussion to take place on relevant issues of administration. The Minister had merely restated his agreement with UNESCO, adding some frills.

We half resigned but Alec was later told that such an outcome would be a tragedy – John Bowers including me in the Delegation's praise which surprised me very much!

After a week of unhelpful chaos the Delegation left Baghdad. Quite suddenly and quietly, three days later on Dec 19th, our Minister was transferred to be Minister of Finance and the Fundamental Education team inherited a new one. There was cautious optimism. The Chief of Mission paid a courtesy call and reported our new boss to be pleasant.

We had, after all, a very good Christmas. One of our female Iraqi staff, Medina, had departed on a scholarship to Denmark. The team had acquired a very good new one, Kowkab, who had agreed to to work in Dujailah. We had an invitation to a Christmas Party in Kut.

Five days before Christmas, E. R. Chadwick, our Patron saint from Nigeria now recovered from his sleeping sickness, was to pass through Baghdad from a visit to India. He would be in the airport from 10.15 pm to 11.15 pm. When the plane came to a halt, Chadwick, looking immensely tall and ten years younger, climbed out. His first words were 'See how much I love you!' We retired to the dining room of the dreary airport hotel to have thermos coffee and U.N. gossip. The visit to India had been thrilling for him: their Community Development programmes and literature were wonderful. We sat by a flickering light while Chadwick spoke almost in a whisper, glancing over his shoulder for spies. When the plane took off again into the night we felt cheered by his friendship and encouragement.

The next morning we left for the Christmas party in Dujailah. Kowkab, who had left the city in tears on being told she was expected to work with the small community still left in the desert, had done wonders. She had set up a sewing class for little girls. They danced and mimed enchantingly for us and suddenly the whole atmosphere was transformed. Here something was growing and blossoming – activity, happiness, construction. She showed us soft toys and artificial flowers made by a group of women she had got together. Something gay and different was coming into the drab lives – the start of an attempt to create along different lines to those which had always been laid down.

In the afternoon the school in Kut put on an excellent show before the Mudir Nahiya. The children were alive and bubbling, the teachers joined in. Alec showed them his one mysterious 'magic' trick and then there was a meal. For the first time we felt hopeful. One Iraqi young woman had caught a spark and blossomed.

There was a Christmas tree in the school dining room with fairy lights. Kowkab had prepared the feast, spiced meat balls, fish, rice, tomato and bean soup, salad hobuz, and in the middle on a bed of rice, a whole lamb and kousi. Besides ourselves, the sisters and Dr Lutfi, most of the Iraqi junior staff had come; the Mudir Nahiya, the Chief of Police and the Postmaster were all there. We sat stiffly on chairs in a small side room while Mustapha handed round cigarettes with a beautiful football scarf round his neck. When the food was ready we all filed into the dining room and fell on it – almost literally as it was a case of using our fingers and one spoon. Kowkab rolled up her sleeves and plunged briskly up to her elbows in the lamb, ladling out portions all round. It was delicious – no one spoke. All present took the business of eating very seriously and in no time the board was cleared and water provided to wash our hands.

Then we sat around again and Alec Dickson told stories. Meanwhile the five thousand had come into the back premises and had fallen on the remains – guards, schoolboys, fellahin – only the women were absent. Sweets, apples, cigarettes went round. The Mudir Nahiya began to thaw. Even the Chief of Police smiled once or twice.

The tables were cleared away and a small stage set up at one end of the room. Three of our Iraqi male staff and some of the schoolboys produced a very entertaining play on an age-old subject – husband, wife and mother-in-law. The audience rocked with laughter and so did we. A highly successful day and, for the first time, barriers had been crossed.

The next day I went with Kowkab to visit some of the women. It was a perfect morning, the Persian mountains snowcapped on the horizon putting an end to the normally endless plain. We walked through the village calling the women to a small hut which had been built by the teachers for Kowkab. There was glass in the windows and mats on the floor. Fifteen or twenty women of all ages were assembled. Some were sewing mats or samplers, some clothes. The older women just sat, saying that they worked enough anyway, why should they work more? I practiced my Arabic. They laughed a lot and were full of life. A new wife was expected in the village that day and they were preparing to welcome her.

My Arabic was beginning to elude me. I started to sketch the women which they accepted politely. Afterwards, when shown the drawings, they pretended to be indignant. 'But we are beautiful', they said. 'Why did you not make us beautiful?' I thought I had but perhaps our ideas of beauty were not the same and few of them had ever seen a reflection of themselves.

Exhausted but exhilarated we had begun to look forward to 1956. On January 5th, Victor Slee, our missing Crafts expert, arrived. He was a quiet unassuming Englishman, new to the Middle East. In a sense his coming became a turning point for all of us. Very early on Victor Slee perceived, as we once had done, the artificiality of all that went on.

The atmosphere for the team had been improved by the transfer of the original Minister. His successor, though no less entangled in both international and local politics, was agreeable as well as courteous. Over the months we had become accustomed to the limitations set on any activity and in the stand-off that ensued it seemed that the new Minister was ready to accept small endeavours outside the city walls to which he could turn a blind eye.

The permission to enter schools had resulted in an implicit acceptance of the Fundamental Education team's right to leave the city and travel round both rural and Liwa schools. This was an enjoyable exercise. The background of the Iraqi Fundamental Education junior staff was educational; most were teachers. While they felt themselves to be of a higher grade than those actually employed in the classroom, they were satisfied with the prospect of running simple courses in Village Development, Literacy, Games and P.T., leaving Home Economics and Rural Health to our seconded women staff under the Mexican sisters.

The schools were a source of national pride and effort. The teachers were often charming and committed, the children ready to be active. Away from the professional, political, and often cut-throat atmosphere of Baghdad, the freedom and contact with simple rural people was less frustrating than the devious and often incomprehensible dealings with Ministries and Government offices.

We knew now that UNESCO in Paris preferred to remain outside the implementation of any practical work. They had said openly 'experts are always replaceable, host governments are not'.

But for the team's genuine experts and professionals, Dr Lutfi, the Mexican sisters and now Victor Slee, who cared about handing on their functional expertise, the situation was very painful. It did not take Victor Slee long to discover that, as a consultant he was expected only to say in the Ministry what he thought should be done but never to have the chance of planning or executing any of it himself, particularly hard for a craftsman whose language lay in his hands.

Alec Dickson's expertise, on the other hand, was to inspire – a talent which neither the Ministry nor the team understood – but to which some of the schools reacted. Lack of recognition led equally to despair but we both now knew that disappointment did not stop fruitful mental discovery and stimulation. He had a way with words and could inspire audiences. At this time, based on experience in some of the schools, he was writing to UNESCO trying to persuade them that international youth groups would be of more value within the simple context of village schools than over-qualified experts. In one rural school when he had ended, while the staff clapped discreetly, the pupils had cried 'When do we start, Sir?'

Of all the team, I myself, who did not officially belong to it though associated as an accessory, was the only one who was relishing life. Free of household responsibilities, enchanted by visual pleasures, colour, light and the variety of human beings active with individuality (even in a black 'aba'), my focus had changed. The first manuscript, whose subject was Nigeria seen through the pioneering work in the Cameroons, was temporarily in abeyance. Originally I had thought that Baghdad might provide a like subject, the development of creative work within a foreign setting, but there was no work to be described, only a multitude of human activities. I was satisfied to be exercising my gifts: maybe this gave a stability to Alec and to our YMCA home. I made friends and had a small exhibition in the YWCA and gave a talk at the British Council on 'Art and the Married Woman'. Of all this production on my part my husband was extremely proud. He embarrassed me and nearly caused a parting by being responsible for an article about it appearing in the local paper.

At intervals pinpricks still occurred. In March the Minister came to visit the Fundamental Education office. He was brisk and efficient but when he left the sum total seemed to be that nothing would happen until October – then the team could think about a full time academic course in Fundamental Education. In fact none of us had anticipated dealing with the academic but rather directly with those at the other end of the learning scale.

In this same month a letter came from Hans Peter Muller of UNESCO's Youth Department in Paris, putting forward the idea that Alec Dickson might be interested in doing some work in India. Combined with the meeting earlier with E. R. Chadwick at the airport, this was a suggestion that Alec Dickson was more than willing to consider.

Then, after six months delay due to the refusal of the previous Minister to allow the purchase of needed transport for the Fundamental Education team, suddenly two new cars were delivered at the office. Opportunities for the whole team to get about freely were opened up. The three small groups established outside the city could be regularly visited and the chances of discovering possible project areas further afield explored.

Plans were made to run a simple course on Village Development at Dujailah. Hasim and some of the other Iraqi staff went there with Victor Slee. Contrary to all expectations the course prospered reasonably and a session on games and physical training suitable to take back to rural schools was well attended. Alas, without results. A crowd of small boys under Victor Slee, in an atmosphere of haphazard enjoyment, attempted to make a culvert to enable the cinema van to negotiate an almost non-existent road. Sitting round in the desert in a bitter wind among the poverty and the camel thorn we watched a film, 'Children's Village, a cartoon on community effort.

From Dujailah, with Mr Slee, Mustapha and Habib of the Iraqi staff, we drove south to Amara, a town on the Tigris close to the land of the Marsh Arabs. We were to spend a night with a senior Sheikh in one of the villages far inside the marshes. River transport had been commandeered for our onward travel. Lying on carpets at the bottom of our canoe, an Arab paddler at each end alternately punting or paddling, we listened to a body servant of the Sheikh singing and clicking his fingers to entertain us. He was a black man whose ancestors must have come from East Africa.

It took four hours, through ever narrowing waterways with reeds seven or eight feet high on either side. Every now and then the head of a huge, prehistoric water-buffalo glowered at us from among the reeds. At last the little cavalcade drew up alongside an island on which a village was built. The Sheikh, our host, stood alone on the bank above us, a magnificent figure in long black robes and a black and white turban. He greeted us courteously and led us off into his splendid guest house. Seven arches composed of golden russet, bundled dry reeds, supported the pillared framework. Over them lay a skeleton of joining canes, then mats, all tied together with papyrus. The result was an awe-inspiring vaulted chamber, dazzlingly gold, lit by electricity – the Sheikh having bought his own small generator.

Although too polite to make it apparent, I was an object of curiosity – and probably, behind the scenes, of consternation. The company was entirely male – any member of this sex in the village was entitled to join the gathering and partake of the strong black coffee cooked over a fire of dung. I asked if I could visit the Sheikh's wife. In fifteen minutes the message came that she was ready.

Leaving my husband alternately telling stories and trying to make plain the principles of Fundamental Education through the interpretation of Habib, I was led away and ushered into the presence of Sabiha.

Accustomed to a crowded harem, it was disconcerting to find only one wife sitting on a carpet in her best black aba and headdress. Her husband made the introduction and left. She spoke only Arabic and that with an accent that was strange to my ear. The conversation started, however, with routine courtesies. Then when those were completed she indicated my handbag. For the first time I was not ashamed of the large number of objects it contained. Having disposed, by sleight of hand, of a disreputable toothless comb, the contents were taken out one by one and spread between us on the carpet: a sketch book in which she was interested, money, dinars and British small change, none of which she had ever seen as well as driving licences and photographs. The variety was endless and my vocabulary just sufficient to explain the functions of most things – except a railway ticket.

Suddenly she was gone. One minute she was in front of me, the next she was out of a back door. While I was wondering what had happened her husband and an unknown man appeared. The Sheikh addressed me in Arabic, but confused by Sabiha's disappearance and my own embarrassing situation on the floor, I understood not a word. He repeated them. Then the two men began to laugh. Roused to defiance I stared back and was caught by something peculiar in the second man's eyes. They were blue! It was Alec, dressed up in the Sheikh's second best robes.

When they had gone and I had translated the Arabic spoken to me, 'Madam this is your husband', Sabiha came back and the joke had to be explained to her. After that the visit was a great success.

As night drew on, the problem of sleeping accommodation began to exercise me. Obviously all the guests slept on the floor round the fire. As the number had swollen with visitors from other villages and all were male, my presence was going to make difficulties. However, the Sheikh himself resolved the situation. He took us into what was clearly his own bedroom and, to our amusement, we found ourselves sleeping in scarlet chiffon sheets.

Those expeditions were interesting and enjoyable but no real creative work was going to come out of them. Not long after our arrival the year before we had been taken to the Holy Cities of Najf and Kerbela deep in the southern desert. Thousands of Shia pilgrims came at the time of an important Festival to Najf to commemorate the death of Hussein, Mohammed's grandson, with dramatic fervour and intense passion. It had been an awesome experience, particularly nerve-wracking for me because, as a woman, it was felt essential I should wear the 'aba'. Sweating under its voluminous black silk, aware that it only needed one close look to divine that I was a foreign female, I was not as engrossed by the sights as was everyone else. At that time I had not yet recognised the immunity growing out of disinterest and disdain that my foreign femininity conferred on me.

Now once more, nearly a year later, we were once again in Najf to visit the Provincial Director of Education. About this time, Alec Dickson had become certain that UNESCO's whole strategy of Fundamental Education was wrong. Briefly, he was convinced that it should be Iraq's students who undertook the work as Arabic was their mother tongue. Even if they were only second year they would, each in their own faculty, be able to make a contribution to better irrigation, better sanitation, a wider expansion of literacy and meet a multiplicity of needs.

He had succeeded in getting a meeting with the faculty of Baghdad

University but was received with incomprehension. By chance, about the same time, a circular had been sent out from the Ministry of Education suggesting that an experiment might be made in using intermediate schools as a spearhead in Fundamental Education. Four days before we arrived, and out of the blue, the Ministry had received a sole reply from one school in Najf saying that 30 boys and 4 teachers were ready to respond to their circular.

We drove up to a very dilapidated barracks of a building. Alec Dickson talked first to the staff, who clicked their beads furiously. It may be that the nature of the immediate response to their reply to an official circular was beyond comprehension. Then he talked to the boys whose only answer, after he had outlined the horrors of hard work was, as once before 'When can we start?' This was encouraging but after nine months experience we had no real hope that Baghdad would support us in any genuine activity. Nor did they.

The UNESCO contract was for one year only, with possible renewal. The temperature was rising steadily and with it, for those for whom escape was mandatory, an atmosphere of anticipation. At the back of Alec Dickson's mind lay India to which he was attracted by the vigorous reputation that the Government of India's programme in Youth Work enjoyed and the absence in Iraq of any policy on UNESCO's part.

Arriving back in the capital, an irritable spirit began to manifest itself in the office. The Iraqi staff, part of whose motivation for joining the team had been possibilities for scholarships to Europe and elsewhere, were restive and losing their up-to-now perfect manners. Quetta, the senior Mexican sister, was manoeuvring an excuse to go home. Dr Lutfi and Mr Slee were low. Alec Dickson came back with his resignation in his pocket no longer provisional but with the date set when his contract would end in June 1956.

Before then, taking Dr Victor Slee and Mustapha with us, we set out for the last time to explore the delectable northern lands of Kurdistan in our new scarlet Ford station wagon. The Kurds as a people stretched over three international borders, Iraq, Iran and Turkey and owed true allegiance only to themselves.

It was the Eid, the four days holiday following Ramadan and much of Baghdad was also setting out to enjoy the beauty and cooler temperatures in the hills. It was to be a magical few days in wonderful country of rivers and gorges, steep snow-covered mountains and tiny, hidden sloping villages in lush valleys aglow with brilliant flowers. To one of these we took Ibrahim, who worked in the YMCA, for his annual leave. This gave us access to his home village and a warm, if bewildered, welcome from his Assyrian family.

Some two hundred miles across the desert, where the heat was already rising to its summer excess of dust and sweat, past the flaring oil fields at Kirkuk, our first stop was Erbil, the oldest continually inhabited city in the world. The inhabitants of southern Iraq are mostly town dwellers. A nomadic past has given them few rural roots such as other nations have.

In Erbil we spent the night in the high city, crowning a gigantic circular mound which thousands of years of alluvium and detritus had built up. Among the excavations for a new road I was given the shard of a 3,000-year-old pot, many of which were being ground up to form a fresh surface. On the streets, little girls in holiday clothes of the most gorgeous colours, magenta, scarlet, orange, green and turquoise twittered and scampered like flocks of birds, perhaps capturing one flamboyant display before their public adult lives made them anonymous in sombre black.

Mosul, on the road to Syria, was also a night stop. It had a railway station built of white marble, large and luminous within and without and haunted by senior schoolboys, themselves clad in white, lounging languidly studying their books on benches, twirling a red rose or walking hand in hand with a blossom between their lips or behind an ear. We were of no interest to them. The contrast between this exotic setting and the local hotel in which we were forced to sleep, all the better hotels being full of holiday makers, was startling. In the latter, filthy bedclothes, constant noise until the small hours and the hazards of a stinking lavatory unequipped except for a minute handbasin and two footmarks in concrete on either side of a hole had nothing in common with the spotless station.

Contrast took over when the scarlet Ford headed at last into Kurdish lands. Here the country became blossoming valleys and rich fertile meadows enclosed by craggy hills with snow-covered mountains on far horizons against a deep blue sky. Tibetan-like perpendicular villages clung perilously to steep hillsides. The nearer the Turkish border the less innocent the reputations of those villages became. By day they were calm, by night the ferment of organising for smuggling or setting up ambushes took over the narrow streets.

Rowanduz Gorge was stupendous. Even Mustapha, who had remained detached, agreed. Enormous crags filled with caves rising clear on either side, the foaming river shared the rock-base with Captain Hamilton's famous road built in 1915 through Kurdistan. On the other end was the plain of Diana, a circular bowl with magical mountains on every side.

We decided to spend the night in the little town of Diana. We picked up two small Kurdish boys who delightedly made faces at their friends as they hurtled by. We entered the village bearing hostages who directed us to the house of Rais Thoma, Chief of the Assyrian community in this place. His brother greeted us and took us to a big room furnished with rugs and chairs with photos of the Queen, Winston Churchill and George V on the walls. A large wooden bed occupied a third of the room. Presently Rais Thoma himself, a little old man, arrived and introductions were made.

Before he left London Alec Dickson had visited a joke shop, resulting in a rubber banana, a huge black spider and Achmet, a small coiled rubber snake who, when a bulb under his coil was pressed, extended his neck like a cobra. With small boys and some adults, including Mustapha, Achmet when operated by his Master had proved a distinct success. Now in Diana to the huge entertainment of the boys who gathered to view us but also to Rais Thoma's friends and household, Achmet, half magic, half real, lived up to his reputation elsewhere.

Meanwhile, the women gathered outside. A chicken was killed, dishes clattered and a small charcoal brazier began to glow. At last a meal arrived – rice, meat, chicken stew, hobuz on gleaming trays. When all was eaten a sudden bustle of activity took place. Iron beds appeared. Clearly there was only one room for all to sleep in. Mustapha, who had his own idea of propriety, began to crack his fingers. Victor Slee looked put out. Alec and I were politely asked if we would like two beds together. A third bed was brought in and made up, then two mattresses laid on the floor. The ancestral wooden bed remained and Mrs Thoma threw the old Chief's pyjamas on it.

In the meantime Mustapha was rapidly undressing. When all the other men courteously went outside so that I could take off my clothes, Mustapha remained, unabashed and unaware. I said, 'Barra, Mustapha!' Clutching his pyjamas he fled. In 60 seconds I was in bed. It was a peaceful and pleasant night.

We dressed in the reverse order, with a little more difficulty as both Mustapha and Victor Slee were very slow. Mrs Thoma was setting breakfast before I felt it safe to emerge. We washed in big basins in the compound and visited a very respectable latrine where Mr Slee's lavatory paper, perched on a pot, looked peculiarly civilised; then we had an excellent breakfast of eggs.

It was still a public holiday, everyone wearing their best clothes. In selected villages on the Iranian border many had come up from Baghdad. We turned off a little side road to the mountain village of Zino which might have been in another world – a world of poplar trees, a stream and Kurds all sitting along the road watching for what might happen. What happened was our enormous scarlet motor climbing slowly into view and disposing of its passengers at the ford.

Ceremonially we were conducted up the street and into the big airy room of the Chief, the floor covered with Persian carpets. We sat round drinking tea, Kurd, Assyrian, Arab, Scottish, indulging in leisurely conversation. 'Our country was like theirs – mountainous and poor'. 'What did we do?' 'Kept cattle and sheep'. 'How, if our country was poor, were we rich?' 'Because we came to Baghdad – like many young men'. 'If we didn't like Scotland, could we exchange?'

As we left, the men ran to mount their horses and rode down behind us – a splendid sight. Later we learned that this was one of the rich smuggling villages.

We returned by overnight train to Baghdad from the beautiful marble station, leaving the car to Victor Slee who had other places he wished to explore. It had been an excellent four days.

At the end of May Malcolm Adesaishah, Director General of UNESCO, flew in from Teheran, Kabul and Russia. Straight from the airport he drove out to look at one of the Fundamental Education groups outside the city walls. From another direction an Education expert arrived from Amman.

In the evening the team gave a dinner for our guests. Officially for this occasion I was Mrs Dickson, a wife with other preoccupations. I said no word, leaving myself high and dry on the desert sand. Inside I was full of resentment, knowing myself to be as intelligent as anyone present and having as much knowledge of the Iraqi situation through long discussions with my husband. Never to be appealed to for an opinion or asked a single question was humiliating: to be driven back to the YMCA while official discussions continued till nearly midnight was depressing.

Very late Alec came home and my anger was cancelled. He saw no reason why he should not take me with him next day on the official conducted tour so that the Director General should see what a good team we were. When, furious and humiliated, I had been driven back to the YMCA the late meeting in the office, convened by the Director General, had been faced by a staff revolt. The resignation of the Chief of Mission was already in the Paris office. The Mexican sisters Henriquetta and Maria Lopez had been unhappy for a long time. Both had talked of resignation, as had Dr Lutfi who felt unappreciated by his Arab hosts. Victor Slee, new to the country, was bewildered by the whole situation.

Confronted by the bullying tactics of authority, Maria Lopez had begun to swither. The threat that he would have to find his own substitute unnerved Dr Lutfi. Quetta Lopez remained unsubdued, adding to her armoury a serious illness of her father in Mexico. Only Alec Dickson remained able to defend his staff and argue a case – the lack of support or any discussion of the work or what was understood by Fundamental Education, either in Paris or the Ministry or indeed visiting experts.

On June 2nd 1956, the Director General flew out for Paris. He left behind him a Fundamental Education team in tatters. On June 6th, when already the heat was contributing to a summer exit from the city, Quetta Lopez came to tell us that she had made all her arrangements to leave and was going home to Mexico the next day. Maria was already changing her mind about staying.

At 7 am a truncated team saw Quetta off. It seemed sad that after four years she should go with so little to show and a smiling face. The great exit had truly begun.

We gave a farewell Masquf party to both YMCA and Iraqi staff. Many things about Iraq we had enjoyed but we looked forward to the future. There were no regrets though there was sadness in the last 'goodbyes'. A great many came to see us off. I was presented with a hat box of manna. We had a feeling that we were leaving a lot of lost lambs.

CHAPTER 17

Interim Two

Edinburgh 1956

A message had come from the Youth Department of UNESCO informing us that, because of the invasion by Britain and France of the Suez Canal, no new British personnel could be appointed to work with any UN Agency in India. It was back to Edinburgh and unemployment. My mother, who had said to Nannie after our wedding, 'She's gone', had little guessed how often we were to return.

The house in Morningside Place had a small sunroom off my mother's sitting room. This she gave to her son-in-law as his own. When he was at work he sat at the little desk with which he had also been supplied, the floor around him covered with papers, his wife squeezed into a corner attempting to correct the final draft of one manuscript, plan a new one and create scraperboard illustrations from a mass of sketchbook material. Every now and again Nannie or 'Ma' brought in cups of coffee.

We were writing, one actively, the other passively, each of us contending silently with the suspicion that we might be unemployable. Alec spent his time with articles, seeking speaking engagements and travelling south to renew contacts with old friends and fresh colleagues engaged in social and voluntary affairs. He needed to find a patron.

Then one winter evening the telephone rang. It was a call from the World Council of Churches in Geneva. They asked three questions. Did Mr Dickson speak German? Had he got an International Driving Licence? Would he take a Mobile Canteen purchased that afternoon over the telephone from the Church of Scotland and drive it to the Austro-Hungarian frontier?

He asked for a moment to speak to his wife.

'Can we go?'

'Yes'.

Austro-Hungarian Frontier

When collected, the Canteen was not the ideal vehicle. It had been designed for British troops in Cyprus so that the sides could be opened up; now it was to be used at night, in temperatures below zero, on the Austro-Hungarian frontier where, as the result of a student uprising in Budapest, refugees were fleeing to the West in considerable numbers.

Once across the Channel, sharing the driving, we drove furiously down the autobahns of Germany convinced, as were many others, that this could be a significant moment in the history of Europe. It might be the end of the Iron Curtain.

One night, in pouring rain and penetrating cold, we stopped at an inn in a town with a thought-provoking name, Katzensprungen. Early next morning in clear weather we took off for Vienna. We were needed. No effort was too great to arrive in time.

It was late and very dark when we reached the Austrian capital and found a given address. The building was deserted. Only after a search, both desperate and despairing, did we find a contact and discover that the WCC staff were having their evening meal in a nearby restaurant. Already dampened in our ardour we found that we were less than welcome and the vehicle we brought with us a positive burden.

Next morning, having been told to look for our own situation on the frontier, we drove out of the city for Eisenstadt, capital of Burgenland in Eastern Austria, where there was a small WCC team unimpressed by our arrival. This was country far removed from any anticipation of the Tyrol, mountain chalets and winter skiing. Level, dead flat country, the beginning of the great Hungarian Plain.

Having found a room in an indifferent, cold hotel we set out to explore the frontier only to find it overwhelmed by the Red Cross of a dozen countries and many different relief organisations, both voluntary and national.

We drove eastward and westward to be told in village after village that they were already supported by the Dutch Red Cross or the Knights of Malta from Southern Germany or some other group who made it plain when we began to ask questions that these were somehow 'their refugees'. Once, longing to be attached to somebody, we asked such a group, 'Could you use a mobile canteen?' They were courteous but the reply was, 'Well we have one already. Let's compare sizes', given by a young man in uniform. In the courtyard stood a vehicle capable of preparing soup for 1500 troops on the move. 'Ja, das ist unsere Goulashkanone'. He laughed as he used the traditional phrase of the Austrian Army. 'The soup kitchen'. We left, humiliated.

One night, more in despair than with any hope of success, we drove down a rutted farm track through a desolate frozen vineyard to a canal which at this point formed the frontier. A rumour had reached us that down there, away off the normal roads and more obvious village frontier posts, a group of students operated as couriers to bands of people who arrived exhausted on the other side of the canal.

We bumped and lurched down the raised embankment of this track, telling each other that this was our last attempt – if this failed we would pack up and return home. Approaching the canal, the shape of a forbidding wooden watchtower gradually loomed out of the darkness on the other side. We doused the lights. Suddenly an Austrian sentry box was there beside our track. Inside it two figures were huddled up trying to keep warm. When they saw us they came out amazed.

They were two of a student group composed of different nationalities from universities of the West – with or without permission – two or three West Germans, a couple of Austrians, a Norwegian, two British, an American from a Paris university, who had chosen to work in this remote spot because they alone possessed the stamina and the enterprise to do so. When they saw us and recognised our purpose there was no doubt of the welcome. Our satisfaction on meeting them was intense. From then on our Canteen and its facilities offered them a support base; they offered us at last a valid and undisputed function.

Next day we left Eisenstadt and, thanks to the help of the local priest, moved our accommodation into the spare room of a widow in the small, desperately poor frontier village of Andau, six miles from the canal in flat, mist-laden country. There was little food in Andau. After some days of near starvation on chocolate and apples kindly donated by the Swiss, a German Red Cross unit offered to give us one meal a day – a wonderful bowl of hot soup with meat on red letter days.

We drove out of the village at 8.30 each night, down the farm track to join the students. On the return in early morning darkness, stiff and tired, our clothes rigid on us, filthy from wrestling with a vehicle quite unprepared to face these conditions, we fell into a huge bed under a mountainous duvet. The room was unheated. It was our responsibility, mostly neglected, to light a wood-burning stove when we returned. The lavatory, in an outside courtyard, was guarded by a fierce Alsatian, 'Hund', chained to a post close to the door. At 3pm, bone sore and exhausted, we crawled out from under the duvet, washed ourselves and the inside of the vehicle in scanty cold water and went to the German Red Cross for a life-saving bowl of soup, then set off for another night by the canal.

Here, after filling it with water, the ten-gallon boiler heated by Calor gas was lit. The Canteen was warm and snug where heat from the gas began to circulate – below the waist the air froze along the floor.

People crossing an international frontier at night, fearing they are constantly in danger of being shot in the back, are not hungry when they first arrive on the other side. They want the comfort and reassurance of a hot drink, somebody to talk to, and to be inside four walls out of the night with its dangers and terrors. We supplied tea, black, sweet, with lemon and rum in it and strong black coffee. For the children, cocoa or warm milk. We gave out jealously hoarded biscuits with cheese or jam, sometimes fruit or chocolate.

We took out a generous gift of food from Britain but some items, notably sugar, were used up very quickly and we had no prearranged method of replacing them. One night about 2 am, two representatives of a Swiss student organisation came to visit our sector. They asked if they could help with food supplies as they had just received a large gift from their own country.

I was tired, cross and unbelieving. In such a situation 2 am was a bad time. Alec thanked them politely and made out a list. The next night, exactly at midnight, a car drew up behind us and the Swiss unloaded bags of foodstuff – apples, cheese, lemons, cigarettes, chocolate, tea, sugar, biscuits, babies rusks, even peppermint leaves. Our Canteen became truly international, dispensing Swiss cheese on British biscuits with Norwegian chocolate, American rum and Swiss lemon in British tea.

crossing the border

Now we were no longer alone. The group of devoted and enterprising young men and women whom we considered 'ours' were always waiting and ready to keep up constant patrols along the Austrian side of the frontier. The canal itself, the final barrier, by some freak of its composition never froze. It ran straight for several miles on either side of our parking spot with no bridge. This was a formidable obstacle for escapees, often accompanied by women and children, from tiny babies to tough little 11- and 12-year-olds.

The babies came on their fathers' backs, wrapped up like cocoons in layer upon layer of sacking and rugs. The knots that held this contraption together were so frozen that they had always to be cut with a bread knife before the child could be unrolled. Often, to keep them quiet, the very young ones had been doped with luminol.

The dilemma of the canal was solved, simply and without fuss, by Einar the Norwegian and Alex the American. They went into Vienna, visited a sports shop and with their own money, bought a collapsible rubber boat. This they brought back on the roof of a bus, hid it in the reeds by day and used it as a life raft by night.

By now, two jeep drivers with vehicles were also standing by to drive people back to Andau, on the first stretch of a safe route to Vienna. For all those whose jobs involved standing round in bitter cold for long periods, we were also able to supply hot drinks and an occasional break in the warmth of the van. Everybody possible had to come inside the Canteen. To operate as it had been designed, with shutters up and counters down, would have been impossible in the cold so every bit of surplus equipment was jettisoned or stowed away or made to act as seats. Only the absolutely necessary remained. Our customers were pushed or hauled through the doors and squeezed into every corner.

We never knew when they were coming. The door would open suddenly and one of the patrol, a German, a Norwegian, the Austrian Boy Scout, would whisper, 'Customers coming up!' Almost immediately, behind them out of the gloom would loom up a group of people, tired, wet and sometimes still unsure whether or not we were friends. If it were a large group, Alec would say, 'Women and children first inside' and begin to hand up small bewildered bundles of clothing which turned out to be toddlers so wrapped up that it was sometimes difficult to tell which end was which. The ten-year-olds climbed in under their own steam, eager and interested in spite of a fifteen or twenty mile walk through snow from the nearest railway station. The women, frozen and frightened, had to be shored up and pulled up the steep step, calmed and reassured with hugs and clasped hands before they could believe that the nightmare was over and the frontier actually crossed. If there was room the men came inside too but on nights when the group was too large, they stood around the open doorway drinking tea and stamping their feet while we tried to ascertain where they had come from or whether any had been left behind.

They carried with them a minimum of baggage. To be seen at a bus stop or at a railway station with luggage could mean courting suspicion. A plastic bag or a dispatch case was the most that would pass muster. In this restricted space family photographs were almost universal with a house, perhaps a dog, to remind them of home. One woman wore a cherished broad-brimmed summer hat which she could not bear to part with; an elderly man stood outside the Canteen clutching a 'cello, defying anyone who offered to guard it while he had a hot drink. Their professional diplomas, the open sesame perhaps to some job in the West, were all that mattered to many men.

They came over in waves. These were not refugees as we had been accustomed to thinking of them in the past, beaten and demoralised, driven out despairing. The first, who had come before we had arrived in Austria, had been the Hungarian Secret Police, the principal oppressors of the population. With the students' revolt in the ascendancy they had recognised early that if the Government fell they themselves would be in danger. They had ways of leaving that did not include the discomforts of those who came later. Then came Jewish families, recalling the horrors of the Holocaust and fearing the role traditionally thrust on them as scapegoats.

A little later, when Russian tanks rolled into Budapest, the students began to leave. They were followed by waves of middle and working class folk. A people who had historically been travellers, accustomed to seeking their fortunes westward, whose frontiers had been closed over the last years restricting their freedom, thwarting their ambitions, now saw, perhaps for a very short time, those frontiers unguarded. They found their own apartment block half deserted. Rumours were afoot of neighbours silently gone. A frenzy took hold of many citizens, especially when a communist government was first restored, urging that opportunity must be seized. These were a people who had made the decision that they would no longer tolerate the way of life being imposed on them and could now see no prospect of relief in their own country. People who still had their vigour and pride were turning to the West because the West had been telling them over the radio, 'Come over to us. We can give you a free life.'

They were a whole cross section: pastor, postman, policeman, professionals, students, schoolboys, soldiers, weavers, mechanics, miners, musicians – sometimes in small trade groups, sometimes in family parties.

One night a batch loomed out of the darkness having walked fifty miles. My husband said to them, 'You must be tired', whereupon the only one who spoke German replied, 'Tired! Not at all. We're sportsmen.' 'What is your sport?' asked Alec. 'Swimming' replied the lad, adding with pride, 'First class'. When asked which country he wished to go to, he answered with passion, 'Anywhere, anywhere where I can swim!'

Very few of the refugees spoke any language but their own. Occasionally there was someone who understood German and could talk with my husband but lack of communication was the great frustration. One quiet night, out of the darkness, a woman answered my greeting in English.

I exclaimed, 'Where did you learn English?'

'I learnt it in Budapest. I've been teaching myself secretly. This is the first time I have spoken to someone who understands'.

As time went on our students grew more adventurous. Crossing the canal, they roamed further and further across the Hungarian Plain on the other side, alert for any sounds that might indicate people in distress.

Then, towards the end of January 1957, two things happened. Up until now the wooden watchtower had not been manned. The seriousness of the uprising in the capital had resulted in the recall to the city of many troops from outlying places. Suddenly one night the moonless darkness was shattered by Very lights tearing aside the cover to which we had become accustomed and exposing to our horror, on our side of the canal, a military patrol accompanied by dogs. In the village we discovered that the frontier, which we had always taken for granted ran down the middle of the canal, lay in fact along the bank on which the Canteen had nightly been parked. The next night when we arrived I insisted that before we did anything else the vehicle be turned round facing back towards Andau!

A few nights later Einar the Norwegian, out on a sweep across the Plain, did not return when all his companions were back. While we waited for him distant gunshots were heard. It was the first time danger had taken on a sinister reality.

We returned to Andau in the morning and after a disturbed sleep drove back down the farm track as usual. Einar remained lost to us. A message came from the authorities in Eisenstadt, to whom we had reported what had happened, saying he had not been shot but taken to Budapest. A few days later he was sent back by the Hungarians, shaken, but saying that his captors had been courteous and treated him reasonably.

It was the beginning of the end. Already the fierce January weather had affected the flow of refugees. Now only a few of the young and very fit were undertaking the challenge of the icy cold. Everyone in our group recognised that our time on the frontier was nearly over. One after another the students left to return to university. Alex sold back the now second hand rubber boat in Vienna.

We were very tired. On the last morning we drove down the farm track to the frontier in daylight to see the landscape in a different guise. The watchtower looked surprisingly innocuous in the flat grey country. In the Austrian sentry box there was, as there had been on the night we had arrived, a shivering figure. We got out of the van to investigate. The young man rose to his feet, his tremors now denoting fear. He wore only a beret, jacket and trousers and carried a straw bag. It was clear from the state of them all that he had swum the canal.

We asked no questions, put him at once in the van and drove him straight back to the refugee reception Centre in Andau, explaining to the woman in charge where he had been found and telling her that we would return in the afternoon when he had been warmed, fed and identified. After our last German Red Cross bowl of soup we went back to the centre. There was an orange in the Canteen. We took it as a present. His name, now known, was Bela Horvath.

Later we discovered that he was the only son, aged 19, of a widow who owned a small steading about twenty miles on the other side of the canal. A rumour had flashed round the community that the Hungarian Army was recruiting in the district. When they came to Bela Horvath's home, his mother told him he must leave at once and cross the frontier to the West. They were very poor so he brought nothing with him but she was certain that freedom was preferable to being taken for a soldier.

He sat in the Centre holding his orange but without any understanding how to eat it. A very simple lad, with no language and no experience beyond his own steading, he was tongue tied. The next day he would go to the distribution camp in Vienna and we would start our journey back to Edinburgh. With universal gestures we wished him well; Alec gave him his card, indicating name and address and a general goodwill.

As we travelled home we discussed our experience in the last two months. Without Einar, Alex, Norbert, Don and the others, who had been discovered by chance, the whole exercise would have been a failure for both sides. Our role was to provide a stable base and encouragement for the student group and to enable the young to do what they were best at creatively. We had come to admire their commitment to a cause and their devotion and courage in serving it. They had, in the incident of the life raft, a simplicity uncluttered by qualifications or consequences which is the prerogative of the young. They asked no permission – they went out and did what was needed.

Reflecting on the vast administrative machinery operated by the United Nations, we contrasted this with the student ingenuity which had helped so many to safety. Did we have to wait for a Third World War until some of our young people, at least, should feel that they were needed?

To us and to the students, this was not a refugee problem any more. The situation had become people needing help – not only blankets, food, medicine, or material goods. Much more important was friendship, the right to work, a feeling that they were accepted by any community that took them in. These people had come over a frontier looking for a better life. They still did not know how many frustrations lay in front of them – camps and queues, queues and more camps, a gradual dying away of interest and sympathy with their cause. Many hugged and kissed us on leaving as they went out to the future and we went back to the darkness and the cold to wait for those who came next.

At home in Edinburgh my mother and I trod warily in a loving vacuum. My husband, occupied with articles which he had little difficulty in getting published and the increasing development of accumulated ideas to which the Hungarian experience had added a new dimension, was stimulated by the announcement that in 1958 military conscription for 18-year-old males would end. Suddenly, possible alternative realities began to take shape. He was oblivious of my increasing unease at the lack of a personal home life.

Being innocent of any experience in the literary and publishing worlds, my imagination was filled with dreams of rejection slips and the impossibility of finding a publisher for the increasing piles of manuscript.

Edinburgh 1957

One morning Alec received a letter from a small London publisher, Dennis Dobson. He was interested in Mr Dickson's time at Man O' War Bay. The firm specialised in Africa (and in Music). He felt that the pioneering work in the British Cameroons/Nigeria might produce an interesting book. Would it be possible for Mr Dickson to come south sometime for a talk?

I laughed, remembering that on return from Man O' War Bay my husband had scornfully rejected the idea of partnership in a book. 'He's got another think coming', I said. 'No', Alec replied, 'I'll write and say I am interested and could I make an appointment to come and see him? Then we'll go together and take your book!'

A week or two later, with my manuscript and illustrations – nearly ninety of them – wrapped up in brown paper and tied with string and carried by Alec, we arrived on Dennis Dobson's doorstep in Kensington.

Greeted warmly, my presence explained simply as the wife, the interview began. It went well. Alec Dickson, when talking about his work, was a compelling speaker. Fascinated by listening to him I sat silent. It was obvious Mr Dobson was impressed. 'I was right, Mr Dickson, to think that there is a book in this. Your description is gripping. Would you be ready to sign a contract?'

With a charming smile, my husband extracted the brown paper parcel from beneath his chair, explained that he himself was much too occupied to embark on a book, 'But . . .', laying the bulky parcel on the desk, '. . . My wife has written one!'

It was clear that Dennis Dobson knew he had been conned. Nevertheless, he was a gentleman publisher. He slid the parcel under the desk with little sign of annoyance, thanked me and said he would have a look at it.

On the doorstep I said, 'I bet it comes back to me in three months with not even the knots of the string undone.'

In Edinburgh other things preoccupied us.

Bela Horvath

Alec's older brother, Murray Dickson, now Director of Education Sarawak, had been pressing us to visit him since we returned from Iraq. However, before any decision was reached, the telephone rang one afternoon. It was Bela Horvath.

He had acquired some very simple English through which he managed to convey that he was in Britain, in Yorkshire, and very unhappy. With some difficulty extracting from him an address in Barnsley, Alec promised he would be in touch and visit him on his way to Edinburgh from London in a week or two. When arrangements were decided, Bela was sent a date and time of Alec Dickson's arrival in Barnsley. When the day came Bela was on the platform as the train drew in.

The story when it emerged through an interpreter was not unusual for that time. In the camp in Vienna a bewildered Bela Horvath had heard that representatives of the Coal Board in England were looking for recruits among the young Hungarians. Alone in a strange land, without relatives or friends, the only contact he possessed was the card my husband had thrust into his hand as we parted at Andau, so he opted to come to Britain and signed the Coal Board form. He was a strong lad with no conception of what happened down a mine.

With a group of fellow Hungarians he arrived in Barnsley to find that the local miners, not having been consulted, refused to let those aliens work in the pits. There were hostile headlines in the newspapers which contributed to local attitudes. In a dreary miners' hostel the refugees sat day after day isolated and unhappy, playing cards and smoking. Some English tutoring was provided of which Bela was ready to take full advantage.

Alec Dickson saw immediately that this was no decision to linger over. He told Bela that as soon as he got back to Edinburgh he would start to find some kind of farming job. When that happened he would send money for a train fare. The local management would be only too pleased to be rid of one of their recent liabilities.

Finding work for a young refugee whose only reference was that we had found him in an Austrian sentry box on the Hungarian frontier was not easy. But having once committed himself to action on behalf of a young friend, Alec Dickson never gave up. Eventually the Factor on one of the Duke of Buccleuch's border estates agreed to take Bela for a re-afforestation project.

Instructions and the railway fare were despatched to Barnsley where the tutor had agreed to see that Bela Horvath understood. Two days later, my mother and Nannie welcomed once again a young man from a country they knew little about and supplied him with a meal and a bed before we drove him next day to Selkirk.

The start to his new life was not an easy one, either for Bela Horvath or the Factor. It lasted a comparatively short time. Bela, more interested in tractors and machinery, once in a country setting was very soon looking for a more congenial job. Over the years, keeping in touch with us, he rose to be a manager with Tarmac, married a girl from Wales and settled down to raise a family in his new country.

CHAPTER 18

Interim Three

Sarawak 1957

Murray Dickson, Alec Dickson's older brother, now Director of Education, Sarawak, had waited a long time to have his invitation to Sarawak accepted. Now, in the early summer of 1957 we decided to go.

The two brothers were of very different temperaments but each admired and loved the other. They were accustomed to speaking freely and having their opinions listened to. Murray Dickson was a classical scholar, a quiet loner, and after Oxford he had spent time as an Able Seaman on a small trading ship. He then joined the Borstal Service in Britain, becoming much respected by his colleagues and modest in any description of his own achievements. He was unmarried.

When the War came he joined the Norfolk Regiment. In 1945/46 he found himself first in India, then in Sarawak, reporting officially on the results of the Japanese occupation. Before the War, Sarawak, on the northern coast of the large island of Indonesian Borneo, had been the property of a White Rajah for several generations. A benign regime, the Rajahs had firm ideas about ruling. A third of the population was Malay. They had political power and composed the administration of Government. The Chinese third was the business community. The up-river indigenous people, living in longhouses in the 'ulu' and generally known as Dayaks, remained in the forest as they had for centuries; self-sufficient but without access to twentieth-century education or ideas. It was said that in Japanese times they were reborn headhunters. All transport was by river, except for a few miles of road outside the capital, Kuching.

indigenous native

This was our first visit to the East. Having changed planes in Singapore we landed in Kuching on a flat green space cut out of the jungle in the brilliant clarity of a new day. Climbing down the steps from the tiny plane we searched the welcoming groups for my brother-in-law. No sign. For all our excitement we were taken aback but we should have known better. As we came nearer to the terminal I saw a face I knew lurking quietly at a window in the reception lounge. We should have remembered that even the arrival of his nearest and dearest after a journey of thousands of miles was not going to cause what Murray Dickson would call a 'fuss'.

From the first moment, Sarawak enchanted us. Kuching was a very small town – from every viewpoint it seemed possible to see surrounding hills. The colour in the lucid light was brilliant; reds and purples, yellows, oranges or turquoise of the women's clothes, set off by black hair and eyes and the darkness of shadow in the tiny Chinese shops. Banana trees, palm trees and others that we did not recognise in myriad shades of green, many laden with scarlet, or mauve or yellow blossoms. Traffic was by rickshaw, bicycle, feet and the occasional car. Murray Dickson travelled only by bicycle which some of the European community thought eccentric for a Senior Government Servant. Nevertheless it very soon became clear that there was great respect and affection for him, eccentricities and all.

A Dayak

His large white wooden house on top of a steep hill would have housed a family of children instead of a single man. Along the roadside at the foot of the hill Murray had begun to plant rice and to put into the soil young, quick-growing trees. The former to make him as far as possible self-sufficient, the latter to shield him from the public gaze. Without inclination or ability as a gardener or a farmer, he was a keen observer of nature and a lover of trees.

In the rear of this house which overlooked the golf course lived Bol, his Malay servant and housekeeper who from the moment we arrived objected to our presence – the amount of laundry we needed, the fact that sometimes we wanted a lunch, all of which interrupted the easy flow of his Master's house which lay entirely under Bol's command.

It was known to us that Murray, admiring his younger brother though he did, was nervous of the effect that Alec's outgoing, demanding temperament would have on his own friends and colleagues and on Bol. Fortunately at the time of our marriage he had told Alec publicly that this was the best decision he had ever made in his life so I knew the role assigned to me.

This was a busy and harrassing time for the Education Department, its Director and his colleagues. On July 1st 1946, the days of the white Rajahs came quietly to an end. Sarawak became a Crown Colony under the British Government – though not without some local opposition. The Rajahs had been just and revered rulers, having a special relationship with the up-river peoples. When a Commission from the British House of Commons came after the handover to try to gauge public opinion some of the Dayaks asked them 'Does the King intend to live in Kuching?'

'No, we do not think he will live in Kuching.'

'Has the King any sons?'

'No. He has no sons.'

'Has the King a brother?'

'Yes, the King has a brother, but we do not think it is likely he will live in Kuching.'

The Dayaks explained to the Commission that this was an important question to them. Hitherto in order to reach the Ruler they could go by canoe and perhaps get a lift in a boat to Kuching. The cost was 6 dollars. 'What would be the cost of going to London?'

'More than 6 dollars, but there would surely be a King's representative in Kuching'.

What Murray Dickson inherited as second Director of Education in a new Colony was a confused educational system. The Malay population had been

Public Works Department N. Borneo

absorbed into a new Government controlled Education Department without difficulty. In the times of the Rajahs, the Chinese had formed tight-knit communities, raised money themselves to create schools for the education of their children and started their own societies to keep alive their traditions. In the country of their adoption the majority of Chinese remained unassimilated. Though mission and government schools, in which the language was English, absorbed an increasing number of young Chinese, there were many Chinese schools outside the Education Department using Mandarin or Cantonese and looking to mainland China as their mentor.

The Rajahs took the view that the up-river peoples should be allowed to develop in their own traditional ways. If they were to be able to play a genuine part in their own country it was vital that primary schools be established in the 'ulu' and longhouse teachers trained.

basket carrier

Murray Dickson was faced with setting up a new teacher training centre in Batu Lintang, a former Japanese prisoner of war camp. It would provide short courses for illiterate young Dayaks without any knowledge of English, each chosen by the elders of his own longhouse, to travel to Kuching and learn to be a teacher.

In the spare time which he did not possess Murray Dickson was teaching himself Mandarin in order that he had some understanding of the arguments and decisions made by staff meetings in independent Chinese schools, to which he was not invited but was accepted on sufferance if he came. In the Education Department much time was consumed in meetings, introducing fresh ideas to local staff consisting of young Malays, handsome, artistic, accustomed to life at a leisurely pace and mission educated up-and-coming Chinese.

For all his quietness Murray Dickson was not easily overcome. Moderate, willing to listen and to devote unlimited time to resolving difficulties, once he had come to a decision based on what he knew to be right – sometimes illustrated by a classical Greek story – he could not be swayed. Fortunately there were also a few senior Chinese staff who well understood the dilemmas being faced by the Director and were committed to supporting him.

It was a measure of my brother-in-law's affection for us, and of the abiding influence of the mother that both had greatly loved, that family matters were always paramount. It might have been more convenient to cancel our visit or, once we arrived, to abandon us to our own resources but that was not Murray's way. Knowing our interests he had made meticulous plans for us to go into the interior and see three community development projects. This was a fateful decision.

Padawan

It was very early in the morning when we started on our first 'ulu' adventure to Padawan, a Land Dayak Community Development Centre up the Sarawak River. Nurse Nichol, young, red-haired and very organised, had been down to Kuching to collect stores. We were to accompany her back.

Murray saw us off by Land Rover on the first section of the journey. Being a man who travelled very light himself, I took it for granted he looked askance at our luggage. It happened that a letter from him had arrived in Edinburgh as we were leaving, advising us to bring an Army kitbag and plastic bags for underwear. Too late. It did not seem important but now I was to discover how unsuitable were suitcases, however small.

Alec, whose only requirement of any house was that it had a pillarbox at the end of the street, now refused to start until letters were posted.

Outside Kuching the tarmac road stretched for about thirty miles. Then it dwindled into a forest track, blocked at intervals by enormous machines digging piles of glutinous red earth to lay the foundations for an extension.

The Land Rover stopped and we scrambled out. Nurse Nichol took up her baggage and set off along a slippery red earth bank. Trying to follow her, I saw the reason for the Army kitbag – a rigid all-corners suitcase was not the same. A few yards on we came to a village perched on the bank above a wide brown river. Down a steep path a boat awaited us. It was a long, narrow, open canoe with an outboard engine and a Malay crew – the District Officer's boat lent in our honour. We lay back buttressed against our baggage, a paper parasol

open canoe

land Dayak

behind us, on a level with the water, cushioned in comfort. Sometimes we passed a group of women washing their black sarongs, cleaning a baby or filling water jars. They smiled, we smiled back.

It was the dry season. As the river narrowed the water became clear and shallow over rocks and little stones. The engine had to be hauled up and the crew took to poling. Then passengers were jettisoned. Leaping out, the boatmen and Nurse Nichol pushed and heaved at the boat. The water tugged and gurgled at our shins, the riverbed stones cut our soft feet. As assistant pushers we were a dead loss.

So the day wore on. The journey was slow and painful. At last, in the late afternoon, the boat rounded a bend to meet rocks and rapids. Here we had to disembark. It was a relief to get out and stretch our legs and to walk into the village. There Nurse Nichol, known as 'Muk' (Land Dayak for woman) was greeted as an old friend. She knew this area; had walked over it doctoring the sick, delivering babies, talking with the women about their homes and families.

The children were astonished to see me. When I asked why I was told that until this moment they had imagined that all western women had red hair. The only two they had ever seen were the female Education Officer and 'Muk', both bronze haired. Meanwhile, boat and baggage were being manhandled up the rapids. Minutes went by; hours went by; the sun began to go down. No boat arrived. A message came that it was stuck on rocks.

Muk began to organise a rescue party to give extra pushing power. By the time the canoe was free of the rocks it was nearly dark and we were both very tired. It was only when the luggage began to be disembarked that we realised there was a walk ahead. It was the baggage we had waited for, not the boat!

When suitcases and bundles were sorted, we were allowed to carry only the smallest pieces. Muk's sidelong glances showed that she was anxious about us; Alec in his early forties, me close behind. The last trek had been up Mt

Cameroon before we were married. The anticipated porters were a line of tiny girls gliding along, each one under a load considerably bulkier than herself.

There was an hour to walk and hazards to be overcome. The first appeared immediately. The river had to be crossed, which lay now in a deep cleft in the rock. The Land Dayaks were bridgemakers, though not bridges such as we had ever seen before. Basic materials were bamboo and lianas. Two or three thick bamboo stems tied together formed the walkway, with a handrail of bamboo laced with liana on one or both sides. This bridge was harnessed to overhanging trees by more lianas. The whole precarious structure responded to the users steps, swaying and dipping like a live thing.

Only the darkness saved us both from being shamed. Muk's brisk firmness as she stepped on to the bridge in front of me made hanging back impossible. The cool scrutiny of the small Land Dayak girls stung my pride. I could not let it appear that red-haired women were superior to the dark-haired ones of my clan.

young Dayak

We arrived at last, shattered by the experience, only sustained by Nurse Nichol's cheerfulness. When she said, 'We're here', there was no sign that we were anywhere. No lights. No sound. Only one small house lit up by Muk's torch. She climbed the steps, opened the door and we staggered into a tiny room. Any feeling that we were visitors of some importance ebbed away through our dripping, sweaty clothes. By the time Nurse Nichol had come back we had drawn a second wind. Having come so far, with such pain and humiliation, we had determined to enjoy our visit. A wash and bacon and eggs prepared by Muk herself restored us. The clock, which we had expected to show 2 am or 3 am proved it to be only 9 pm. Then footsteps outside the door announced the arrival of Canon Peter Howes, creator of the Padawan Community Development Training Centre.

He was tall and very thin. Long legs in ancient shorts and a taut corded neck supported a head lit by eyes at once alive and remote, introspective yet sharply aware: a black beret crowned the whole figure, a shifting representation between monk and elderly schoolboy, foreign workman and English eccentric. He greeted us as though he had met us by chance on the street and had only a few moments before hurrying on to catch a train, a greeting which warned us that what we learned here would be the results of our own efforts, the fruits of our own questioning. Nevertheless, this air of rakish unconcern, the impression gained of a man whose whole mind was concentrated on the work he was doing leaving minimum attention for extra troubles like ourselves, made us warm to him. There is a strong attraction about the single-minded man. Canon Howes was single-minded about Padawan.

He had been in Sarawak many years and had come to have a special knowledge of and devotion to the Land Dayaks, a remote, timid people, quiet and unaggressive, guarding their own way of life rather than interfering with others.

When the war came Peter Howes was interned by the Japanese in Batu Lintang along with other missionaries and Government servants. He told of the courage and devotion of indigenous people who risked their livelihood and often their lives to bring the prisoners a little extra food, a message or some outside news.

Next morning all uneasiness was forgotten. There was a freshness and clarity in the air and the sky had the blue of a more temperate climate. Now we could see that there really was a Centre here with wooden buildings round a flat grass space in which goalposts were set up. In the distance, hurrying about his jobs, was the tall figure of the Canon, blue shirt blowing behind him, his beret at a rakish angle. Although it was very early there was a great deal of activity going on. All round the houses and playing fields groups of boys were working, cutting grass with 'parangs' (the all-purpose knife), collecting rubbish, sweeping, tidying, working with stores or boats. Those were the trainees. To our eyes they seemed too tiny, too fragile to be anything but little boys. They were not only working. They were singing and the tune was familiar to us.

'Che sera sera' they sang. 'Whatever will be will be', 'The future not ours to see'. They sang for us as well as themselves.

Beginning to explore the compound and talk to the boys, we were struck by the seriousness with which they took every aspect of their daily lives and of Community Development. We brought with us from Nigeria understanding of community development training, serious in aims and exercise, but lightened by laughter and fun which was natural to many of our West Africans and to Alec Dickson. We knew the value of this element within the training, slackening tensions, creating a basis for friendship and understanding, sometimes in moments of shared fun easing the approach to shared problems.

These were a different people, belonging to a different culture. They were also in many ways very young. It was not that Land Dayaks could not laugh. Indeed as we grew to know them during our short stay, to talk with them of their lives and to tell them of ours; as we sang with them and played with them, Alec told them jokes and stories. I crossed 'parangs' on the floor of the large open dining/recreation building to show some of them a Scottish sword dance and they laughed a great deal. Barriers broke down and we felt that they were not accustomed to having visitors from outside doing these things with them. Of course this was true. The Europeans they knew were earnest and devoted, working long hours to establish Padawan as a Centre for the future. There was little time for relaxation. We were passers-by of a kind they had never seen before. Even the fact that my hair was not red and I could draw pictures of them caused enjoyment, added to their knowledge and were remembered. Of such simple things are links made and on both sides horizons widened.

This small point had some influence on Alec's thinking later on. We felt then that it would be fun for these small Land Dayaks to have young Britons working alongside them and that both groups might find a measure of understanding in sharing simple pleasures. We were aware that we were middle-aged and we thought how enormously some of the young people we knew at home would enjoy this experience and could easily visualise them making friends with these enchanting young trainees.

There was a Garden of Eden quality about Padawan and the reserve with which the Canon treated any such ideas when Alec Dickson aired them, without then any real purpose, did not surprise us.

Amin and Maug were among the twelve or fourteen boys who lived wholly as boarders. Many more children of varying ages came daily to school from the surrounding longhouses. For the trainees, the intention was that eventually they go back to their own longhouses ready to give a lead on improving conditions. They had an insight into and an interest in the whole working of the Centre, the layout of the ground, the planting and growing of crops, carpentry and the putting up of buildings, hygiene, the siting and making of suitable latrines, the order and checking of stores, care of boats, helping in the dispensary and so on as well as straightforward schooling. It was expected that they work hard – indeed they seemed to have an unlimited capacity for hard work. It was our advocacy of the light-hearted and entertaining as a relaxation that was revolutionary.

Amin and Maug took us on a walk to visit one of the longhouses. They walked single file in front of us down one of the narrow forest paths. Occasionally we met travellers coming in the other direction and discovered that there were certain ritual greetings:

'Where have you come from?'

'Where are you going to?'

'Have you eaten?'

For us when we walked on after such an encounter, there was no conversation at all. Amin and Maug took the responsibility for us seriously but they did not know how to entertain strangers.

We reached the longhouse and climbed up on to the raised platform of bamboo which formed a central street with small wooden homes on either side. We were led to a shop at the far end where we each drank a 'Green spot'. A few of the village children gathered round us shyly. One or two women came in to make purchases, smiled and hurried silently away.

On the way back we tried some questions.

'Can you sing a Land Dayak song?' Alec asked.

'No', replied Amin.

'Can you tell us a Land Dayak story?' Pause. 'Do you have dances, then?'

Amin turned round and said slowly, with a certain exasperation, 'No. Land Dayak people not very clever.'

We were rebuked. It was a defensive answer to keep us at bay. In one instance at least we knew it was not true. We had noticed, in the shade of the

Borneo house

roof of the recreation room, two boys sitting deep in thought. A third, Suwim, stood intently looking on. Curious to find out what engaged their attention so profoundly, we approached. Punjabi and Agoye were playing chess.

In the cool of the early evening my husband took out of his baggage the rubber ring with which we had provided ourselves in London. He collected together on the football field some of the older boys to teach them Ringing the Stick, a game which could be played in any village without equipment and with an indeterminate number of players, on any size of ground. The ring could be woven out of twisted palm strands.

Two of the smallest boys stood perched on stools at either end of the field, holding long bamboo poles on which they would catch the ring that their team mates threw at them. At the height of the excitement these small goalkeepers sometimes forgot their position and stepped off into mid-air, rolling on the ground among friends and opponents and hysterical laughter. In the midst of their slender brown bodies Alec looked like some large white elephant with a hat on – being bald, having lost most of his originally red hair, he needed protection from the sun. But his sleight of hand and the tricks he used to baffle them as to the direction he intended to throw the ring caused enormous pleasure.

That evening after supper by lamplight, with the trainees in the open dining hall, we stayed on when the Canon and Muk had gone to work on tiles. The boys were ready to attempt any game that might be suggested but had no thought of taking the initiative. We sang 'London's Burning' and 'Red Sails in the Sunset', both of which they knew, and 'Que sera sera'. I produced Achmet, the little rubber snake, and we rejoiced in the shrinking boldness of those who agreed to activate him by pressing the bulb. Alec had a trick which never failed to baffle and entrance audiences in any part of the world. A Nigerian student had once taken him aside and offered money to buy the solution. Seeing it for the umpteenth time I still felt a shiver of surprise when the name written unseen on a piece of paper appeared traced in black on Alec's upper arm.

Though we had been so short a time with the Land Dayak people this evening we felt at one with them.

The next morning we left early to return to Kuching. This time we were being given a lift directly from Padawan in the commercial canoe of a Chinese trader. At the first village of call his young employee landed to collect a cargo; kerosene, rice, beer and then fifty young citrus trees, squeezed into a corner of the boat. We were aware that this journey was not going to be without its hazards.

The next uncertainty was the breakdown of the outboard engine. When with much trouble a substitute had been acquired, a thunderstorm, accompanied by darkness and driving rain, convinced the Chinese-in-charge that he could go no further. He landed us and our baggage at a village still eight miles from the end of the track where the bus from Kuching arrived next morning.

The village had a small school. We were rescued by the 17-year-old Land Dayak teacher who courteously offered us the hospitality of his house which he shared with the Malay tractor driver working on the new road.

Apologising for the little he had to give us, Edward Sian showed us into his own bedroom. Then he and his Malay friend, having consulted together as to the food we might be able to eat, prepared a wonderful meal; rice with meat topped by fried eggs and they provided us with spoons to use in eating. While the thunder crashed about the village, the rain on the roof and among the leaves joined with the noises of the night and brought the jungle very close. With two village elders who had come in to scrutinise us we had a safe, enjoyable evening and an unbroken sleep.

In the morning Edward Sian laid on coffee, provided a carrier for our bags and walked with us to the huge red scar in the jungle where the tractor driver worked. The bus was waiting to leave. No sooner had we arrived back in Kuching than we were preparing to leave for Budu Community Development Scheme up the Krian River.

Budu 1957

The Budu Scheme had been the pioneer child of a remarkable man, John Wilson, whom we had known since meeting him at a conference in Britain. In fact it was partly the lure of Budu that had led us to accept the invitation to Sarawak. In 1957 John Wilson was in Scotland on leave and he rang us up in Edinburgh and asked if he could come to tea.

'Of course', Alec said, 'And tell us how things are with Budu'.

When the car stopped at the gate we saw that he had not come alone. Two brown-skinned dark haired boys clambered out. Ma began hastily to count the tea cups. This was our first introduction to the Sea Dayak Ibans of Sarawak.

Their names were Luke and Jawie and over the years to come we were to retain a strong bond with them. Struck by their physical attractiveness – small and fine-boned, they were by no means fragile. Their manners were perfect; their self-possession caused us to wonder about the nature of the background that enabled them to face so quietly and easily the transition from Borneo to Britain.

It was a beautiful early summer day, cloudless and sunny, so we had tea in the garden. We were astonished to observe that Luke and Jawie did not appreciate this rare treat but unobtrusively moved themselves round to take advantage of any shade. Later we came to know that for forest peoples the sun could be an enemy rather than a friend.

Now we were actually boarding a Government launch in Kuching to visit Budu.

John Wilson was a teacher born in Glasgow. A man of enormous determination, he had served in the Royal Air Force during the War, suffering a fractured spine when shot down. Medical authorities were dumbfounded when after a year in plaster and the prospect of life in a wheelchair, by sheer willpower he was passed fit for active service in the final year of the War.

In 1949, at about the same time as Murray Dickson, John Wilson joined the Colonial Education Service and found himself in Sarawak. He came to Kuching with ideas about education radically changed from those of his pre-war experience. Teaching, he was now certain, should embrace a far wider concept – that of community and not something that just happened within four walls.

This was the time when Murray Dickson, as Director of Education, was considering setting up a primary school system of education in the longhouses of the 'ulu'. At Batu Lintang, under the authority of John Wilson, special teacher training courses for 17-year-old youngsters from upriver were started.

A natural pioneer, John Wilson was not content to plan courses in the Training Centre. He travelled extensively by foot or 'prahu' through the remote Dayak country. It soon became apparent to him that to open schools in backward areas was not enough. A necessary step it might be, but unless there was also parallel development in the surrounding communities, the school could bring depopulation rather than progress.

One day in 1953 John Wilson told the Director that he was resigning his job as Principal and walked off into the jungle to work out his own ideas. He abandoned secure employment and a pension, taking with him enough food to keep him going for several months, and a vision. At the other end of his pilgrimage were a number of ex-Batu Lintang Iban students doing their best to face an immense challenge in tiny inadequate 'ulu' schools.

It was significant that Murray Dickson wished him well and let him go instead of having him deported back to Britain as a more orthodox Colonial Servant might have done. Although such pioneering enterprise was not in my brother-in-law's own nature, a close relationship with his younger brother, Alec Dickson, had acquainted him with the urgency that needed to be instantly accommodated when the call to action came.

For months it was as though John Wilson had vanished into the 'ulu'. Then gradually, rumours began to filter out from a place called Budu on the Krian River; remarkable things were happening in community development.

By 1957 when we climbed into the Government launch, Budu had become famous in the territory of Sarawak and known in Community Development circles outside. Still fiercely independent, with two new members of staff, Arthur Thwaites and Tom McBride recruited directly from Scotland by John Wilson, the Centre was acknowledged to be worthy of support.

The initial part of the trip took us round the coast to the mouth of the Krian. We were accompanied by the Government Community Development Officer and a young teacher recruited from Canada on his first visit to the 'ulu' as well as the inimitable Bojang, a Malay Jeeves, who came along as cook and bottle washer, entertainer and friend.

We thought we had learned lessons about baggage from the expedition to Padawan. For my husband, the fundamental requirements on any journey were pens, paper, documents and a hat. He was astonished to find that the case containing those essentials was frowned upon. He took it anyway. I too had my 'essentials', sketch books, pencils and paints and was willing to jettison surplus clothes instead. However, I produced convincing arguments for retention. We were in holiday mood and enchanted with Sarawak. It was the launch that was cast off rather than our surplus.

Alec exchanged stories and jokes with Bojang and teased John the Canadian, who having no experience of a colonial regime, anticipated the worst and was mystified by an air of camaraderie which included Bojang. I got out a sketch book and made a portrait of him. The excitement of going to see Budu for ourselves, which John Wilson and the Ibans had between them built up out of the jungle by the power and passion of their own dedication, infected us both.

At Kabong, a Malay fishing village built on stilts at the mouth of the Krian, we changed to a District Headquarters launch from the upriver town of Saratok where we were to spend the night. There were now many hours of travel. The river was very quiet and we watched the banks slide by with an occasional small village then, later, forest. The sun had set before we reached our destination.

In the morning we transferred to a 'prahu' with an outboard engine. The river narrowed; rocks and rapids began to appear. We lay drowsily under the canopy while Alec wrote notes and the steep tree-covered banks reverberated to the shouts from the look-out on the prow to the man in charge of the engine, warning of broken water ahead.

After the last Chinese trading centre we entered Wilson territory at Nanga Enkilili, a small Budu outpost with a cooperative shop and a store, where some

prahus on river

of the trainees were to meet us. Then, suddenly, the 'ulu' quiet was shattered by shouts and laughter. Two canoes expertly handled came round a corner and guided our 'prahu' into the bank. In their own country, rather than in an Edinburgh garden, the Iban boys looked splendid and virile and not particularly small. On land they greeted us courteously and announced their names: Liman, Belun, Inyang, Gentan.

With great efficiency they began to transfer our baggage to their boats. Stores from the cooperative shop had then to be loaded, a complicated operation taking both time and knowledge. When at last passengers stepped in there was little room for comfort. Each space left had been exactly calculated. The boys took their places at prow or stern, vigorously poled their 'prahu' into midstream and we were off.

This, however, was not the final stretch. In mid-afternoon, after pushing and hauling the laden canoes up rapids, while passengers contributed little and snagged their toes in rocky water, we arrived at Nanga Budu, also a substation, this time with a school, a cooperative shop, a dispensary and several small plantations, pepper, rubber, hill rice and other minor crops. All the work was done by the trainees.

Here we met for the first time one of John Wilson's staff, Tom McBride, 'Mac'. In fact he was the only one from Scotland to be at Budu during our

trading centre

visit. John Wilson himself was still on leave as was Arthur Thwaites. Ex-Royal Navy sick bay attendant, Dr Lees from Nairn, only arrived shortly after we left. Mac's specialty was agriculture.

John Wilson's methods of recruiting were like himself, unorthodox. When it had become plain in the early days that someone with a medical background was needed to establish a dispensary in the Centre, look after the health of longhouses in the area and train the boys as assistants, Wilson went back to Scotland. Here he put an advertisement in the press asking for a young man with some medical training, willing to undertake arduous work under very difficult conditions, a minimum of pay, local food, inadequate accommodation, no allowances for wife or child, no leisure or recreation. He then sat back and waited. Replies began to trickle in – then a flood. Nearly a hundred young men applied.

Kabong boy

When weeded out, the interviews started. Now the basic realities of the situation being offered were revealed. 'Are you prepared to eat rice at every meal? Never to go to a cinema or any recreation for two or three years? To sleep on the ground? Live communally? Work twenty-four hours a day, seven days a week? Walk five, six, eight hours through the jungle and back again if need be before you rest?' In the end, only Arthur Thwaites from Warrington remained. When John Wilson sailed for Singapore on the way back to Sarawak, Arthur went with him.

That was the beginning. Four years after Wilson had walked into the jungle he had three young men working with him as disciplined and devoted as himself.

Now the time had come for going out. A number of the original chosen trainees, fully nurtured, had arrived at the stage of secondary education. Though Wilson had visualised a senior school on the site, it was not yet practically possible. It was envisaged that eventually each trainee, whether remaining within or returning from without, would work in the 'ulu' helping his own people. Wilson would not countenance secondary education in Kuching or indeed in Sarawak where the bright lights and the temptations to desert their upriver roots might be overwhelming. He had contacts in the small town of Nairn on the Moray Firth in the north of Scotland and knew the Rector of Nairn Academy, Mr Robertson. Life in Nairn, John Wilson was convinced, was still based on a united community and had a stability and rugged strength not unlike the 'ulu' communities of Sarawak. Daily life could be hard, but peaceful. Education was respected and rigorous. The town was still small enough to accept without divisions a group from the other side of the world. Northern Scots had themselves sent many of their own young men out to seek their fortunes in other countries and would understand that these young Dayaks were trying to get themselves fit to help and develop their own communities.

John Wilson's vision and the depth of his convictions finally convinced the citizens of Nairn. They agreed to try. Though we did not fully realise it at the time, Luke and Jawie, my mother's garden guests, were on their way to Nairn with John Wilson, taking the first steps on a path which others were to follow.

Tom McBride, very tall in contrast to his young trainees, fairhaired and naked except for a small pair of white pants, greeted us in a strong Scottish accent. 'Hello. So ye got here safely all right!'

He was a man of few words but he also spoke Iban with an accent indistinguishable, it was said, from that of Budu-born natives. Confusingly, many of the Budu boys spoke English with a strong Scottish accent. Until he found his visitors harmless, Mac regarded us, the Dicksons, John the Canadian and Bojang, as a cross between an inquisition and a circus but he had done his best to provide comfortable guest quarters where we spent a second night.

The next day it was disconcerting to find that Budu was an hour or so away by foot. I had hoped that Mac would find space for me in the 'prahu' but this he firmly refused to do. It was shallow dry season water in the river and heavily laden as they were, it would take the boys all the strength they had to get the boats up to the Centre. So accompanied by Mac and some of the trainees who had been working at Nanga Budu and having discreetly lessened our baggage surplus to be picked up on the way back, we started – Alec retaining his papers and I my paints.

The trail wound through thick jungle, a single track, slippery, covered with rotting vegetation and made dangerous by the snags and snares of barely concealed roots. We were walking along a steep hillside which every now and then descended to ford a small river and then climbed up the other side. For unaccustomed Europeans with unsuitable shoes it was horrific. For Alec Dickson, not naturally agile and suffering from the heat, it was only the much worse situation of Canadian John and the need to encourage him that kept them both going.

Early after we set out I was taken into the charge of the smallest Iban boy we had yet seen. His name was Gentan. He slid his tiny hand into mine, put his sharp eyes at my disposal and guided me across the many river fordings with a total confidence which he transmitted to me. We soon left the others behind. The track was empty and almost unnaturally silent. Gentan allowed no rests and I came to realise that the steady pace which he made me keep was valuable. Eventually we came to the nineteenth river crossing and saw on the other side a stretch of well-kept grass, some white buildings and the open cleared terracing of rubber and pepper plantations. I took Gentan's hand for the last time and stepped into the water.

On the other side a bigger boy with bushy hair and slanting original eyes was coming towards us. He advanced and held out his hand. 'How do you do?' he said, 'I am Henry. You must be Mrs Dickson'. I agreed that I was. Sometime later, shattered physically and mentally exhausted, under the tender care of the Iban boys with them and the robust encouragement of Mac, Alec Dickson and Canadian John staggered out of the final river crossing. Fortunately, when Alec had made sure that his documents were safe and after a period of prostration, the resilience of achievement brought them both to life again.

The physical appearance of Budu after the untamed wildness of the jungle track was striking: the neat grassy expanse, the white wooden buildings, the school, dispensary, shop, store, tiny houses inhabited by staff – an atmosphere of orderly brightness lay over it all. The only untamed ground was in the pig pen with its grunting occupants. Young trainees working everywhere were clearly absorbed. They greeted us cheerfully but never idled on the job to talk. Budu had been built on self-help and that was how it survived. Every boy, however young, had his responsibilities to undertake. Each knew that the Centre depended on those being properly carried out.

The Centre, however, was not enclosed. From the first, Wilson had looked out to the surrounding community. That evening we were taken to the nearest longhouse for a ceremonial greeting and once again we waded across the river. The boys who went with us were in clean white shirts and shorts, Mac fully clothed, the rest of us in the best that we had salvaged from our baggage. We climbed the ladder on to the verandah, the main street and meeting place of the house. At the top a group of elderly men greeted us in Dayak. Mac replied.

Lamps cast an intermittent light and darkness engulfed the far end of the verandah. We sat down – two or three of the elders sat opposite us and scrutinised us closely with kindly humorous wrinkled old faces. We looked back unembarrassed. It was our sole way of communication. From both sides we must have liked what we saw and the atmosphere relaxed. We all picked up the glasses we had been given, bowed and drank a toast.

A white cock was handed to the senior elder who clasped it under his arm while making a speech. It was an emblem of his sincerity and truth talking.

Mac translated and responded on our behalf. Then Alec produced our toys and tricks – the little rubber snake resulted in shrieks of terror among the girls, the older boys were challenged to touch it. The disappearing matches; the thoughts read and then mysteriously revealed among the ashes of burned paper; John's reply to a question, 'Was Canada also America?', all this dissolved the strangeness. We requested that our hosts now entertain us. After a long silence the old men turned to the row of young men behind them and ordered one of them to dance. There was muffling and scuttering in the dark then a youth stepped out into the light dressed in crimson cloth sewn over with glittering silver bugles. The plaintive whispered notes of a stringed instrument sounded. Shyly, softly, he began to dance. Suddenly he stopped as he had begun, covered with confusion, and nobody else could be persuaded to take up his steps. It was the end of a memorable evening.

We woke in the morning to the grunting of pigs and went down to the only bathroom, the river, to wash. I struggled again with the many difficulties of

the little dancer

washing adequately, clad in a sarong held together in my teeth while I wrestled with earth-covered or elusive soap. Then we went into breakfast prepared by Bojang.

The next afternoon when chores had been done and we had somewhat recovered from the soreness left by the trek the day before, Alec asked if he could teach the boys some games. Mac, who did not wholly approve of the effect that our lightheartedness might have upon his charges, stayed to watch. I took my paint bag and accompanied by Gentan went up the hill to make a picture of the Centre below. Gentan was reluctant to leave me, clearly doubting my ability to find my own way back, but at last he was persuaded to go down and join the fun.

Sitting overlooking Budu, I could hear the shouts below me and see the riot of small bodies scurrying around. Alec had started to teach them some of the exercises that had made the Mobile Propaganda Unit in East Africa such a success. When he arrived, Gentan, my faithful friend, was in demand to be the triumphant top of the human pyramid or at least the man crawling through the tunnel of human legs. Then they played 'Ringing the Stick' and loved it though they played very badly being quite unaccustomed to team games. Henry who was tall, lanky and fiercely enthusiastic, flung himself wildly on the rubber ring and hurled it madly in all directions, regardless of the way his team was playing. The young ones jumped and screamed and got in everybody's way. Perhaps it was as well John Wilson was in Scotland. He might have considered Alec Dickson a serious threat to order and discipline!

The last evening, the boys collected in the school and we went up to sing, play games and tell stories. Alec Dickson was a natural storyteller, indeed whether he was sitting on the floor of a remote longhouse or on a platform passionately addressing an adult audience, the subject matter was always based on known examples of human action from which conclusions could be drawn and challenges flung out. The boys sang, led by Henry, whose breaking voice growled and soared in the lamplight. They knew Scottish songs, 'Roaming in the gloaming by the bonny banks of Clyde' 'Loch Lomond' and many others. Sitting in the flickering light of a Tilly lamp with the 'ulu' surrounding this small oasis, such mixed feelings came over Alec and myself of fear for the future and of faith in it too; of the impotence of man and his tremendous spirit, that we were glad of the darkness which hid the tears that gathered in our eyes.

Baram River – The River of No Return

Coming back to Kuching we had a free week before Murray Dickson himself was going to travel with us up the longest river in Sarawak, the Baram.

River Baram boy

This expedition was to be a very different experience from the visits to Padawan or Budu. With the Director himself paying his first official tour of inspection to new schools up the Baram, we would be away ten days, travelling 250 miles by canoe to Lio Matu which was as far as the river was navigable by boat. Accommodation would be in longhouses, except for one stop at Long Lama about a third of the way up, where there was a school and a development centre. The District Headquarters and administrative offices lay between Long Lama and the mouth of the river, at Marudi, where the District Officer with the delightful name of MacSporran held sway from the town to the remote north. Our first night would be in his house where we would meet the elite of the District – teachers, preachers, clerks, administrators and wealthy businessmen, wives and daughters; Chinese, Malay, English, Scottish, Irish, Dutch, Dayak. In the morning we would leave for Lio Matu in the official boat by courtesy of Mr MacSporran.

This time I had learned my lesson baggage-wise, paints and papers excepted. I had also discovered that there were other essentials which we had not carried. The bare bottoms of canoes and the ribbed bamboo floors of longhouses loomed large among the discomforts and for me the necessity of having personal sarongs to assist my ablutions. With silent pitying scorn for our softness my brother-in law lent us two inflatable mattresses.

In scale this was a bigger river than we had yet seen with dangerous rapids on which, but for the skill of local crews, 'prahus' could be overturned, resulting in casualties, occasionally a drowning, certainly loss of cargo. In between lay long stretches of broad, flat, deceptively deep waters lined by thick perpendicular jungle. Longhouses were few, inhabited by people we had not yet come in contact with,

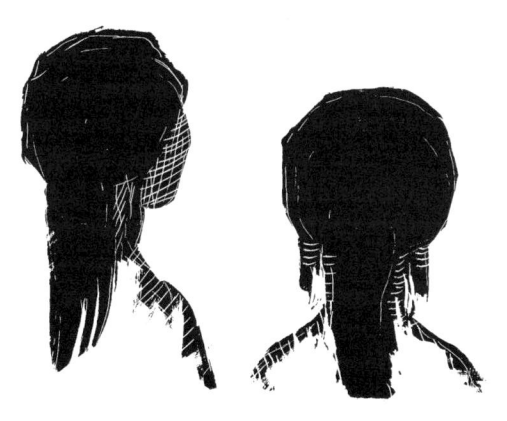

Long Lama women

at the mouth of the River

Kenyah, Kayan, Kelabit. The boys wore their black hair in a circular cut with one long lock from the crown down the centre of the back. From quite a young age the women had their ears pierced and gradually extended by brass rings until in older women the lobes lay on the collar bone adorned with heavy brass circles. Here too, in some of the longhouses we saw for the first time new primary schools with shy seventeen-year-old teachers who had come back from the unimaginable adventure of a Batu Lintang training course.

A bush telegraph had gone upriver that the Director of Education was coming on a tour of inspection. The longhouse was a-twitter with excitement. The school band with instruments made of bamboo, looking and sounding not unlike recorders, was on parade in spotless shirts. The elders and teacher waited anxiously for the first head of the little cortege climbing up the steep bank from the 'prahu' to appear over the top. Then the teacher conducting the band piped up.

It was at this moment that the Director's retiring temperament resulted in difficulties, both with the hosts and with his brother. Murray, who disliked any public recognition, insisted on being last out of the boat so that it was his younger brother Alec, ready to meet any new experience, whose head and shoulders set off the music. It was only when Director of Education Murray Dickson, half-hidden behind accompanying boatmen, finally made the school ground that a whisper of agitation went round the adults there, indicating that they were confused about the identity of the Director. When Alec Dickson realised what had happened he was upset and annoyed. Speaking sharply to his brother about the importance of the occasion being treated as a ceremony he brought him forward and introduced him. However we knew Murray's quiet temperament too well. On every other school arrival, in spite of his brother's anxiety to push him in front, the Director of Education, Sarawak, was adept at concealment.

Every evening, about 4 or 5 pm, the canoe stopped at whichever longhouse was seen on the bank. The bush telegraph had done its work and we were always expected. As we drew into a jetty of two planks and climbed thankfully out of the boat one or two men came out of the house to greet us. One was the 'penghulu', the Chief, probably wearing in his long pierced ear lobes hornbill ivory earrings.

We were greeted courteously and taken up to the longhouse over a path of logs laid down on mud. All the longhouses stood on stilts though their designs varied. The inhabitants smiled politely but except for the very small children, the normal work of the house went on around us. Some of the old men sat on the verandah in a circle. Drinks were brought in little plastic glasses. There would be a joke about Baram orange juice – after a while we knew that it would turn out to be potent rice wine.

After a short talk about education from the Director we all went out to visit the school. The Headmaster and teachers were all rolled into one, the gentle shy seventeen-year-old who greeted us. In the school his pupils were sitting on wooden benches, their anxious blank faces and huge black eyes under round caps of dark hair. Alec would have liked to ask questions and make jokes but he recognised that things on the Baram were not conducted that way. The inspection took its course almost in whispers.

Afterwards when all were gathered outside on the grass, proud fathers watching their offspring, Alec suggested games. But it was not until he took off his own shirt and showed them how to 'tumble' and one or two team games that the tiny boys slowly came alive. When the Fox began to chase the smallest chicks the first laughter bubbled and the children were ready to accept anything new while their sisters sat on the school steps and giggled.

At last, exhausted, the adults began to drift back to the house – then my ordeal began. Forewarned about sarongs I had them in my baggage. Now the reality of toilet facilities and the river were staring me in the face. Equally

Baram hats

daunting was the lavatory, a small hut on stilts with a hole in the floor and underneath, waiting, the longhouse pigs.

In front of the longhouse everybody, male and female, was going for the evening bath. Clutching towel and toothbrush, grasping soap and concealing as best I could the large safety pin which had become the last resort in keeping a sarong anchored, I clambered down the ladder and made my way along the logs to the river bank. It was still light and the river was full of splashing, soaping men. The women had all finished their ablutions and were in the house preparing the evening meal but the children were an audience for all that was going on. I was only too conscious of my conspicuous looks – a great deal taller than the average in Sarawak, taller even than my husband and brother-in-law, my sarong just covered me from my armpits to above my knees. The flesh revealed was white and goosepimpled through nerves and anticipation of the water's cold. Reaching the river and climbing precariously out on the slippery little jetty I put towel and soap on the end of a canoe and plunged in.

Baram River man

The water was deep with a swirling current that threatened to carry away the sarong. Grasping the safety pin with one hand, with the other held on to the canoe, I strove with the current and my cover in despair. My own compatriots, out of decency and kindliness, had moved to the other side of the boat, refraining from providing any shield. I could only help myself.

Realising that European respectability was out of place – even if the sarong was swept away only my own kith and kin would be embarrassed – I released the hand holding the safety pin and with a convulsive kick climbed up on to the canoe. Nobody took the slightest notice. Struggling along the boat to shallower water I abandoned efforts to use the 'ulu' way of washing. Sitting safely on a log I cleaned myself as well as I could.

Later, regaining the house and my clothes, I realised that no Kenyah inmate, with their instinctive courtesy, looked even remotely aware of my recent difficulties. My husband and my brother-in-law, with the cowardice of men brought up in a tradition where privacy was important, simply said, 'Are you alright?'

After that the evening went well – as it did in every longhouse in which we stayed. The meal's staple component was rice, then we all gathered for a night's entertainment. The women who had been out of sight until now, appeared in large numbers, not to sit silent as I had imagined, but to play a major role in the programme. The Kenyahs were prepared to make positive efforts to amuse us. The young men and girls played games, not unlike the games we had played in our childhood. After the first one they insisted that their guests join in. We sat in a circle with a cord on which a ring was hung running through our hands. An 'it' sat in the middle while the concealed ring was quietly transferred from hand to had. When 'it' cried stop, the hands stilled and it was the turn of 'it' to identify the hiding place of the ring. I was invited to be 'it'. After that we all joined in the games.

Then the dancing began, the girls with fans of black and white feathers and beautiful slow movements. The young men had their own dances, often performed individually to a stringed instrument, the 'sapeh'. A melancholy tune floated gently into the darkness with a flavour of sadness and resignation. The atmosphere was transformed. Into the circle of light stepped a dancer crowned by a headdress of black and white hornbill feathers; he stood quietly, eyes averted, trembling slightly. The 'sapeh' player plucked out his grave tune. Softly, unexpectedly, the dancer moved. First his fingers, then his arms, finally his whole body began to flow and undulate with the utmost grace. Under the splendid feathers his face was withdrawn and remote. The gentle fluid lines of the dance were strengthened and given shape by the firm placing of feet or a sudden leap or crouch, the more startling for its unexpectedness. The whole house watched entranced. Then the spell broke, instantly, without reason. An awkward self-conscious youth was left hurriedly retiring into the shadows.

Now it was our turn. Alec diverted the audience with riddles and puzzles. The Director told stories adapted from Heroditus, at once recognisable in their humanity by an 'ulu' audience. I drew portraits. The old men sat beaming in the lamplight.

When we left this first longhouse, Long Ikang, Alec and I had had an experience that was hard to convey; the warmth of community, the sense of belonging which surrounds people who have always lived on family ground, lack of physical privacy compensated for by a mental delicacy which turned the interest taken in the habits of strangers into the concern of friends because of an affection felt for their owners. Astonishment, amusement, approval, openly met with no need of defence against ill will. It occurred to no one that hospitality could be refused or abused.

In a sense we had a revelation. We had seen something of the reality of our

dancing at Long Kesih

own Christian values; for the first time we had caught sight of the meaning of the phrase 'members one of another'. Our view of social relationships was changed by the Baram. This change remained with us. If the vision that had begun to take shape in Alec Dickson's thinking was to be fulfilled, we would remember and make use of Sarawak.

Travelling up the river, staying at more longhouses on the Baram, we saw more schools and talked much with Murray, Director of Education, about the problems of schooling in areas such as this. Everywhere there was a cry for schools but this education challenge, the welding together of old and new, seemed at that moment too heavy for the organisation to bear. It was not simply the difficulties of distance and lack of adequate staff that created problems. Alec Dickson could see here the early start of an educational system whose ultimate results we had tried to counteract in West Africa: an excessive emphasis on academic qualifications, a divorce from the land, a contempt for manual labour and a selfish preoccupation on the part of the young with their own advancement. Here the field was still virgin, the way open to learn from past mistakes if the nickname of this river was not to become sadly relevant – The River of No Return.

It sickened Alec Dickson's heart to look forward a very short distance and see longhouses disrupted, community life broken up, a traditional sense of values lost – as John Wilson had feared when he walked out of Batu Lintang.

With an effort of imagination this seemed the very moment to recreate the educational system so as to give the young Kenyah or Kayan a fair and equal right to the advantages of the modern world, while retaining the old values; to make it plain that some in other cultures still recognised that communities could be interdependent; that those who were not gifted academically were just as important and necessary to their nation as the clever, while the latter, because of their very gifts, were needed back among their people.

Even here, in an area so remote that only echoes of the outside world still reached it, the pace of education was set by political pressures. The ultimate object of these tiny new primary schools was to produce young people who could go forward to secondary school and eventually hold their own in Government with the sophisticated Malays and Chinese. The Director, an education professional, was uneasy with his younger brother's ideas though he recognised the dilemma as expressed and seen from the outside. Nor did he realise how important it was to Alec Dickson that his dreams had an outcome in practical action, which meant discussion, adaptation and the open attempt to convince opponents – not always successful but never abandoned.

As we travelled on towards the headwaters of the river and the border with Indonesian Borneo the rapids became more frequent and more turbulent than anything we had yet met. It could be a terrifying experience to the uninitiated.

Sheer rock and jungle banks made it impossible during the worst passages for visiting travellers to leave the boat while amid the thundering water the canoe breasted steep narrow liquid rock-lined slopes. The engine strained and sputtered, the extra boatmen taken on at Long San rejoiced in the battle, shouting, taking furiously to their paddles. Each time it seemed the 'prahu' would lose, each time it won.

At the farthest point on the river to be reached by canoe, Lio Matu (The Thousand Isles), we had our last night in a longhouse before the return down river. This was Kelabit country. It was also the country of the Punans, a nomadic people who owned no animals, no houses and very little property; each man had a blowpipe to hunt with, some eight feet long, and was immensely skilled in using it.

Punans were rarely seen by outsiders. The forest life was self-sufficient and they moved from place to place in the shade which they preferred to sun, ruled by dreams and omens and the flight of birds. If the birds were unfavourable the men had to wait until the forewarning changed.

We were fortunate to meet a group of Punans just after arriving at Lio Matu. While the boat was being onloaded, Alec went off with Andrew, the boatboy, to look for fruit. I followed them. Suddenly, on the fringe of the forest, we were surrounded, very silently, by a group of tall, pale-skinned men who looked as curiously at us as we at them. We were astonished, being accustomed by now to a land where most people were small. Their skin was as pale as our own. Having spent all their lives in the thick cover of the jungle they disliked clear open spaces. After the exchange of mutual smiles they showed us their blowpipes. It was plain that they had no fear of us. Then, as suddenly and invisibly as they had come, they were gone.

early morning on the River

After a night in the longhouse it was from Lio Matu that we began the backward journey which, with the exhilarating downstream current, took only a quarter of the time taken on the way up with one overnight stop at Long Lama, a new Government Training Centre.

Long Lama was under the charge of Mr Southwell whose wife was on leave when we arrived. A middle-aged couple with long years of missionary service in Borneo behind them, including a period of Japanese internment, they had three adopted children. Kakim, the eldest, was away at school in Kuching. Her father was Chinese, her mother Kayan, a slave wife of one of the Kayan chiefs. When small and badly treated Kakim had been sold to the Chinese. However, her father had succeeded in getting her back and asked the Southwells if they would adopt her. Mina, whose mother had died giving birth to her and Luket, the only boy, survivor of twins, were both Kenyah. In no case were the children legally separated from their parents. The intention was that they should eventually return to them.

We landed at a makeshift jetty, climbing a perilous mud bank on a narrow plank into a small settlement; an old fort in which we were to spend the night; a ramshackle bazaar with Chinese merchants sitting outside their crowded shops and a large Chinese school where a game of basketball was in progress. The trainee students who met us, aged 15/16, came from longhouses all up the river. Some wore hair cut in a round flat fringe, long swinging ears weighed down by heavy brass rings and exotic, splendidly coloured body-tattoos.

Long Lama differed from the other Community Development Centres we had seen, Padawan and Budu. In their own ways and reflecting the characters of their founders both of those projects had something of monastic dedication about them. It was the Centre that ruled over a wide area and laid down policy. Long Lama did not seek the control that John Wilson used, however subtly, to bring the longhouses into the Centre's sphere of influence. Here, though all the students were boarders, it was the Baram River and its mixed populations that had more importance than the Centre. Traffic came down the river and went back up again but it was no part of Long Lama's plan that some boys might be prepared for greater things in the outside world.

Mr Southwell was a man of high principle and gentle nature. Mrs Southwell contributed a robust domestic common sense. The atmosphere was lighter and less filled with tensions than in the other two Centres and the aims were not as ambitious. Hopefully all the trainees would return to their own longhouses and villages to contribute productively their simpler skills; blacksmithing, carpentry, some agriculture and the technical expertise learnt in building their own Centre.

We returned to Kuching with much to think about. Visually enamoured with my first visit to the East, I was busy creating a Book of Sketches as a 'thank you' present for Murray our host. Alec saw in the reality before him the other side of a puzzle he had wrestled with for so long. Here in Sarawak, were men with visions complementary to his own. In their projects he found situations where there were needs that young people from outside could meet – the giving of friendship, the value of their own mother tongue, a kind of young Briton that so far overseas countries had rarely seen – without authority, an open spirit ready to do what was asked of them and to receive a reciprocal experience alongside young people of their own generation and men with dedication to a different future.

fish trap on the China Sea

CHAPTER 19

Interim Four

Edinburgh 1957

We returned to Edinburgh with very mixed feelings. We had been two months in Sarawak. The visit had quickened Alec's thinking and given him glimpses of a way forward. To return to Scotland where there were few contacts with whom he felt at ease began to sow seeds of depression. He flung himself into travel, to visit John Wilson's Dayak boys, now four of them in the longhouse 'Grianach' at Nairn, well looked after by Mrs MacTaggart: to Gordonstoun and Outward Bound schools of which Kurt Hahn had been the inspiration: to Northern Ireland and to London. For me there were different pressures. I had arrived home to good news. Two letters awaited me from Dennis Dobson, the London publisher who many moons ago we had persuaded to take the Nigerian manuscript. A momentous decision lay behind the order of opening – fortunately I got it right. The words were warm and courteous; behind them I sensed an element of surprise. They might have read, 'Dear Mrs Dickson, when we got around to reading your manuscript we were astonished to find that we liked it'. The only query was would it be an economic proposition to produce a book with 70–80 black and white illustrations? When the Finance Department had been consulted, the answer in the second letter was positive.

Alec was delighted. I was delighted. My mother and Nannie were delighted. New vistas were opening up for me but, like my husband's visions, breakthrough lay in the south.

We had been married for six years and so far lived a nomadic life. I suspected that my mother had had enough of it. I was becoming increasingly unhappy and I needed a stable independent base – so did Alec. Not for the first time I knew that the decision would have to be mine. It was to be a significant one – a turning point for us both.

Once our departure was certain I took charge of the preparations. For Alec, all that mattered were his papers. He would look after them himself; clothes were left to me, household goods we had hardly any. One or two pieces inherited when my mother-in-law died were all in store, along with a mountain of cases and tin trunks containing practically a lifetime's accumulation of those things that Alec – a magpie collector – had never been able to throw away. Everything else – suitcases, some of my pictures, books, odds and ends – went into my mother's garage, as did also her small, much-used car.

On return from the Cameroons we had brought the Chevrolet back with us, but before leaving for Iraq in 1955 we sold it. My mother was generous with the loan of her car and ours had never been replaced. It never was to be – from now on we adapted to being without a personal vehicle.

PART IV
TRUE PARTNERSHIP

CHAPTER 20

Acacia House

Mortlake 1957–58

The kitchen table

Boarding the London train at the Caledonian Station Edinburgh, our journey south had still a nomadic feel to it. In a sense we were both escaping rather than adventuring.

No plans were made. Though many Dickson kin lived in the south, no closer family were there at this time. My brothers were in Africa; of Alec's family, his older sister was married to a tobacco planter in Malawi, his older brother a regular soldier with the Army in Malaya, Murray in Sarawak. Perhaps it was as well. We had asked elderly Dickson connections to put us up for a week while we looked for somewhere to live. While hospitable, they were of a generation who were without understanding of my husband's unorthodox views. The first morning we left the house early on the search.

It so happened that our only possible lead drew us to a small private agency. The two sisters who ran it, Gytha and Iva Hughes, had lived in a basement flat in Kensington underneath Alec's mother and had become close friends so we had made an appointment to see Iva Hughes. I was reminded as the interview went on of my own contact years before with the Universal Aunts which had unexpectedly brought me to the door of my future mother-in-law.

Iva Hughes made plain that their Agency did not deal with property. She gave us what advice she thought helpful but glancing at my husband I could see that his heart, like mine, was steadily sinking. Then Miss Hughes remembered something and began to look through her papers. She knew a Miss Flora Hastings who lived in a Queen Anne house on the river at Mortlake. Miss Hastings inhabited the ground floor and let out, furnished, the basement and the two top storeys. It so happened that her tenants from the two-roomed first floor flat had just left and she was looking for replacements. We looked hopefully at each other.

'There is just one difficulty,' Miss Hughes said. 'She is very choosy about her tenants. She will need to interview you.' We asked if an appointment could be made.

The next afternoon at 4 pm, in answer to an invitation to tea, we stood nervously on the top step before the front door of Acacia House, Mortlake. An elderly lady, with purple hair in a bandeau, whose appearance instantly stamped her as the owner of the historic house, opened the door. She ushered us directly into an interior which had been carefully kept in period. The drawing room, looking out on a walled garden along the riverside and filled with a mild green light, had pictures and furniture complimenting the house's past. Beside the fire, tea was already laid out. I recognised some of the pictures as being by W. P. Frith. Miss Hastings told us that she was his granddaughter. After that the ice was broken.

We were taken up to see the flat; a sitting room with a chaise longue, a double bedroom with an old chest before the window and a small kitchen in which meals could be eaten. The bathroom was to be shared with the single lady who was tenant of the large front room across the landing above the drawing room. Rent £5 a week. No guests to stay the night.

Downstairs an agreement was arrived at. Miss Flora said we could take possession at the beginning of the next week. She gave us the key of the tenant's entrance in the basement. Aware that we were in the presence of a miracle we accepted gratefully. Desperate to be settled we moved in two days early which did not please our landlady and offended the relatives who had been our hosts.

Acacia House had a feeling of its own. It was hardly possible to turn round in the flat – but it was ours. I went at once to see the publisher. It was to be another year before 'New Nigerians' was to appear in the bookshops but I came back from the interview having persuaded Mr Dobson to accept a second manuscript, 'Baghdad and Beyond' – Sarawak too was already underway.

Alec found himself immediately immersed in an atmosphere in which the ideas he cherished of 'volunteers' and 'service' were already in circulation, stimulated by an important event. Government had announced the abolition of National Service in 1958. In future, Britain's defence would have to be assured by a professional force. The economic and strategic implications were endlessly discussed by Parliament and the media but there was another aspect. Thousands of young male school leavers would now be released from any obligation of conscription in August 1958 and would therefore be available for possibilities of service of a different kind – more challenging, more inspiring.

Already known in London, Alec Dickson took a natural place in public meetings and discussion. In the autumn a Study Conference on Community Development was held by the Colonial Office at Hartwell House, Aylesbury; the object to produce a Community Development Handbook. Mr and Mrs Dickson were invited, so too was John Wilson then still on leave, and a number of senior overseas social and community development officers from various territories as well as the Social Welfare Adviser at the Colonial Office. We already knew most of them. To my surprise I was asked to illustrate the Handbook and accepted.

An open meeting under the Chairmanship of UNA was called at Caxton Hall in London. Forty-eight voluntary organisations and public bodies sent representatives. Again we both went. Discussion, often agitated and argumentative, sometimes passionate, barely with any agreement, took place, ending in the appointment of a Steering Committee. There were many axes to grind and differences aired.

For Alec Dickson the way forward had now become quite clear. Uncertainty and depression had lifted. Experiences in Sarawak, on the Hungarian border and at Man O' War Bay now took their place in the jigsaw. All at once there were those few willing and able to use influence where once he had thought himself alone. Among them John Marsh, Director of the Industrial Welfare Society, who had behind him the experience of working on the infamous Burma/Thai Railway during the war; Janet Lacey, who as Director of Inter-Church Aid had promoted refugee relief worldwide and was now eager to put her organisational resources at the disposal of some new worthwhile endeavour, and, lurking quietly in the background, Launcelot Fleming, Bishop of Portsmouth, Chairman of the Church of England Youth Council.

For me also life had changed. I recognised that I was needed as a full-time backroom partner in any work which would engage my husband. There would always be an essential precariousness in life with him; experiment, change and uncertainty were in his nature; optimism and perseverance in mine. Now I knew the areas in which my contribution could lie. I had discovered in myself an unexpected talent for organisation and had cultivated flexibility in the use of time. Self-discipline came naturally.

One Saturday when we had been some time in Acacia House there was a knock on the door. Alec answered it. The heads of several grey haired ladies started back with profuse apologies. They were a local Historic Houses Society and had not been told that this flat was out of bounds. My husband flung the door wider. 'Have a look, Ladies. This is where history is made!' It was, as yet, a ringing challenge to the future. They gazed at a floor completely covered by papers in some amazement but they enjoyed it!

We left for Edinburgh to spend Christmas with Ma and Nannie in a very different frame of mind from when we had earlier come away.

On our return to Mortlake, Acacia House already felt the centre of an active universe. Out shopping in Sheen, I began to knock on the doors of widows or elderly couples, some of whose names arrived by bush telegraph, asking whether they had a spare room. After describing some of our personal history the question was: Would they be able to put up, for one night or two, a young visitor? As a reference Acacia House was powerful, that Miss Hastings would not accept overnight guests believable. One or two overcame their natural hesitations and gradually the network expanded.

We had acquired a view of the world drawn from and based on individuals, not on groups or masses. Alec had written to John Wilson now back in Sarawak, 'We are drenched with Dayaks'. Already Mrs Mactaggart at Grianach was hostess to several extra Budu boys whose home in Britain was Warrington with Arthur Thwaites' mother. Passing through London, Acacia House had become a staging post for them. Then, to train as nurses, Chundie and Rabing arrived at the Dreadnought Seamen's Hospital in Greenwich.

It was never certain who might be visiting. Maurice, our Seamanship Instructor from Man O' War Bay being one, Brian, once a court-martialled officer for whom Alec had stood as Sc in Kenya, another. A Pakistani student, now a doctor, met in a work camp in Egypt when we were en route to Iraq, a third.

Alec had the bit between his teeth, travelling widely to talk to schools at the invitation of Headmasters who had heard of Dickson and of an idea which interested them on behalf of their boys. The Bishop of Borneo, a man of great energy whom we had met in Kuching, was home on leave and determined to have a part in any action that might concern his diocese. John Wilson had written a letter saying he 'thought a scheme sending young Brits would work but if the Bishop of Borneo were involved, No, No, No'. John himself would think up all the snags and report, 'Budu might be able to take twelve boys! Probably Canon Howes at Padawan could be persuaded'. Sixpenny airletters flew hither and thither.

Meanwhile the Steering Committee set up in Caxton Hall was sinking into depression, unable to find any real accord among the multitude of organisations ostensibly represented by it. The Colonial Office remained aloof on the sidelines. Alec came home one day furious because a particularly jaded young civil servant had drawled, 'After all, what have they to offer – except their pimples!' Ruthlessly he abandoned as allies the uncertain, the timid, the quarrelsome and was scornful of the British Council who went about recruiting a few boys from the top schools to spend a year teaching in elite academies in South America and India. Jack Marsh, Janet Lacey and, in the background, the Bishop of Portsmouth, recognised that the fervour and spirit of Alec Dickson's activities were based on experience and months of thoughtful conception and gave their support and resources to what was going on in Acacia House. Meanwhile I worked in the kitchen designing a cover for 'New Nigerians' and clearing the small table for meals. Through the door the sitting room floor was littered with Alec's peculiar filing system. Letters began to come in from boys, from Headmasters, even from the occasional parent – usually Mums. Our local school, Sheen Grammar, had a committed Headmaster who already wished to have one of his boys at the top of any list that might eventually surface.

Dick Hancock, Headmaster of the City of Portsmouth Grammar School for Boys, had been at Caxton Hall. Launcelot Fleming was his Bishop. In February 1958 they came together, the Bishop seeing an opportunity to test his increasing interest in Alec Dickson's theories. He asked Dick Hancock to arrange a meeting of senior boys from Portsmouth schools. The speaker was to be Alec Dickson, the Chairman, Launcelot Fleming, Bishop of Portsmouth.

Meantime Murray Dickson, who had been wandering about Northern India on his way home for leave, arrived in Mortlake to spend his time with us and to the welcome of one of my local widows. The Rev. Dr Hubert Thomas, Minister of the small Congregational church to which we belonged, a Welshman with a charismatic tongue, became and was to remain a tower of strength.

In the middle of all this hectic activity, Alec made an arrangement for the first two Nairn Dayaks, Jawie and Luke, to go in the summer to Canada on a Commonwealth Youth Scheme. They had had passport difficulties on landing in Britain the year before as Ibans then had only one name because they did not take their Father's name. A lack of comprehension arose between the two boys and the passport officer when the reply to the question 'Name'? was simply Jawie or Luke. It took some time for an agreement to be struck as to whether any additions should be before or after. Now officially they were Jawie Masing and Luke Wilson.

The Portsmouth meeting took place on Feb 19th. Alec Dickson was always nervous before speaking and spent the train journey making last minute notes on the backs of envelopes. He used to tell an anecdote about Disraeli: 'The day when my knees don't shake as I rise to speak in the House will be the day when I know the time has come to retire!' But like Disraeli, once launched, Alec Dickson was riveting. A speaker who did not talk of theories or seek to convince with intellectual arguments, he spoke of experiences, his own and other peoples, from which insights had arisen, challenging audiences directly so that they were unable to escape the relevance to themselves of what he was saying. A lateral thinker, he had an instinctive ability to translate actions from their accustomed settings to fresh situations where imagination revealed the personal consequences. Very often when he sat down there was a breathless silence.

Afterwards Dick Hancock commented, 'You don't need me to tell you what an impression you made'. From that moment the Bishop of Portsmouth was a convert.

'What next?' he asked.

The journalist in Alec Dickson surfaced. 'A letter to *The Times*,' he replied. 'You sign it, I'll draft it.'

Letter to *The Times*

Every aspect of the letter had to be carefully considered. There must be mention of Prime Minister Macmillan's Commonwealth Tour which had given birth to the catchword 'the Wind of Change'. A confident assertion that, with the demise of National Service, a number of headmasters were anxious about what would now happen in the unexpected vacancy to some of their most gifted students when they left school. Some of those Commonwealth territories which Alec Dickson knew from personal experience offered chances of service in exacting conditions for limited periods – followed by a description of urgent appeals from Sarawak, Uganda and West Africa – not for money but for volunteers. Practical examples of what could be done by young people and the care that would be taken by their hosts – Government, missionary and social service councils – was carefully laid out. Finally the need for our own young people to have a period of transition which would challenge their spirit and reveal their potential.

A letter was carefully crafted. Alec Dickson knew that each assertion made could be substantiated, if only because the recipients would be ashamed to deny involvement. The floor in Acacia House was littered with abandoned drafts. The Bishop was consulted. So was I. Janet Lacey and John Marsh were fully committed. Launcelot Portsmouth signed the letter. *The Times* refused it.

Casting them into outer darkness, the Bishop had a fresh top copy prepared and sent off to *The Sunday Times*. On March 23 1958, *The Sunday Times* printed it, whole column, centre page, under the heading 'The Year Between'. It was immediately apparent that *The Sunday Times* had one great advantage over its daily stablemate – the time lag before it next appeared. On sixpenny airmails, in envelopes with local stamps, Alec Dickson worked late into the night stirring up everyone he knew who had (so far) paid lip service to take up their pens for action, to provide the Colonial Office with the 'public opinion' which they had always insisted was missing. The correspondence went on for six weeks. For Alec and myself the most difficult conversion job was still to come.

The Year Between

Murray's retiring character was refreshed from his solitary journeyings, part of the charm of which had been for him the lack of responsibility. Much of his time was spent in our sitting room enjoying the stress and activity of other people. The brothers admired and respected each other; their everyday relationship was warm but Murray, having detached himself from business in Sarawak, was determined not to be involved with his younger brother in a way he considered nepotism. He knew Alec's 'extremism' when one of his ideas took hold and Murray's natural instinct was to remain aloof.

After a stubborn refusal he was eventually persuaded to cable his Governor, Sir Anthony Abell, suggesting in very mild tones that the Education Department would be prepared to accept six of this new type of young assistant. For the next day or two we watched our brother wrestling inwardly with a wish that the Sarawak Governor's reply might be lukewarm.

When it came Murray opened the cable slowly. We waited with bated breath. He handed the slip of paper to us. It was enthusiastic. 'Take twelve'. Signed Governor Abell.

The momentum had become unstoppable. Under pressure from Alec, Dickson Whitehall, whose acquiescence at least was needed if volunteers were to be sent in any capacity to dependent territories, agreed that they would not object to such a project but no practical help, no funds, were yet forthcoming. However Janet Lacey at Inter-Church Aid pledged office help, an administrative member of staff to assist – Geoffrey Clarke – and began to search for funds.

Alec Dickson approached Gulbenkian. The Bishop of Portsmouth offered to act as Treasurer and in small amounts money began to come in. Nuffield sent £2000 with a note saying that they were only giving it because Alec Dickson had a track record. The Bishop put pressure on the Dulverton Trust who had originally refused. He had contacts there and was a Governor of three schools, Marlborough, Canford and Wellington. The Bishop of Borneo was an old boy of Marlborough. The Headmaster, T. R. Garnett, began to think he owned the Sarawak affair.

CHAPTER 21

VSO

Voluntary Service Overseas 1958

The erstwhile Steering Committee was transformed into a support group under the Chairmanship of John Marsh whose sister, I had just discovered, was married to my brother in Capetown. Correspondence both to the Bishop and to Acacia House accumulated. Geoffrey Clarke, a small quiet man, suddenly found himself out of his depth.

Meanwhile the other Bishop, Borneo, was making his own spectacular way through the semi-chaos. He had his contacts including a brother who it was intended should keep an eye on developments in Britain when Borneo returned to the East. Then Acacia House heard with some dismay that he had recruited a volunteer of his own and was personally going to fly him to Kuching. He was anxious to call the, as yet unnamed scheme, Sarawak Voluntary Service, thus annexing priority on the ground.

Suddenly it became plain that the time had come to take practical steps on our part otherwise we might be stymied by Bishop Cornwall or the British Council. The name, conjured out of the air when it was agreed to set up selection boards, was a straightforward statement – Voluntary Service Overseas.

When news got around various old friends and contacts began to get in touch. E. R. Chadwick, no longer working in Nigeria, came to see us; another contact retired from Northern Nigeria was Gilbert Stevenson who had been the senior Colonial Service Officer when we were evicted from spending a night in Kano city in 1953! Murray came and went from visiting friends in Scotland and England as did Chundie and Rabing from the Dreadnought Seamen's Hospital, wanting relief from pressure; once, Bela Horvath, whom we had found on the Hungarian frontier.

In July a Sarawak Selection Board was arranged in a room lent by the Royal Commonwealth Society. This suited Launcelot Fleming who was in London for the Lambeth Conference. On the Board also were the Bishop of Borneo's brother, Major General Cornwall of the Royal Marines, Dick Hancock from Portsmouth, a retired Colonial Office Administrator, Murray and Alec Dickson.

Alec had asked me to act as a receptionist/clerk, chatting to the boys while they were waiting outside to be interviewed and when they came out. Those were perhaps the most revealing moments in the whole selection process. Suddenly they all seemed desperately young; some worrying about A level results still to come, some were going to have to be rejected and I could not bear it, some even to be accepted and I wondered secretly if that would be wise. For both Alec and myself that first Selection Board would lay seeds that would bear fruit later. In 1958, with the youth culture not yet over the horizon, the choice for those who failed was probably a junior position in Daddy's office or stacking shelves in Marks and Spencer.

Then the fortunate eight who had been selected began to become familiar to us. In Acacia House, among the clutter or having coffee on the kitchen table where I hurriedly cleared away my own manuscripts, briefings began. There was to be a later briefing on British Council premises – travel arrangements, clothing lists etc. – but neither the boys nor Alec could wait for that. David Fisher from the local school Sheen Grammar, whose Headmaster had been an early convert determined to have 'his boy on top of the list', was one of the first. Flora Hastings, our landlady, might well have thought it too much when she heard the continual tramping of hefty young feet on the basement stairs but she also, in a detached way, seemed to have been drawn in.

The briefing was practical and straightforward, based on our personal experience. Only one or two of these young men had ever been out of Britain. They were going now without any enfolding authority – taking without reserve the whole of themselves. Guests of the communities who had asked for them and whose hospitality they would enjoy; prepared for friendship; ready to learn as well as to help.

Their loyalty would lie with those among whom they were working, an allegiance also to whoever was in charge of the project. Their help had been asked for – they had volunteered. They had not been invited to change the communities to which they were going, that was for the people themselves to do, but to accept and respect their hosts and come to know them as friends.

Appearance was important: in the East the young generation were fastidious about clothes and cleanliness. Carry photographs of home/school/relatives and picture postcards of your neighbourhood and country. There would be great interest in your background. If you can't swim learn before you get on the aeroplane. If you play a musical instrument take it with you. In a longhouse the entertainment is dancing, games or telling stories. Look for helpful small books and be prepared to make your own contribution.

There would be no such thing as personal holidays. When the school term ended, go back to their longhouses with the pupils and give them the pleasure of being hosts.

The briefing was also a challenge. As yet there was no official training, the emphasis was on self-preparation. Those young men who climbed Acacia House stairs or met Alec Dickson in a Lyons Corner House or Geoffrey Clarke's office at Inter-Church Aid were the pioneers and on them the future depended. Alec Dickson's driving conviction affected them but it did not leave them cowed by responsibility. There was also another aspect to his inspiration. They sensed that he had complete confidence in each and every one of them and went away determined not to let him down.

It was made plain that they were expected to write to us, describing, criticising, telling the reality as it was – and their own ideas. On this correspondence future developments might depend; our ability to be of help certainly would.

If he was with us at any time when the briefings were taking place Murray would introduce himself, assuring them that in the case of difficulties the Education Department door would always be open. He was due to sail for Sarawak on the *Carthage* in the middle of August and would be there to meet them when they got to Kuching in September. Before he left he presented us with a photocopier which took pride of place on Flora Hastings old chest in the bedroom. The young man who came once a month to service it and renew its liquid innards never got used to having to do so in that room. He thought it a great joke.

Alec himself had an invitation to the Gold Coast in August. Life had always been so unpredictable that extra opportunities were to be considered, not set aside. He knew I was capable of keeping Acacia House afloat, Geoffrey Clarke could appeal to John Marsh, Janet Lacey or the Bishop in any crisis. In fact the first crisis was mine.

One late afternoon the telephone rang in the sitting room. On it a distraught young voice whom I recognised said that he had got his A level results and had failed an important subject. He would have to go back to school. While thinking all the time about a replacement, I comforted him with the prospect of next year and wished him well – then I telephoned Alan Tyne.

Alan, from a Grammar School in East Anglia, was a candidate who had divided the selection board. I suspected the Bishop had voted against him. I knew Alec would support my judgement. He was a cheerful open boy desperate to be chosen and devastated when told he would be the first substitute if anyone fell out. Talking with me afterwards in reception he had had no faith in this possibility nor could I give him much encouragement. Now, when he answered the phone at home, he could hardly believe what had happened. When I asked, 'Alan would you still be able to go to Sarawak?' he had no voice to answer.

He would have to be ready to leave in a few weeks. I gave him information about vaccinations, where and how; Geoffrey Clarke's address; the Bishop's phone number; told him to come to Acacia House when Alec returned etc., etc. Then I rang Launcelot Fleming. He was hesitant but being a man of gentle temperament he gave his agreement. So Alan went to Long Lama on the Baram River. To me he remained always 'my' volunteer.

In mid-September eight young men in various stages of trepidation left by air for Kuching. Some had said goodbye to their parents earlier, some were supported by family until the last moment. Even this first journey by air was an adventure. We went back to Acacia House exhausted, to think about the next two going to Man O' War Bay and two more to the care of Alec's friend, Peter Canham, Headmaster of a school in the Gold Coast.

VSO was an instant success. It suited the times in Britain. The slow change over from a wartime regulated country had at last come to an end; the start of a youth culture to come was encouraged by the growth of new young organisations and a fresh stirring in traditional older ones. In overseas countries the experiment of receiving a new kind of Briton to whom they could stand as hosts was attractive.

By this time Murray Dickson, in his capacity of Director of Education, had received a message from his opposite number in North Borneo (Sabah) asking where some of his excellent young men could be found. Soon after, an indent for several volunteers arrived at Acacia House. Robert Sutcliffe was on his way to the Livingstone Institute in Northern Rhodesia (Zambia). Arthur Thwaites at Budu was asking for girls: John Wilson and Raymond Snowsell at Man O' War Bay both reported well of their boys. Murray, having quite overcome his initial hesitations, was meeting, placing and hosting the volunteers as they arrived. In early 1959 the Duke of Edinburgh paid an official visit to Sarawak. He mentioned the UK Volunteer Scheme in his speech from the throne to Council Negri.

The Royal Commonwealth Society which had been watching VSO's development with interest now offered Alec Dickson a job – Secretary of the Commonwealth Studies Committee – which already had an immensely efficient secretary (with a small s), June Walker. Wary of entrapment, knowing himself to be a hopeless committee man, Alec Dickson made it plain during an interview that he would accept the job in order to have an official base but intended to continue working with VSO. He knew that the main bargaining counter was his. The RCS agreed. They wanted the connection with VSO and knew that the secretary who went with the job was more than capable of running their work herself. In fact June Walker enjoyed the extra responsibility. She also became interested in VSO and a lifelong Dickson friend.

Though Alec Dickson may have intended moving the office completely from Acacia House – all the early papers except the 6d airmail correspondence which we shared – it did not happen that way. In his diary the word 'tidy' was written on the weekend spaces with an increasing number of exclamation marks after it. His papers were sacrosanct. He had his own system. Instead he found in Mortlake another devoted secretary, Marjorie McCaw, who became as enthralled in the work at Acacia House as did June Walker at the official end. I, too, knew the importance of papers and of sketchbooks, not so much as a record of facts but as vital foundations of inspiration and significant signposts to future growth.

Alec was working tremendously hard, out all day travelling to talk at schools or conferences, often with industries who might have apprentices that they would be willing to release to go overseas. The first Chairman to be approached, AEI (Associated Electrical Industries), was so surprised not to be asked for money that he agreed, almost without argument, to give us some of his young men.

When we had first arrived in London in 1957 with the idea of getting a project going, our previous experience had been entirely overseas. Advice given by friends included warnings that nothing happened in Britain without the interest of those in high places because they had influence and brought in the money. This may have been true but as far as personal relations, which were all important to Alec Dickson, he did not find the results very easy to deal with. The open door, inner sanctum, of Acacia House which suited the young and unorthodox had little scope for adaptation. Since school and the Army, Alec Dickson had distrusted those with power. Experience in Iraq had not endeared the professionals to him. Neither in the Gold Coast nor in the Cameroons had he been accepted as part of the regular Colonial Service. He was uneasy with Committees. A born teacher, he was neither detached nor a despot.

Fortunately, in June 1959, E. R. Chadwick became the first member of staff in the Royal Commonwealth Society office. He had been Alec's patron during the establishment of Man O' War Bay. They had retained a relationship of affection and admiration but had never worked as closely together as now in the RCS's two small rooms. Chadwick had been a successful Head of Community Development, Eastern Nigeria, visiting at intervals the Cameroons where his protégé, Alec Dickson, was pioneering a new kind of citizenship training centre. Each man had his own space.

With Alec frequently absent from Acacia House, my books were going well. 'New Nigerians' had been two years in gestation, now publication was nearly in sight. 'Baghdad and Beyond' had been accepted and on the kitchen table illustrations were supplanting the typewriter. Because Dobsons was a family firm, their productions being not only books but children, I became accustomed to being summoned over the Thames on a Number 9 bus to assist in page designing, proof checking and discussions on covers. Mrs Dobson, producer of beautiful babies as well as handsome books, might be lying in bed suckling the latest arrival with page proofs of my own *oeuvre* scattered across the quilt. I was new to both sides of this life and found it exciting.

Alec was a risk taker as indeed are all pioneers, always reaching out to the next frontier to be crossed. I was not a taker of risks but I understood the need he had both for foundations and for freedom. Not all the young were takers of risks but almost all were inspired by the prospect.

One evening, returning home from the opera, we were astonished to find in our sitting room a young man, casually clad, with a glint in his eye. How he had got past Miss Hastings remained a mystery. A greater one still was how he had persuaded her to let him stay there. This was Colin Henfrey from the same school as one of the boys we had seen off to Sarawak. He wasted no time in explaining his purpose.

'You sent my friend to a very exciting project,' he said, 'I want you to send me to the most difficult and adventurous one you've got now'.

He ended up in British Guiana with the Amerindians of Orealla on the Corentyne River.

In those next years the world began to open up to young volunteers. Alec the risk taker was in full flight, leaving the more cautious souls of the recently set up Advisory Committee uneasy. The Grenfell Mission with Eskimos in Labrador was a success. Timbuctoo, where Alec himself had visited, was not – partly because the standard of French needed by the volunteer had been miscalculated by us all. The young man who went to Vietnam was remembered years later when his sponsor who ran the project accosted Alec Dickson in the London Tropical Diseases Hospital. Fiji and the Solomon Islands; by this time we had girls setting out for Kenya and Sarawak, and one from the Midlands for the New Hebrides. She spent the night before her journey with one of my local widows. At supper we discovered that her ticket had been left at home and her mother had gone away for the weekend. Very early next morning mother was tracked down, persuaded to go home, find the ticket and take the soonest train to London and the airport. In a ferment of anxiety I stood with her daughter at the departure desk trying to convince a reluctant hostess to make out a duplicate ticket in case mother did not arrive in time. At last the pilot said on the intercom that he could wait no more. Clutching her handbag and fresh ticket, suppressing tears, Diana disappeared through the departure lounge. Two moments later her mother appeared at the top of the stairs waving the lost ticket. For Diana, nevertheless, it was a successful year.

Reading an educational paper one day, Alec saw an advertisement asking urgently for itinerant teachers for the Falkland Islands. He answered it and two VSO horse riders sailed south on board the Antarctic survey ship.

In September 1959 an announcement appeared in *The Times*. A reception was to be held in the Royal Commonwealth Society to welcome the return home of the first VSOs. Friends and supporters welcome. It was a time of great excitement. Talking with Alan Tyne, David Fisher, Chris Tipple, John Seely and the other returnees was so exhilarating, a vision fulfilled, that Alec decided to broadcast their experience: a Press Conference, a Reception, radio items! At the reception those of their successors who had not yet left Britain would have a chance to meet and talk with their predecessors.

A day or two before the event a telephone call from the Admiralty asked if the First Sea Lord, Sir Charles Lamb, would be permitted to come. Of course the answer was 'Yes'.

For us the meeting was thrilling: the freshness of the boys' presentations, the delight of supporters and friends. The enjoyment of the tales told, the nervous queries of those about to go, the self-confident rejoinders of the newly returned. Exhausted at the end we said to each other, 'No Sea Lord!'

At that moment from behind a pillar, a small man in a dark suit came out and introduced himself. 'I am Sir Charles Lamb, Mr Dickson. Come and see me at the Admiralty tomorrow. The Royal Navy could be at your service'.

Next morning agreement was reached. If the destinations of Royal Naval vessels coincided with the needs of VSO to transport volunteers the Admiralty would be glad to help. The young people would travel as ordinary seamen and it was expected that they would work their passage taking part in any jobs required. For one of them, en route to the West Indies, this meant giving simple literacy lessons to some of the very junior sailors as well as swabbing down the decks.

The Navy started the ball rolling. Some weeks later a senior official in the Air Ministry asked for an appointment. The Royal Air Force would be prepared to help with transport to Singapore and the Far East.

At this moment VSO's finances were still very slender. Janet Lacey had said that Inter-Church Aid would be responsible for volunteers to Kenya, including apprentices. The Colonial Office, now under an enthusiastic Alan Lennox-Boyd, had given a grant of £9000 but the young organisation lived from hand to mouth. Alec Dickson had an established theory. Money should not come first. Top of the list should be a good idea; second, a practical experiment – does the idea work?; thirdly, when there was something to show, the money would come in. Somehow both publicly and privately, though often close to failure, the theory seemed to work for him.

Now, primed by those prestigious offers of help, Alec Dickson began to canvas civil shipping companies of which there were a great many, using the Royal Navy and RAF as motivation. One by one, from the Union Castle Line or P&O, British India to Elder Fyffes or oil tankers, they agreed. Volunteers had to be prepared for last moment arrangements depending on cabins being unoccupied just before sailing. Edwin was the first volunteer to go to Fiji. He was taken out of school in the last week of the summer term with the willing cooperation of his Headmaster and his mother and put straight on to a Royal Naval Auxiliary vessel bound for Suva – a seven weeks sea journey. This passage was offered suddenly, by telephone, a few days before the ship left. For Edwin this was to be an idyllic year. In the middle of it he wrote, 'At present I would willingly give up my British heritage to be a Fijian boy living in a village'.

There were 61 volunteers going out this second year, half of them on free transport. With a group for the Far East on an oil tanker, the Captain considered it too risky to use them for work so they lay on top of the tanks for three weeks of tropical sunbathing.

For some there was another aspect too. We had a Chinese friend, Peter Joe Chia, in Singapore. Alec had met him at a Scout Jamboree. Singapore was a centre for VSOs going by train to Thailand or Malaya or other destinations in the Far East.

Alec Dickson felt strongly that on arrival in the country to which they were going to serve the volunteers first introduction should be to local people, not to a British expatriate. Peter Joe Chia, newly married, was asked if he would be VSO's overseas arm in Singapore. He agreed at once. While this arrangement lasted, in September/October, he met volunteers at Changi Airport off RAF planes at 2 am or at the docks at all hours. The Chia's neighbours who were sometimes called in to help did not always appreciate ebullient young Britons sleeping on their floors. When some years later I saw the tiny tower block flat in which Peter and Pat lived I recognised what a strain the request must have put on them.

Mysterious visitors, small groups of two or three rather earnest Americans, now began to appear in the office. Their real reason for coming, apart from the human interest, was never disclosed. Each group had its own focus – how were projects in overseas countries found and approached? financing? training of potential volunteers? overseas supervision? The group focussing on the latter seemed bemused by the 6d airmail letters – as indeed did the group asking about training who were told that so far VSO had no 'training' only 'briefing'.

Alec was speaking all over Britain, summoning Headmasters or Chief Constables to meet him at local railway stations; addressing meetings; UNA, Chatham House, Commonwealth Studies Group, Colonial Office Youth Group.

The future of VSO was beginning to concern the Advisory Committee – to be part of an already established organisation or independence? Rifts were starting to show. Unsurprisingly Alec often returned from such a day with a migraine.

He also became uneasy about the VSO selection process and would spend the evening after sitting on one querying the acceptance of certain candidates. Had we taken that sophisticated boy when a member of the board thought he must be intelligent because he had a copy of *The Times* under his arm? How did we know that he had not bought it on the way in and flung it away when he left? Even if he read it did it indicate an ability to deal with the problems of an upriver Dayak school? Or the rejection of the quiet boy from Scotland, tired and inarticulate from a night train journey? or the pretty girl who charmed the male board and was accepted practically without questioning? For those rejected he had a humane heart. What could they now do? Having had the courage to apply for VSO would their self-confidence be eroded by rejection? Alec Dickson himself knew the pain of being discarded.

The correspondence had grown when the new volunteers began to be in touch. So too had problems although a pattern of experience had emerged which could be passed on from Acacia House.

Fred wrote from a Middle school where all the pupils were Chinese. 'The form I had difficulties with was Senior 1. They seemed to think they could tell me what to do and I am now in the process of making it clear to them that in the classroom I am in complete control. "I shall succeed" I say, gritting my teeth every time I walk in to teach them! Thus I started off over-confidently, degenerated to complete slackness and have now achieved a state of happy apprehensiveness.'

This pattern became known to me as a general one whatever the job. Arrival: often in a state of euphoria and confident anticipation. Reality: a month or two later when their own contribution seemed to bear little resemblance to the need. Balance: when both sides had come to terms. Looking back the volunteer could see that after all appreciation and even friendships were being achieved.

Charlie, an apprentice from the Clyde, going to Aden to be the handyman in a small mission hospital, spent the night before he left at Acacia House. While he was talking to me in the sitting room before I took him over to one of our hostesses, Alec took a look in his small attache case lying open on our bed. It contained his tools, given him by the company and overalls, his Boys' Brigade cap, his trumpet and his Bible. What better baggage to take on the adventure on which he was embarking Alec said to me after he had gone. Towards the end of the year he wrote that he had become home consultant to the local Sheikh about the education of his daughters!

In 1960 my first book made its public appearance. So much had happened since the manuscript had been accepted after we had returned from Sarawak in 1957 that my mind was already occupied by its successor and the one after that but 'New Nigerians' was particularly important.

Since our marriage I had been preoccupied with a new kind of life concerned with nurturing skills never guessed at till then – from catering for a husband who was not interested in food, to supplying meals for a group of hungry men who were very much aware of its importance. Without Lucas, our excellent cook at Man O' War Bay, I would have found the task impossible. And Lucas, though daily demonstrating his own capabilities, also unmistakably showed that he needed to have confidence in mine. A current ran between us when we met each morning, the shared knowledge of Master's domestic incompetence. At the same time I was also adapting myself to play a public part in a world so far unknown to me. It was not easy. There were moments in the early days when I went behind a banana tree and took off my wedding ring but I had wanted this man and made a commitment and anyway in Cameroon there was no way of escape – so I put my ring on again.

Always in the background Brian Thomas' words as I left Art School whispered in my mind, 'Never forget to carry a sketchbook and remember the great work'. The first had not been difficult, the second seemed very far away.

Now ten years later and almost unexpectedly the 'great work', on however small a scale, lay in my hand. Though I feared my former mentor would despise it Alec was proud and I knew it to be a success. It represented the reality of a conviction that had grown in me over the years when a popular slogan 'there's no alternative' had begun to be widespread. I knew now that there was no truth in it. There were always alternatives. This one gave me a life of my own to balance my husband's life to which I was also committed: it eased the guilt which he sometimes felt when his own concerns were all-consuming. Confidence in the ability to find as yet unknown self-potential, to juggle with time, to use opportunities, to discipline myself and yet remain flexible, became a way of life. A well of satisfaction which lasted even in the face of separate stresses.

When they began to appear the reviews were good. Mrs Dobson was pleased though warning me that one book did not make a 'list'. I began to long for an appreciative letter that did not come from family or kin – even to sit in the underground train beside someone reading 'New Nigerians'. Alec, understanding this wish, told me that in his journalistic days he had hoped to do the same beside a traveller with the *Yorkshire Post* who would exclaim, 'Now that was a good editorial!' Neither of us ever had this personal satisfaction.

In the first year of VSO when we ourselves knew the projects and had spent time and consideration in equipping each boy for the situation he was likely to encounter, we wanted everyone to be not only excited by the challenge but convinced that the project he was going to was his particular niche for which he was peculiarly fitted. It was this care and effort that contributed in large measure to the very small rate of failure in the first years.

In the flood of correspondence that overwhelmed us as time went on this could not last. Originally there had been hesitation about putting school leavers into projects in regular schools. But the flood of requests for teachers made it obvious that there was a real need and it became clear that an overseas school gave volunteers a stable background and a recognised job which could make the fullest use of their gifts – and sometimes a chance to infiltrate ideas of their own. Through the school they could enter the wider life of the village, the district, the country and go out from the institution taking their pupils with them.

Christopher in an Anglican school in Sarawak wrote, 'I have had a very eventful term and am utterly exhausted. I have been appointed boarding house master, responsible for 160 boarders. My duties are very varied, anything from catering to curing minor ills to collecting fees and seeing parents. I am becoming quite a farmer. We are turning a good bit of our swamp over to rice in the summer; we have started rearing chickens and except for a nasty moment when they nearly all got fowl pest and I had to inject sixty on a Saturday morning, they have supplied us with some good curries.'

Keith in a different school had strong views on some of the educational ideas. 'There is an appalling idea here of a 50 per cent pass or fail mark which is hideously discouraging for the boys and girls themselves. My educational theory is based entirely on personal experience at the receiving end. Surely encouragement not discouragement is the correct approach?'

The extra activities that volunteers became involved in astonished us as much as they astonished them.

Angus was musical. He went to teach in the Solomon Islands. There he set up three different choirs, writing harmony and arranging the music himself. Keith inspired splendid crepe paper costumes and produced the school concert in Sarawak. Michael in Aden wrote that he was 'deep in the blood of Julius Caesar'. Oliver in Sabah started an Art Club and took classes on sketching expeditions. Dick went hitching and camping round Swaziland with one of his students – his object was to show European car drivers that such a partnership was possible between white and black. No Europeans stopped to pick them up though they had often done so when Dick was alone but Dick and Joseph became firm friends. In 1959 Bronwyn went to the YWCA in Kenya, the first girl to serve in Africa. She started informal education groups in two villages in spite of talk of the improprieties of letting a girl into the Reserve alone. When she left the request came for two to replace her.

Back in the London office things were also moving fast. There was now £10,000 in the bank. The Advisory Committee in discussion about the future was not unanimous about the way it should go: to constitute VSO as a separate organisation or to join with another patron. The Chairman, John Marsh, had reservations about the former. Alec Dickson had never thought of the present Inter-Church Aid umbrella as anything but temporary. His own instincts told him that VSO had lifted off and left patrons behind.

1960–61

Selection boards started early this year taking place from February to July. There were requests for 86 volunteers from 25 different countries. As yet the hearts of all concerned were with the young.

Alec Dickson's mind was on the future, thinking ahead with his boys (and now girls), seeking ways to expand further with those overseas and experimenting with projects at home which would also be a challenge for some who would never be selected for VSO. It was at this time he met George Webb, a manager at Michelins, who was thinking on the same lines and who made it possible for three of his apprentices to undertake short pilot projects. One went to a leper colony in East Africa.

Peter and David were the first two volunteers to go to Somaliland, a British Colony but within a year to become independent and leave the Commonwealth. The request had come from a country, small and Moslem, in which we had few direct contacts. It specifically asked for a Scout. Peter, a Queen's Scout fulfilled that need. The boys became firm friends and successful teachers.

A week or so before independence a cable arrived from the British authorities in Hargeisa asking for the volunteers to be removed as the British were leaving the country. Consternation reigned. Alec Dickson, discovering that the general feeling was that the volunteers should be withdrawn and enraged at such pusillanimity, insisted that the boys themselves should have the final decision. So a cable went off to Peter and David asking them to tell us if they wished to stay and if it should be possible for them to do so. They replied instantly – on no account did they want to leave at a time when 'a total sell-out' would be taking place and their services most badly needed because of a shortage of teachers.

Arrangements were made to accredit them to the new Government which gratefully accepted the offer. At the end of the school term the new Somali Director of Education put a Land Rover and driver at their disposal for eight days in appreciation so that they could see more of the country before they left.

At home there was dissension among the Advisory Committee.

Later, as a direct result of a previous visit by Alec Dickson to Vietnam, a request came for a volunteer to help with the teaching of English in the University of Hue, a walled city in the north of the country very close to the line of a civil war then going on. The only person who accepted without hesitation or reservation the decision that he should go was the volunteer himself with his parents in agreement. John went and was a complete success. Although no such arrangement had been made the University insisted on paying him a salary.

Within VSO, on one side it was felt that to move out of the comfortable background of countries which had an historic connection with Britain was to expose volunteers to immense hazards. On the other, Alec Dickson had a small group who believed with him that the prospect of moving out of the British sphere of influence was an exciting possibility. Alec also accepted that experience indicated that dangerous situations for volunteers lay not in 'foreign' countries but in subtler and more corrupting tensions which could confront them in lands with racial strains such as Rhodesia.

Within VSO the rift grew larger – perhaps due in some part to success.

The office now had a very good secretary who dealt with the increasing administrative load. She did not find Alec Dickson easy but he liked her and she returned his liking. September was the time for the exodus of the 1960 volunteers still dependent on a mixture of transport. The girls all went by air – some of them regretting that they were deprived of an unusual and exciting start to their volunteer year. A number were on HMS *Bermuda*, those going to the East had a lift to Singapore by the RAF after which the boys going to the Solomon Islands were given an adequate supply of money, introductions and told to find their own way, nobody in London having any idea how to get there. By a miracle of confidence on both sides all arrived safely.

On November 7th 1960 Alec Dickson was invited by Derek Heathcot-Amory, now retired Chancellor of the Exchequer, to have lunch with him in the House of Lords. Lord Amory had always been interested in youth affairs and at the suggestion of Lennox Boyd he was considering joining a proposed Grand Council of VSO.

Both personally and for VSO itself 1961 was to be a year full of events.

'Baghdad and Beyond', my second book, appeared in bookshops (though never on an underground train) and was well received. There was 'A Season in Sarawak' on the way and I had a feeling of being established.

An announcement had been made in public that, by agreement, 150 American teachers and graduates were arriving to fill vacancies in East Africa schools. In March President John Kennedy announced the setting up of the Peace Corps, an all-graduate overseas service fully paid for by the US Government. There was consternation in the clubs of Pall Mall about the first African invasion. Within VSO this explained at last the visits of exploration to the London office the year before and brought to the surface the discussion, hitherto latent, of graduate volunteers versus untrained youngsters. Using competition as an argument for the latter, Alec Dickson went to the Colonial Office to persuade them to give both open and financial support to VSO in a way they had so far refrained from.

At this moment the British Council decided to close down its own small overseas service scheme and merged with VSO bringing a dowry of £5,000. The Foreign Office alerted all its diplomatic posts to be on the lookout for possible projects for volunteers. The Government was soon to come up with a grant of £17,000. VSO was growing in significance and strength. In 1961, 38 countries had asked for volunteers and there had been requests from other countries about running such a service themselves – Germany and Canada were two of them.

Alec Dickson had always been international in his thinking. Those announcements did not shock him or induce a mood of pessimism. In a sense it was a compliment. VSO had led the way. There was a battle to be fought and he was ready to rise to it. The Americans were welcome to enter the field but they should not threaten VSO's school leavers, as indeed they had no intention of doing.

From the beginning with Alec Dickson there had been no question of VSO's young people being any kind of a substitute. The philosophy behind their contribution was quite different from and complementary to what adults might bring. The young could speak to those of their own generation across racial or cultural frontiers. It was a reciprocal message; a life change for those who went out as well as for those they befriended. It was building on the experience and knowledge which these young people had provided and persuading countries on the verge of Independence that their own young people could also give as well as gain.

In February Gilbert Stephenson joined the office. With E. R. Chadwick, his background was also the Nigerian Colonial Service but unlike Chad, whose work had been centred in the Eastern Region particularly with the democratic Ibo peoples, Gilbert Stephenson's career had been in the autocratic Muslim North.

Our most memorable meeting with Gilbert had been our expulsion from the walled city of Kano when we were forbidden to spend the night there with our MOWB student's family. It is unlikely he ever thought much of it but we remembered.

In March, the Governing Council met for the first time under Lord Amory. A shiver ran over Acacia House at the name being given to a group of people with little understanding of the origins of what they were supposed to be governing. But Lord Amory was a man of humour and a long interest in youth affairs. He and Alec Dickson had met several times. Alec trusted him and recognised that his influence was valuable in the circles into which VSO was now moving.

Gilbert Stephenson, ostensibly in charge of public affairs and fund raising, was an administrator by nature and career. He had been a Senior Colonial Administrative Officer with whom the Colonial Office was at ease. Soon after he arrived I found myself being asked by him to bring my husband to heel as far as the duplicate office of Acacia House was concerned. I knew that from Gilbert's point of view he was right and warning signals rang when he approached me. Alec was a lateral thinker in giving birth to ideas as well as in hoarding documents. He felt a journalist's possessiveness of pieces of paper with writing on them and a strong sense of their possible future significance. No paper was ever lost. No one but Alec himself could make sense of his filing system – but no paper was ever lost. Given time he could eventually bring to light the most trivial jotting but I had no doubt where my loyalties lay and no desire to be pig-in-the middle. I answered with a denial, suggesting that he try to work out something with Alec himself.

Meantime Selection Boards were frequent. Any request from a Girl's School, usually Catholic, for a speaker got Mrs Dickson. Our world seemed full of volunteers, past, present or potentially future. There were tensions in the office as it expanded but most offices had growing pains. Alec often came home unhappy and not wanting to talk but that was not an unusual situation and I let him recover in peace.

Then two things happened. An invitation arrived from the Ford Foundation inviting Alec Dickson to visit the United States in the autumn and see something of Peace Corps training and youth work in general. He wrote back an acceptance and added that he would bring his wife. This was to set a future pattern. We calculated – no children, no car, no mortgage, neither of us drank spirits, this would be a priority expense. As time moved on the only Government ever to invite Mrs Dickson in her own right was Nigeria. When it happened it reinforced my affection for that country and its people.

We were revitalised. So far we had never visited the USA.

We had come to know Sir Edward Ford, the Queen's Private Secretary. The Palace was interested in what was happening and Sir Edward felt this gave him licence to come and make his own enquiries. At one meeting Alec suggested that HM might like to meet some of those who had come back. Sir Edward was surprised that the cautious answer he got from the Palace was more positive than expected. In due course an invitation arrived for a Reception at Buckingham Palace on September 25th at 3 pm. There were 120 returned volunteers, members of the Council and of the Advisory Committee, including John Marsh who had been the first Chairman. At that stage Alec and I knew every one of the young people. They were drawn up in two parallel lines. Alec took the Queen down one line introducing each one to her, telling her where their projects had been. I took the Duke of Edinburgh down the other line. Then we changed over. Afterwards we asked the volunteers which had impressed them most. Without hesitation they answered, 'The Queen. She knew where we'd been. She asked intelligent questions and took us seriously.'

Almost immediately afterwards Lord Amory revealed that he was resigning the Chairmanship of the Council to be High Commissioner in Canada. He would have been with us only six months. A few weeks before, meeting casually in a corridor, he had asked me if I would think of becoming Deputy Director of VSO. Astonished and flattered though I was I had no hesitation refusing. I never told Alec about this curious conversation. I am sure now that Lord Amory being the man he was and coming across me unexpectedly, he had suddenly thought that it might be a solution to problems he foresaw and went straight into action – perhaps even without thinking much.

USA 1961

We landed in New York after a night flight on November 2nd. I had not much wanted to visit America. If given a different choice it would have been East not West. The reason I put forward was that it was dull to travel where the universal language was English. We were soon to discover that I was wrong about this.

Alec on the other hand was stimulated by the prospect. He had long been an admirer of the Civilian Conservation Corps associated with the name of Roosevelt. In the dark days of the '30s Depression when unemployment was Stateswide, many in the cities starving and the dustbowl in the centre of the landmass barren, Franklin D. Roosevelt set up the CCC. Like everything in the USA it was on a massive scale, organised by the Army, taking in their hundreds of thousands the poor, the desperate, those with no hope of work to save their families or indeed their country from disaster.

It so happened that in a taxi from the airport to the small hotel on 42nd Street where the Ford Foundation had booked us in the driver was an elderly man. Unlike most New York taxi drivers he was prepared to enter into conversation when Alec asked him if he knew anything of the CCC. At the peril of our lives he turned round, his face alight. 'The best years of my life', he said, and went back to driving. Pressed, he began to expand this statement. He had gone when he was young. With many others he had been taken to a camp on the edge of the dustbowl. The work was tree planting. There he had found hope and pride. 'Half the trees growing in America today were planted by the CCC', he said. 'Last summer I took my grandchildren out there to see where I'd been. These trees were planted by your Grandad when he was a young 'un I told them.'

It was talk after Alec's own heart. We arrived at the hotel ready for adventure.

When we rose from our jet lag dreams, the adventure started in just such a haphazard way as it might have done in Britain. The Ford Foundation had made out a 'program'. When we looked at it in their office it was at once obvious that they had little idea what Alec Dickson did. They took 'Youth Service' to mean dealing with young delinquents, interspersed with two or three visits to universities where Peace Corps Training was taking place, particularly in languages. Clearly Sargent Shriver had been equally ignorant about VSO or maybe dismissive, or we suspected, never even been approached about a visit. But New York was alive – face-to-face anyone we met was outgoing, welcoming and hospitable. Trouble had been taken to let us see their delinquents and no stinting of the ground to be covered in doing so – even as far as California. We accepted the plans laid out before us with anticipation.

It was the polite blankness that first alerted us to our language problem. Our new American friends liked our accents so it did not much matter if often they did not understand what we were talking about. But it mattered to us. Alec used the word 'scheme' in connection with VSO. One day he was asked to explain what it meant. When he told the enquirer there was an exclamation – 'ahhh–pro-ject–plaan'. 'Scheme' in the States had only one meaning – an 18th century one – 'witchcraft', 'planning evil': it was a bad word. After that we were more careful. We began to make it a reciprocal learning process.

Once launched it turned out to be a fascinating visit, full of interest and fresh contacts. Camp Scott and Camp Scudder were two camps for young delinquents in the West where the training was learning how to deal with forest fires. The two officers from Los Angeles Probation Office who escorted us on our visit found us hilarious and naive, almost from a different planet. We were not far from feeling the same when we were handed over to the Camp staff.

The daily routine involved not only normal duties but being continually on the alert for action. The Camps had their own fire engines to be kept at maximum readiness to answer a fire call and join the professionals as directed. In the hot dry season alerts could be frequent and the job extremely disciplined and hazardous but more interesting, the values in those two Camps were reversed. A new Camp member started on arrival as part of the fire patrol but on his report he was marked as routine. He had to work up to a place among the elite and an excellent report when he performed well at Kitchen Duties. The staff recognised that they were chasing ideals. They wanted the young men to go out with a sense of values totally opposed to those with which they had come in.

In a large closed institution we saw, sitting on two adjacent chairs in a bleak corridor, a black youngster and an elderly black man. I asked what they were doing. The answer was that the boy was without any relatives but had many problems. His volunteer Foster Grandad had come to visit him. It was the University visits that were eye-opening and laid the groundwork of a personal connection with the Peace Corps that was to last many years.

Peace Corps 1961

Compared to VSO the Peace Corps was an enormous endeavour, well planned, munificently government financed, aiming at 5,000 volunteers in the first year, going up to 10,000 and beyond. We could only admire. Alec himself knew what it was to dream in thousands but the mouse was never in a position to envy the lion; only to have, if possible, a friendly relationship.

With the best brains giving their attention to language teaching, in one case Thai, we thought of our approach to the School of Oriental and African Studies in London asking if on behalf of VSOs going to countries like Aden they could suggest any simple handbook on spoken Arabic or set up a short course. The reply, icy cold, was that Arabic was a classical language taking at least seven years study.

Our selection process was thought quaint and without value. We were told a wartime story of an RAF officer stationed in the Shetland Islands who had the job of selecting aircrew for a special mission. There were also American aircrew stationed on the island at that time. The RAF officer sat in a ramshackle hut and each man, after a knock on the door, disappeared within. He came out five minutes later with an answer, Yes or No. An American queried the validity of the proceedings. The RAF officer put a finger on his lips and lifted the cloth on the table. Underneath lay a black retriever dog. 'You see', he said, 'If he wags his tail, you're in! He's seldom wrong.'

Of course the size of the States required singular recruiting strategies. Papers were sent out to every state. They could even be had from the local Post Office. The volume of paperwork was enormous; multiple questions with answers ticked in boxes, some of them of a psychological background. At this point ten references were asked for, then one or two of those would be requested to give an extra name and address without referring to the applicant. Everything was done by mail. All replies were sorted out in Washington DC and the clearly unsuitable rejected. The remainder were invited to Puerto Rico, a small US island in the West Indies, for group sessions. This did not mean that they were selected. It was an assessment course at close quarters. Even when they left for home none were sure whether they were in or out. The letter came later – selected or deselected. Then the training began.

In all this activity we had only one real advantage. We had already had volunteers overseas for three years and had accumulated genuine experience to describe. Alec spoke to every group. They listened. Astonishment at the age of VSOs was palpable. They did not hesitate to express admiration that we could consider 18-year-olds responsible and trust them. It was then that I devised the answer which was a foreign language to an American audience. 'It's a confidence trick.'

At Ann Arbor, Michigan, walking across the campus after a discussion we heard footsteps running after us. When we turned it was one of the graduates, a tall young man in his early twenties. 'Can I come with your organisation Sir?' he said. 'It sounds much more fun.' We had to refuse because he was too old!

Columbia University, New York, was training their Peace Corps group for service in Sierre Leone, West Africa. We sat at the back of the auditorium and listened to a talk by a staff member and the discussion which followed. It emerged that the problem which the graduates found most worrying was how they should adapt to living in an all-black community. I was naive and from outside but there seemed to me to be a possible answer. So I put up my hand. The group quietened. It was indicated that I should speak.

I stood up and asked, 'Why don't you take small groups to spend a day or two in Harlem?'

The silence was absolute. The teacher said, 'Ma'am, it's really *wild* down there.'

We left for home on December 16th, stimulated and refreshed. The irony of it all was that many years later and many visits to the USA, when John Kennedy and Sargent Shriver were gone, Alec Dickson, when addressing different American youth and voluntary organisations was often introduced as the Father of the Peace Corps. The Americans are generous people.

In those days the West–East overnight flight always seemed the more exhausting. We arrived at Acacia House very tired. I would have ignored Mrs McCaw's neat heaps of correspondence but Alec, however much he desired simply to fall into bed, always insisted on glancing at the letters first. He took up the piles and shifted through them. There were some official ones and those he put aside.

Suddenly I felt a silence and looked up. Dead white, without words, Alec handed me a typed letter. It was not long. The heading was VSO. Signed by Acting Chairman General Sir Archibald Nye, a man I had never met, it began without any preamble. There had been a reconstruction in the office while we had been away. It would be better if Alec did not come in until he had talked with the Bishop of Norwich, Launcelot Fleming, who would explain the new staffing arrangements. These gave Alec Dickson an advisory and public speaking role in the future.

I hardly read more. I had lived long enough with a pioneer to recognise the pattern. Experience told me that the ultimate aim was to put in place a process which would eventually drive Alec Dickson to resign. And I knew why – as indeed he would. I was conscious of an emotion which was quite strange to my nature and which I had endured only once or twice before in my life. From the moment the letter was read I at least knew that there was no return. Every nerve in my body was trembling with a furious anger at the way this shameful betrayal had been planned and executed.

Still without a word we clung to each other. Some wounds penetrate too deep ever to be expressed in speech. Then Alec went to bed, his refuge in trouble, and I began to open the luggage and set the flat in order.

The next few days remained a blank. Perhaps some of the Dayaks visited us or other friends: maybe we went to family. Of what had happened we spoke only to each other; often not even that. Alec had sunk into a depression without the ability to make any decisions, seeing the future only as personal failure. He was already in limbo. VSO was in the past.

Certainly there must be a meeting but not with the Bishop, the only person suggested. We sensed an element of cowardice that none of those we had trusted as friends contacted us. The decision at last was made that we would go to the top, to the man who had signed the letter, who had taken over from Lord Amory as the acting Chairman of the Governing Council, General Sir Archibald Nye.

We asked him to meet us on our own ground, Alec's club in Pall Mall.

The meeting took place on January 2nd, 1962.

The General was an unpretentious man. It was soon clear that he knew little of VSO's early background and was uneasy in the situation in which he found himself. With no common ground the meeting was very difficult for him, as it was for Alec Dickson. There were others whom he might have met with stinging words but not this unassuming soldier.

For me none of this was true. My unnatural rage still burned white hot. I had words and I wanted to utter them. I had watched my husband devastated by callous official calculation and was determined to wound in return.

'This was a dishonourable action: to come to such an agreement when we were out of the country', I said. 'It may happen in the Army but it was shameful and should never have been considered in this situation.'

I saw at once by the General's face that I had struck home. But I did not care.

CHAPTER 22

Sequel and CSV

Community Service Volunteers 1962

In the New Year Alec Dickson had an engagement to speak to the Headmasters Conference. He left in time to catch the train. Contact was renewed with supporters for many of whom what had happened with VSO was a minor affair. We discovered we still had friends.

The overseas correspondence continued. The decision to resign had been carried out but for the volunteers we knew, for whom Acacia House *was* VSO, the coming and going of letters went on as usual. No divisions were created, the focus as always, being on their experiences, problems and successes. To those who had returned and came to visit us we said nothing of the realities of the parting. In fact, soon enough, future experiments provided plausible reasons for leaving.

It was to be many years before any genuine connection with VSO Headquarters was renewed. Only with David Green, the first early young volunteer to become Director, was the rift healed.

It was our Congregational Minister, Dr Hubert Thomas, who pointed the way forward. A Welshman with words of great spiritual power, he was also a man who had experienced personal disappointment in his own professional career. He admired Alec Dickson and understood his nature so I told him what had befallen us. A week or two later we got an invitation to tea at his home. Fearing small talk about the break with VSO, Alec was reluctant to go but was persuaded.

There was no light chit chat. Hubert Thomas began at once with the future. He was on the Management Committee of a big East London Hospital, Hither Green, which had an excellent forward-looking Matron. He could arrange a meeting with the Hospital Secretary and he then went on to remind Alec of his own unease when applicants for VSO were refused. He reminded us of George Webb's experiment with three of his Michelin apprentices on domestic projects. Almost as though he had had forewarning of the future, Dr Thomas had stored up in his memory conversations with

Alec Dickson, casual remarks, ideas expressed in articles by Alec which he had read. As I watched, my husband began to respond to the stimulation.

When we got back to Acacia House we began to think seriously of the possibilities of a domestic service and of lessons learned from VSO. This time we would get together a group known to us, with similar ideas and experience in the same kind of work.

In a surprisingly short time a group of four met round the small kitchen table in Acacia House to consider a plan known only as Service in the UK. They were Dr Hubert Thomas, Chairman; George Webb, Michelin; and Michael Dower, The Civic Trust and Tim Newell Price, General Secretary, Student Christian Movement in Schools. The Student Christian Movement (SCM) had a Trust Association which also included the SCMS. The Trust agreed to launch the scheme which would have Tim Newell Price as Treasurer and to guarantee charitable status.

When it came to a name, VSO had suffered at conferences or public meetings from always appearing alphabetically at the end of indexes or lists. Though neither catchy nor inspiring, Community Service Volunteers (CSV) answered this need.

A more profound decision arose out of Alec Dickson's unhappiness with the selection process. He was adamant that no young person who made up their mind to volunteer for a period of service in their own country should ever be refused. 'We've no right to say to them, "Sorry, chum, nobody needs you". Everybody has something to give'. So when it began to take practical shape CSV became non-selective, a characteristic of importance to staff as well as applicants – in interviews How and Where replaced Yes or No.

Volunteers should work in projects away from home. Within Britain this could be for them the first adult experience. Growth of confidence could well be eroded if they returned after a day's work to jokes and a dismissive family attitude.

Once again Acacia House buzzed with creative activity. On April 23rd 1962, the first volunteer of an as yet unestablished organisation, Nigel Potter aged 18, left Euston Station, London for an Approved School outside Glasgow whose Headmaster had heard Alec Dickson speak and was courageous enough to accept a challenge.

Nigel had never been in Scotland and knew nothing of young delinquents. As we saw him off Alec said to him, 'There is no organisation yet, Nigel. You are CSV. It depends on you – and on us'.

Two more volunteers followed Nigel, this time to Hither Green Hospital where Matron had persuaded her reluctant Hospital Secretary to accept them. The era of male nurses had not yet arrived and as Matron had anticipated, a fresh-faced young man on certain wards had an instant therapeutic value.

'What did you find most difficult?' we asked Chris when his stint was finished. 'Behind the tennis courts' was the reply. 'Behind the tennis courts?' 'Yes, that was where the young nurses proposed to me!'

Nevertheless, earlier than anticipated, we were hoist by our own petard. One day a letter arrived from a student of St Andrews University. She told of her strong desire to be of use in some way to anyone who needed help. She had applied to every voluntary organisation in Britain and been refused. A fellow student had suggested that she write to Alec Dickson. Then came the punch line: 'You see I'm blind'.

That was Jenny Revel. Now we knew we faced the reality of the challenge.

Her home was in the Midlands and in the Easter vacation we asked her to lunch. The Acacia House door bell rang. Answering it I found a very attractive girl carrying a white stick, having found her own way to Mortlake without assistance. Consulted about what she might do she described how she had only become blind at the age of eight so she knew what it was once to be sighted and also knew that her affliction could be overcome. She might be able to help those who had suddenly lost their sight – in a motor bike accident for example – and were in despair.

My husband got on the telephone. After numerous calls to possible projects who knew us and had affiliations with blind people the reaction was always 'No – she's a receiver of help'. He rang a senior social worker at the Home Office whom we knew and at once she said, 'Yes'. She would accept Jenny as a CSV in a new institution that had been set up to deal with the very problem she had outlined.

The experience changed Jenny's life and ours too. We now knew for real that everybody could be a giver as well as a receiver.

In 1963 CSV was offered a very small room in the offices of Toc H on Tower Hill. It might hold most of the papers and two people although there could be difficulty squeezing in an applicant! I had already set up a card index and basic files, now we needed our first member of staff.

This was for me an anxious time. I wanted to hand over the administration which was not Alec Dickson's forte and had no desire myself to be an official of the emerging organisation but I knew only too well how testing might be the choice of a close professional colleague to work with my husband.

In the event I was prevented by business with my publisher from joining our managing group at the selection meeting. Alec Dickson came home in despair. Without me, on whom he relied, he was haunted by demons from previous experience.

A young woman had been chosen, fresh from training as a medical social worker. For my part I was glad she was female. This was Elisabeth Plummer, aged 23, later to become Elisabeth Hoodless. Her gifts were to prove vital to the future development of CSV and her ability to deal with people, particularly of Alec Dickson's uncertain temperament, was to provide a long-term stability to the growing organisation.

As I handed over my simple Acacia House files, I was able to inform and warn Elisabeth that her relationship with the Director would be a challenging one but, with her help and understanding, could lead to infinite imaginative possibilities.

The speed with which CSV came into being did not mean that it was simple to convince either potential young volunteers or their possible employers that there was merit in this experiment. Because from the start the progamme was non-selective, this meant the widespread opening up of projects to accommodate the variety of young human beings who would come through the office door. It was not easy for social workers to conceive that within their work young volunteers could have any use. We ourselves had brainstorming evenings when we imagined the day's work of varied professionals so that when he addressed such groups Alec Dickson could present them with positive suggestions as to the inclusion of CSVs. Once, at the end of such a meeting, one of the audience stood up and questioned Mr Dickson as to what such a volunteer, untrained, inexperienced and fresh out of school could do in the institute she ran for abandoned children? Quick as a flash Alec Dickson replied, 'He could climb trees with them! Trained social workers are not expected to be seen waving their diplomas from treetops'.

Talking to a school was no simpler. Birmingham was no match for Bangladesh – revealing the hidden life of Liverpool to those who had been dreaming of Lusaka was not effortless.

The early years were hard work but after the successful placing of Jenny Revel we had a different perspective. Problems became opportunities; we read the newspapers each morning with open eyes. How could young people help in this or that situation of social change or local disaster? We were working within our own country and it was here that the needs proliferated. CSV was entitled to suggest, to experiment, to ask for or offer help. As time went on the volunteers themselves had their own ideas and a tact that surprised many professionals, indicating that the young people might be able to extend the range of patients recreation – for instance, one arrived saying he wanted to teach origami (the Japanese art of paper folding) and was successful in involving nurses as well as their charges. As we asked for help in giving some young people knowledge of the reality of problems in their own society, professionals became proud of their contribution to changing attitudes and the new generation working with them came to admire their seniors.

It had been our intention that CSV should be always at the cutting edge of social change: for the volunteers the three Rs were a Role, Responsibility, even an element of Risk. For official bodies change is rarely easy and risk an element to be wary of but for the young the challenge of exploration arouses their spirit and can alter the direction of their own lives.

In 1964, with CSV now in an office in Toynbee Hall, a long-established settlement in London's East End, and expanding steadily, we finally crossed the Thames to a home of our own. When asked what his desires were for a new house Alec made only two requests. Within five minutes of good public transport with a pillar box at the end of the road. My need was for a work room of my own.

Both wishes were fulfilled. I bought the house in Chiswick and moved in, with volunteer help, while my husband was spending three nights galvanising meetings in Canterbury! We were to live there contentedly for 30 years.

For us CSV opened up the world. As the organisation grew, at last moving to quarters of its own in Pentonville Road near King's Cross Station, so too its reputation and outreach widened both in numbers and requests. The growth of a youth culture worldwide in the '60s and '70s resulted in invitations to Alec Dickson to consult with governments elsewhere (Ministries of Education or Social Welfare) and other organisations on how their own young people could be interested in service in their native country. An unexpected one was Japan; emerging from a group of young people themselves JYVA (Japan Young Volunteers Association) who arrived with a video team to record CSV's work in schools. Requests for a return visit by Alec Dickson followed, out of which grew lifelong friendships.

Alec Dickson would not travel overseas without his wife. At first this greatly surprised his hosts, especially the Japanese, but they became accustomed to the fact that Mora-san did not like shopping and Mr Dickson took it for granted that she would accompany him – even to Ministerial interviews. If I saw that sensitivities were scandalized I took notes which bestowed a pseudo-respectability – though the notes often went into a sketchbook! Once, in Hokkaido, a women's group asked me to speak on 'How to manage a Husband'!

In the 1970s an invitation came from the Vice Chancellors of Nigerian Universities wishing to consult about setting up the NYSC (National Youth Service Corps). It was addressed to Mr and Mrs Dickson, with all expenses paid by them, and was one of the very few times I was to be officially included. The first Director of the NYSC was Dr A. A. Ali who had been a student of ours at Man O' War Bay.

Late in the 1960s the Peace Corps asked us to visit the USA again. The warmth and welcome that greeted us was first to overwhelm us and in the next two decades to enfold us as part of the volunteer family.

We became very close to a number of organisations: the Partnership of

Service Learning (PSL), sending college young people overseas for a semester, both to learn and to serve. The NYLC (National Youth Leadership Council), based in Minnesota, frequently invited us to their Annual General Meetings. In the late '80s we got to know well the Pacific Institute in Seattle. Through each of these organisations we became not only part of the ongoing work of volunteer activities in the States but also, through American hospitality, to feel at home within ordinary family life.

Col. Dr A. A. Ali

In the '70s Alec Dickson became Consultant to the Commonwealth Secretariat in London which took us to Sri Lanka as well as Fiji and the South Sea Islands.

The next decade Robert Blackburn, the Director in London of the International Baccalaureate schools, whose curriculum was the only one worldwide to include Community Service as a required subject, asked Alec Dickson to be their Consultant on Community Service. This took us from Korea and Taiwan to South America and proved a fascinating experience.

The British Council had my husband on their list of travelling lecturers. As the years went on there was for me an extra excitement in those overseas visits. I first became aware in Nepal that some of my books were in Council Libraries. Flying from Kathmandu to Pokhara I was told that we were to be met off the plane by the Librarian, at present unemployed because of a political imbroglio which had temporarily closed all national libraries. He had just discovered that I was the real live author of one of his books! Fearful of diplomatic consequences we were hurried past the locked front door and in the back. We sat waiting while he searched for 'A World Elsewhere' and I then signed it – to my pleasure and his pride. The next discovery was in Port Moresby, Papua New Guinea. After that my aim in any strange place was to find the British Council Library and search for Dickson in the Index!

In the '80s Alec Dickson, somewhat reluctantly, resigned as active Director of CSV and became Honorary President. Elisabeth Hoodless took over a thriving organisation which she herself had done so much to develop and to which she had added new dimensions.

Alec Dickson died in 1994. In June 2001, thirty-nine years after CSV had started, at a small reception in Edinburgh I spoke to a Spanish volunteer serving in a project in Glasgow.

'How did you hear of CSV?'

'I met a Japanese student in Madrid. She told me she was coming as a volunteer to Britain to work with Community Service Volunteers so I thought I'd come too!'

She was talking with Jackie – about to enter St Andrews University to study English and Philosophy when her time as a CSV ended.

'I was always academic but in my CSV project I discovered I could also use heart and hands. It changed my life. I became a real person.'

I wished them both well.

the Scottish hills